Japanese Submarines
in World War Two

Japanese Submarines in World War Two

Hirohito's Silent Hunters

Terry C. Treadwell

FRONTLINE BOOKS

First published in Great Britain in 2025 by
Frontline Books
An imprint of Pen & Sword Books Limited
Yorkshire – Philadelphia

ISBN 978 1 39909 422 1

A CIP catalogue record for this book is
available from the British Library.

Typeset by Mac Style
Printed in the UK by CPI Group (UK) Ltd, Croydon, CR0 4YY.

MIX
Paper | Supporting
responsible forestry
FSC
www.fsc.org   FSC® C013604

The Publisher's authorised representative in the EU for product
safety is Authorised Rep Compliance Ltd., Ground Floor,
71 Lower Baggot Street, Dublin D02 P593, Ireland.
www.arccompliance.com

For a complete list of Pen & Sword titles please contact

PEN & SWORD BOOKS LIMITED
47 Church Street, Barnsley, South Yorkshire, S70 2AS, England
E-mail: enquiries@pen-and-sword.co.uk
Website: www.pen-and-sword.co.uk
or
PEN AND SWORD BOOKS
1950 Lawrence Road, Havertown, PA 19083, USA
E-mail: uspen-and-sword@casematepublishers.com
Website: www.penandswordbooks.com

For Wendy, Toby and Sam

Contents

Introduction

The word 'submarine' during the First World War and indeed the Second World War, struck terror into the hearts of sailors on surface vessels. The sinister shape that slid silently beneath the dark waters of the oceans and hunted prey like a giant metal shark, was enough to strike fear into the strongest of hearts. The men who manned these underwater predators were no less human than their counterparts on the surface, the difference being that they lived in indescribably cramped and insanitary conditions and under the constant threat of being sunk and entombed in a giant metal coffin. It wasn't until the First World War that the submarine became recognised as a real weapon of war when it started to sink enemy shipping with its silent approach and deadly sting. At the end of the war the Japanese, who had been on the side of the Allies during the conflict, began to produce their own submarines and by the beginning of the Second World War had the largest fleet of submarines in the world. The downfall of the Japanese submarine force became apparent when the submarine was used mainly in supply and evacuation missions and not as an attack weapon as it was originally intended. When used to form picket lines it failed to intercept enemy warships because of confused communications within the Japanese Naval High Command. The book also tells the story of that development and the infighting between the two military powers, the Army and the Navy, which contributed to the misuse of the submarine and its failure to capitalise on its initial overwhelming force.

Midget submarines and human torpedoes were considered by the Japanese to be among their deadliest weapons, but neither were really effective. The development of the aircraft-carrying submarines, the giant I-400 class, is covered in detail, which would have been more effective had they been developed earlier, although one of the earlier I-class submarines, the I-25, did have the distinction of launching the first, and only, enemy aircraft to drop bombs on American soil. The failure by the Japanese Imperial Navy to develop anti-submarine warfare (ASW), unlike the Americans who had developed it whilst carrying out escort duties on convoys in the Atlantic against German U-boats, became a major setback. The losses and successes of the Japanese submarines are also recorded at the end of the book.

Chapter 1

The Beginning of the Submarine

The recorded history of the submarine goes way back to the time of Leonardo da Vinci in the fifteenth century and the concept probably earlier than that. In 1578 an English innkeeper, mathematician and amateur scientist William Bourne wrote: 'It is possible to make a ship or boate that may get under the water unto the bottom and so come up again at your pleasure. Any magnitude of body that is in the water having alwaies one weight may be bigger or lesser then it shall swimme when you would, and sinke when you list …'

This principle, although there are no recorded efforts to develop it, explained that if the volume of the boat is decreased the boat becomes heavier that the weight of water it displaces and sinks. Conversely, if the volume is increased the boat becomes lighter and it rises.

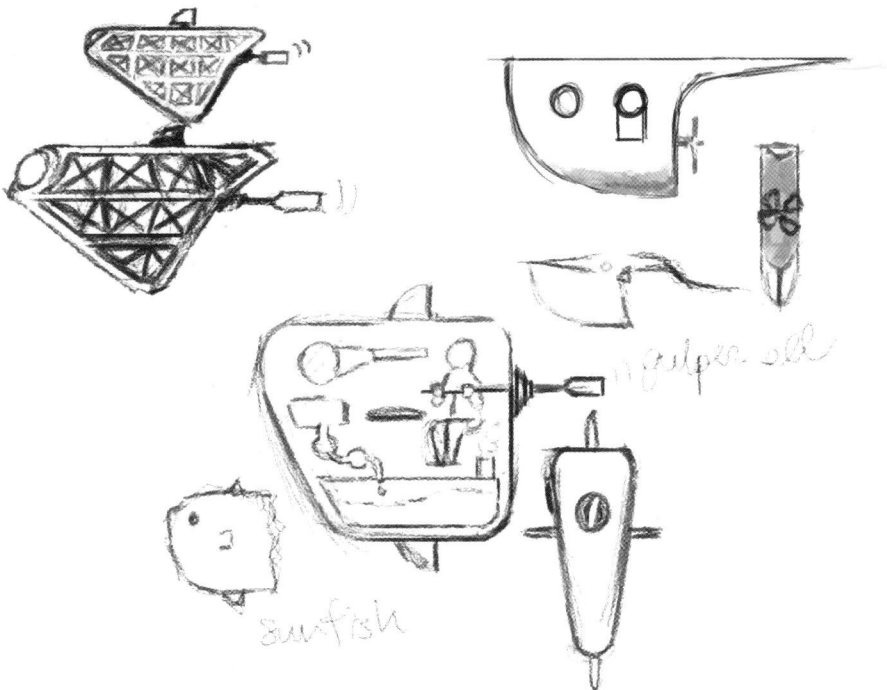

Drawing of Leonardo da Vinci's proposal for a submersible vessel.

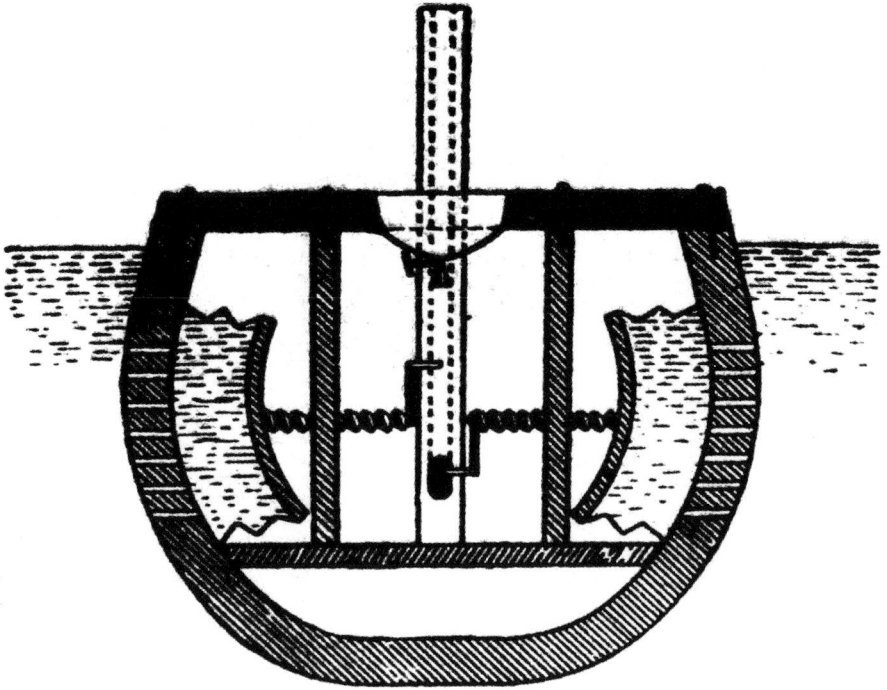

William Bourne's invention of a submersible boat. (*Author*)

In 1620 Cornelius van Drebbel, a Dutchman, who was said to have been appointed as the court inventor to James I, is said to have submerged a boat in front of the king in the River Thames. It was alleged to have been a rowing boat manned by twelve oarsmen who, beneath a covered deck, rowed the vessel to a depth of 15ft. There is no evidence to support this, but it is possible that something like this may have happened, as there was certainly a great deal of interest in the submerging of boats at the time.

The first serious treatise on the use of underwater boats, however, was in 1643, when two French Jesuit priests, Fathers Marin Mersenne and Georges Fournier, published a thesis entitled *Questions Théologiques, Physiques, Morales et Mathématiques* in which Father Mersenne included a detailed design of a submarine. The design incorporated a fish-shaped hull made of copper that

Father Marin Mersenne. (*Author*)

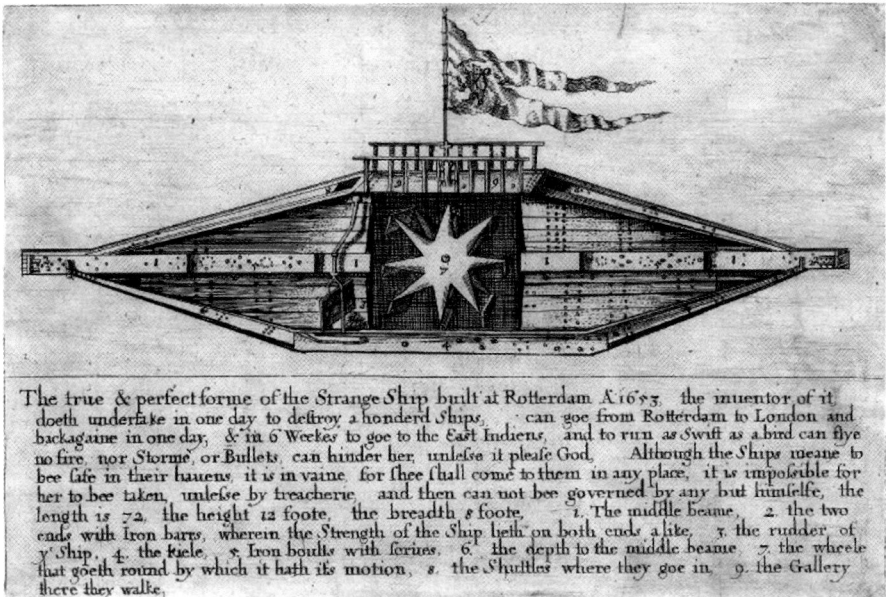

The true & perfect forme of the Strange Ship built at Rotterdam A̅ 1653. the inuentor of it doeth underfake in one day to deftroy a honderd Ships, · can goe from Rotterdam to London and backagaine in one day, & in 6 Weekes to goe to the Eaft Indiens, and to run as Swift as a bird can flye no fire, nor Storme, or Bullets, can hinder her, unleffe it pleafe God, Although the Ships meane to bee fafe in their hauens, it is in vaine, for fhee fhall come to them in any place, it is impofsible for her to bee taken, unlefse by treacherie and then can not bee governed by any but himfelfe, the length is 72, the height 12 foote, the breadth 8 foote. 1. The middle beame, 2. the two ends with Iron barrs, wherein the Strength of the Ship lieth on both ends a like, 3. the rudder of y̅'Ship, 4. the kiele, 5. Iron boults with feriurs. 6. the depth to the middle beame 7. the wheele that goeth round by which it hath its motion, 8. the Shuttles where they goe in. 9. the Gallery there they walke,

'Rotterdam Boat' drawing of 1653. (*Author*)

was spindle-shaped at both ends to enable it to cut through the water smoothly. A large cannon was mounted in a broadside position and when fired, the recoil would hopefully close the gun-port and enable the vessel to submerge and make good its escape – well, that was the theory. The design was never followed up, but the rumblings of this new conception were starting to make a number of other countries aware of the possibility of a new weapon.

In 1648, the Reverend John Wilkins, brother-in-law to Oliver Cromwell, made reference to a 'Submarine Ark' in one of his lengthy discussions with fellow members of the clergy. Maybe it was his close ties with Oliver Cromwell that prevented some members of the clergy declaring him a heretic. Six years later in 1654, a Frenchman by the name of De Son, built a 72ft long underwater vessel named the 'Rotterdam Boat'. It had been commissioned by the council of Southern Netherlands as a submerged ramming vessel with which to attack the English navy. Fitted with a metal bow, the idea was go across the English Channel and punch holes in the enemy ships. When it was finally built and launched, it was discovered to be so heavy and underpowered that it couldn't be moved, and so the whole idea was scrapped.

The publication of a theoretical work called *De Motu Animalium* by Giovanni Borelli in 1680, added more fuel to the speculation that submersible vehicles were a reality not a myth. In 1685 Father Giuseppe Ciminius, a Jesuit priest, offered the King of France a design for a machine that would take a number of fully armed men to the bottom of the sea and transport them undetected. There is no record of the offer being taken up.

Drawing of Giovanni Borelli's design of his submarine boat *Nova*. (*Author*)

Then in 1774, an English wagon-maker by the name of John Day is said to have converted an old sailing ship into a type of submarine by building a watertight compartment surrounded by seventy-five empty hogshead barrels. Detachable stones were hung on ring-bolts on the hull as ballast which could be released from inside. When submerged the craft could be raised by jettisoning some of the ballast, aided by the buoyancy of the barrels. On Day's first dive off Plymouth large stones were hung on the ringbolts and the vessel sank as planned, but did not surface when the ballast was jettisoned. John Day was drowned and became the first recorded casualty of a submarine disaster.

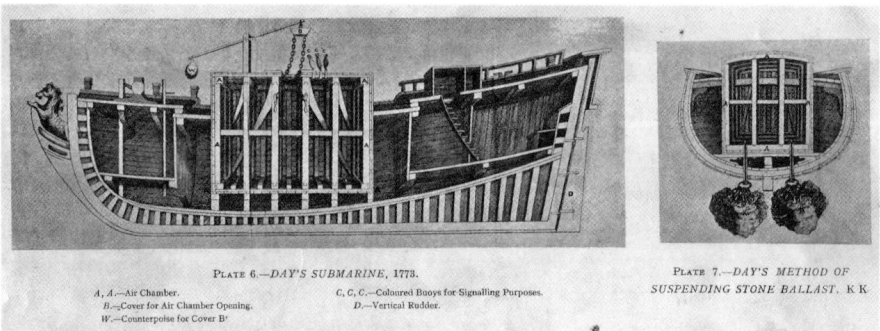

1773 Drawing of John Day's submarine. (*Author*)

Two years later, during the American War of Independence, an American by the name of David Bushnell, supervised the attack on the British warship HMS *Eagle* by Sergeant Ezra Lee of the Continental Army, in Bushnell's submersible called the *Turtle*. Although unsuccessful it did demonstrate that the submarine had a place in war.

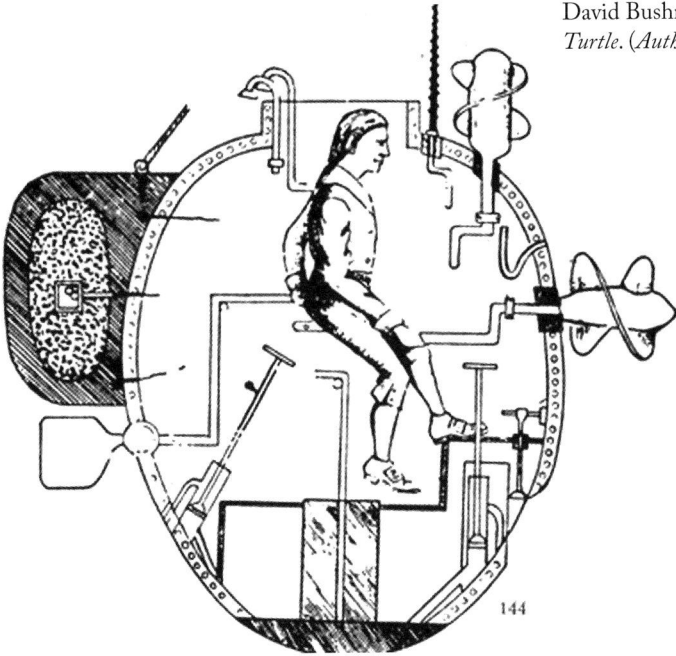

David Bushnell's submersible boat *Turtle*. (*Author*)

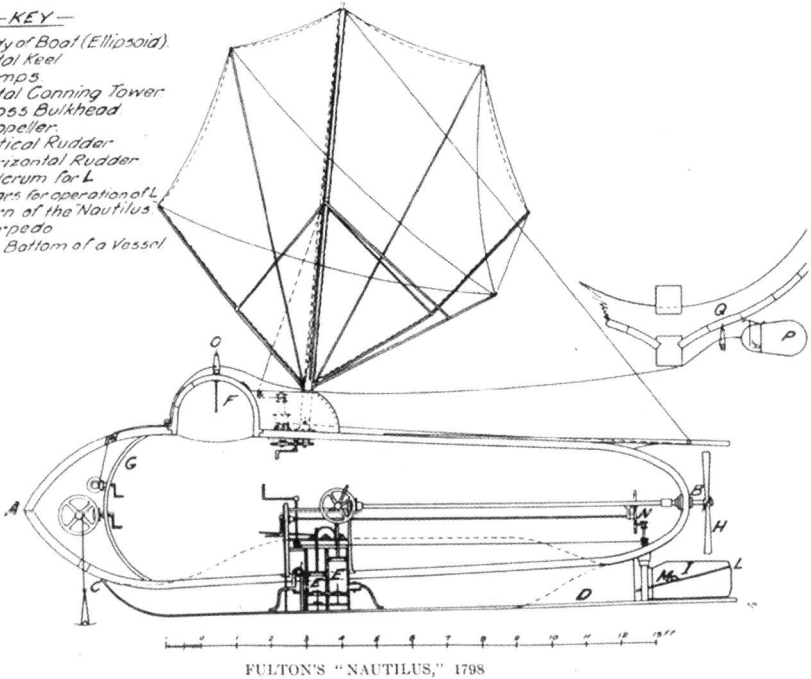

—KEY—

AB. *Body of Boat (Ellipsoid).*
CD. *Metal Keel*
EE. *Pumps*
F. *Metal Conning Tower*
G. *Cross Bulkhead*
H. *Propeller*
I. *Vertical Rudder*
L. *Horizontal Rudder*
M. *Fulcrum for L*
N. *Gears for operation of L*
O. *Horn of the Nautilus*
P. *Torpedo*
Q. *The Bottom of a Vessel*

FULTON'S "NAUTILUS," 1798

Drawing of Fulton's *Nautilus* submarine. (*Author*)

In 1790 an Irish/American engineer by the name of Robert Fulton designed and built a submersible called *Nautilus*. The cigar-shaped vessel was 21ft long and 6ft at its widest point. Its construction consisted of an iron framework covered in copper sheets with a hollow iron keel as its ballast tank and was powered by means of a hand-cranked propeller. When on the surface the boat was propelled by a fan-shaped sail which could be raised and lowered as and when required. The submersible had a couple of unique innovations such as a periscope, bottled compressed air and a snorkel which could be raised to supplement the air in the boat. Having an intense hatred of the British, Fulton offered the boat to the French who turned down the offer, stating that it was an 'underhand weapon of war fit only for pirates'. Putting his hatred for the British to one side, Robert Fulton offered the *Nautilus* to the British Prime Minister William Pitt, who at first displayed an interest but declined after Admiral of the Fleet, the First Earl of St Vincent John Jervis, said of Pitt: 'He is the greatest fool that ever existed to encourage a mode of war which they who commanded the seas did not want and, if successful, would deprive them of it.' Even at this early stage of submarine development St Vincent recognised that this type of vessel could be a deadly weapon in war.

In 1847 an American by the name of Lodner Phillips approached the US Navy with his invention of a submarine. Despite his enthusiasm and ingenuity his invention never progressed past his third prototype and was dismissed out of hand by the Navy.

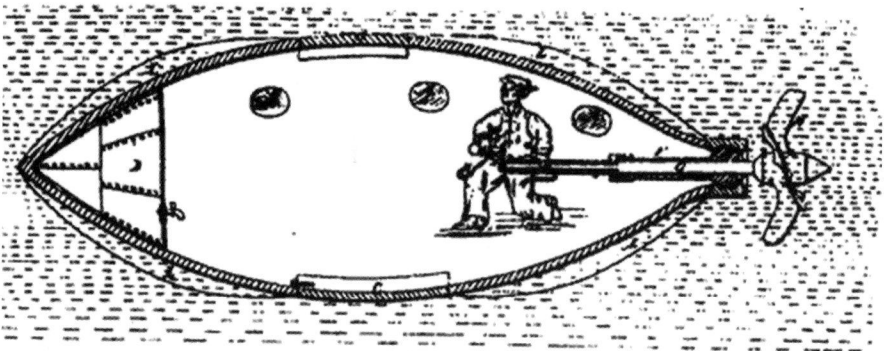

Lodner Phillips's submersible boat design of 1852. (*Author*)

The first recorded 'successful' use of a submersible vehicle in a war situation was in 1850. A Bavarian corporal by the name of Wilhelm Bauer was serving in the Prussian artillery at Kiel during the Schleswig-Holstein dispute, when, during a blockade of the port by the Danish fleet, he came up with an idea to try and end it. A carpenter by trade, Wilhelm Bauer built a submarine, the *Brandtaucher* ('Fire Diver'), by covering a wooden frame with iron sheets. Ballast tanks were placed inside to control the buoyancy of the boat, these being controlled by a water-pump that was hand operated. A crew of four propelled the boat by means of a hand

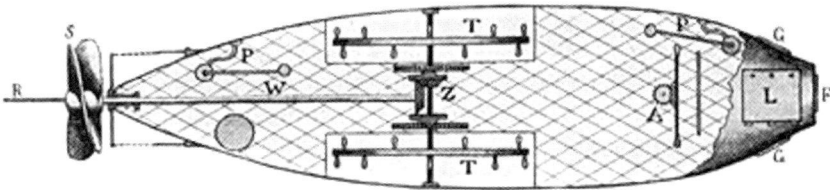

Das Innere, von oben gesehen.

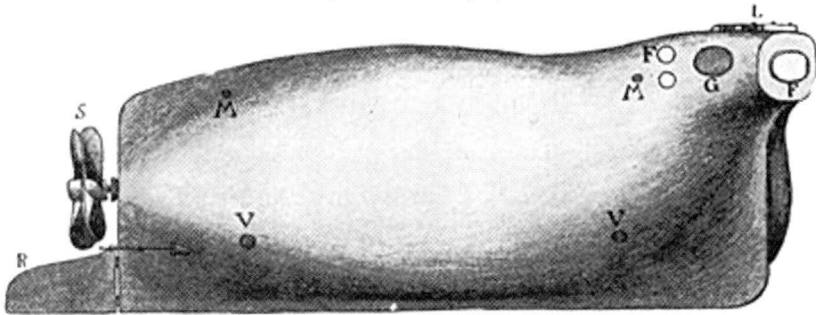

Äußere Ansicht.

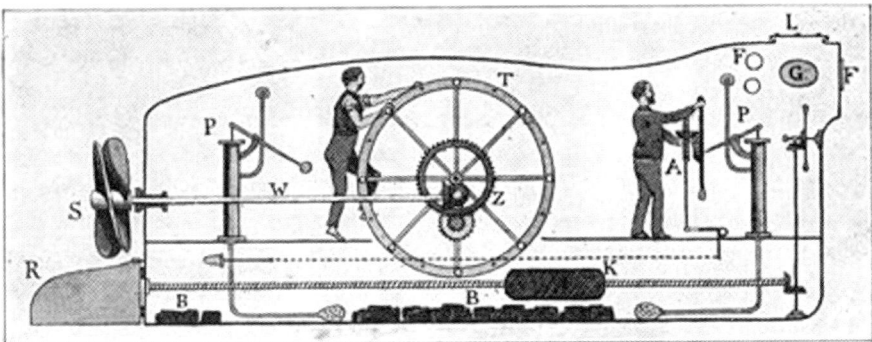

Das Innere, von der Seite gesehen.

Der Bauersche Brandtaucher.

Länge: 7,90 m.   Breite: 2,00 m.   Höhe: 3,00 m.

S Archimedische Schraube.	B Eisenballast.
W Schraubenwelle.	V Ventile für das einzulassende Wasser
R Steuerruder.	M Öffnungen für das auszupumpende Wasser.
A Steuerapparat.	F Mit Glas verschlossene Fenster.
T Treträder.	G Mit Gummi verschlossene Öffnung zum Hinaus-
Z Zahnradsystem.	greifen, um Sprengminen an den feindlichen
P Pumpen.	Schiffen zu befestigen.
K Verschiebbares Balanciergewicht.	L Einsteigeluke.

Drawing of the *Brandtaucher* submarine.

wheel, whilst two sets of leather gloves were attached to the bows, which enabled explosive charges to be placed on the hull of ships. The boat completed, it set out toward the blockade and its very sinister presence sliding silently just beneath the surface of the water was enough to force the Danish fleet to withdraw. Whether or not it would have been able to carry out an attack will never be known. One

Model of
the *Brandtaucher*.

year later Bauer's submarine sank whilst on trials after he had lost control of it. He and his two fellow crew members were trapped 60ft below the surface and could not open the hatch because of the pressure of water on the outside of the hull. Bauer managed to persuade his two colleagues to trust him and opened a seacock and flooded the submarine, thus equalling the pressure inside. This done, they opened the hatch easily and shot to the surface – the first men ever to escape from a sunken submersible.

In 1863 August Prince and Cornelius Scranton Bushnell started to build a submarine based on a design by Stovel Sturgis Merriam, called the *Intelligent Whale*. One year later the company was taken over by the American Submarine Company, and after a great deal of legal argument they obtained the rights to the *Intelligent Whale*. The submersible was completed in 1866 and launched the same year. In September 1872, the then Secretary of the Navy George M. Robeson agreed to purchase the submarine subject to the successful outcome of a series of trials. The submarine was submerged by filling its water compartments, which were then expelled by means of hand pumps and compressed air to raise it. It was claimed that the boat, carrying a crew of six, although it had room for thirteen, could stay submerged for up to 10 hours. The first trial was a catastrophic failure with the crew having to escape after the boat was unable to surface. The result was that the US Navy pulled out of the proposed deal and the project was abandoned. However there was one report that a General Thomas Sweeney, wearing a diver's suit and accompanied by two crewmembers, submerged the *Intelligent Whale* in 16ft of water. It is then said that the General left the boat through a hole in the bottom and placed an explosive charge beneath an old scow (flat-bottomed barge), returned to the *Intelligent Whale* and exploded the charge using a lanyard attached to a friction primer, sinking the scow. There is no official report of this happening however. The *Intelligent Whale* is currently on display in the National Guard Militia Museum in Sea Girt, New Jersey.

The *Intelligent Whale* submarine. (*USN*)

In 1852 the man who is said by many to be the father of the submarine was born – George William Littler Garrett. The son of a vicar, Garrett, who himself was later to become a man of the cloth, was to leave an indelible mark on the world of submersibles. It is interesting to note that up to this point, almost all of the people involved in the theoretical and practical development of the submarine had strong religious convictions and were connected to the church. When one remembers that

One of two *Resurgam*s built by Garrett. (*USN*)

the only use of a submarine at this point was for the purpose of war, and ultimately the killing of their fellow man, one wonders about the thought process of these deeply religious 'Christian' inventors.

Garrett designed and built a submarine called the *Resurgam* in November 1879 and carried out a series of trials. On one of these, he and his crew took the submarine from Birkenhead to Rhyl as part of a voyage to Portsmouth. On the final leg of the journey to Portsmouth the weather took a turn for the worse as a north-west gale sprang up and the crew were forced to abandon the submarine and take to the yacht that was accompanying them. The *Resurgam* was placed under tow, but the seas pounded the submarine and, because the hatch was unable to be closed properly from the outside, water poured into the boat and it was sunk off the coast of Wales. In 1995 a SCUBA diver discovered the wreck in 60ft of water whilst trying to disentangle snagged fishing nets. Since then efforts have been to conserve the wreck by making it protected wreck No. 42 under the Protection of Wrecks Act.

In America, the Civil War was raging between the Confederacy and the Union. During a blockade of Charleston by the Union, the Confederacy developed a

The *Alligator* submarine built during the American Civil War. (*Author*)

Drawing of the Confederate submarine the CSS *Hunley*. (*USN*)

submarine named the CSS *Hunley*. Plagued with problems, the submarine was the cause of a number of deaths amongst the volunteers that tested it, but finally it was deemed to be ready and was launched against the blockade. The CSS *Hunley* made its attack against the USS *Housatonic* with the result that the Union ship was sent to the bottom of the sea, but in the process the CSS *Hunley* was also lost with all hands. Also during the American Civil War the US Navy had their own submarine built, the USS *Alligator*, designed by Brutus de Villeroi, but despite a number of trials it was never a success.

Then appeared what can only be described as the breakthrough in the use of a boat under the water. In 1840 John Philip Holland was born in Liscannor, County Clare, Ireland. As a young man Holland joined the Teaching Order of the Irish

USS *Housatonic*. (*USN*)

The Holland SS-1. (*USN*)

Christian Brothers, not for any religious reasons it is said, but to earn enough money to carry out his own engineering studies. Holland had a built-in hatred of the British after seeing the poverty that was sweeping through Ireland at the time, and the way that British landlords had evicted tenants from their cottages when they defaulted on their rent. In 1873 Holland immigrated to America where he took up American citizenship and started work in earnest on developing his submarine. Financed by the Fenian Brotherhood, the American counterpart of the Irish Republican Brotherhood, Holland started to develop his submarine.

In 1881 Holland launched his submarine, the *Fenian Ram*. It weighed 19 tons, was 31ft long, had a 6ft beam and carried a crew of three – pilot, engineer and gunner. The British Consul tried to stop the project by approaching the American government, but they refused to intervene, saying that it was a private concern

The *Fenian Ram*. (*Author*)

and not contravening any of their laws. Powered by a 15hp Brayton twin-cylinder, double-acting petrol engine, the *Fenian Ram* carried out a series of surface and dive trials. It wasn't until 1883 that trials started on an underwater gun, which was mounted in the bows of the submarine and fired pneumatically by high-pressure air. The trials were a complete success.

The Fenian Brotherhood, who had financed the whole project, were now becoming restless over the length of time the trials were taking and took matters into their own hands. Placing a tug alongside the berthed submarine, they attached a line to her and towed her away but made such a hash of the towing that they had to beach the submarine. They later tried unsuccessfully to sell the boat to the Russians, but failed. Holland, angered by what he termed a betrayal, refused to have anything more to do with the Brotherhood and went to work for the United States Navy.

In the late 1880s French engineer Claude Goubet put forward a design for the first electrically-powered submarine/torpedo boat. It was briefly considered by the French Navy but rejected as being fraught with problems and the idea was abandoned.

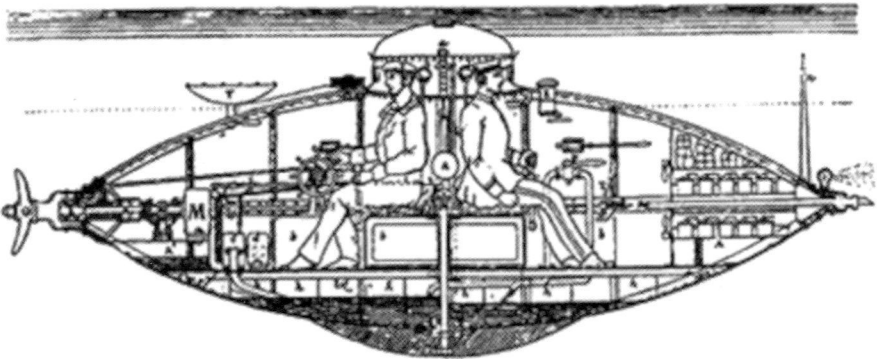

The French electric submarine *Goubet II*. (*Author*)

Chapter 2

The Early Years

I t was around this time that the Japanese Navy began to hear stories of underwater boats, so in July 1897 two Japanese naval officers visited the Crescent Shipyard in Elizabeth Port, New Jersey and saw a strange vessel being constructed. What they saw was the USS *Holland S-1*, a Holland VI submarine being built for the US Navy. They were so fascinated with the vessel after finding out what it was, that they asked to be shown around the boat. On their return to Japan they described the boat to senior members of the Admiralty, who then decided to arrange for two of their senior officers, Lieutenant Commander Count Kosuka Kizaki and Lieutenant Count Takashi Sasaki, to visit the United States and take a more detailed look at the underwater boat.

In 1901 Lieutenant Commander Kōzaburō Oguri, who was attached to the Japanese Embassy in London and had been watching trials with the Holland submarine being carried out by the Royal Navy, reported back enthusiastically about the new invention. In the meantime in America, the *Holland S-1* submarine had been moved to the Atlantic Yacht Basin, Brooklyn, New York, where sea trials

The first Holland I submarine. (*USN*)

Holland S.I submarine. (*USN*)

were about to begin. Lieutenant Commander Kizaki persuaded the US Navy to allow Lieutenant Count Sasaki to be aboard during the initial sea trials. One year later Lieutenant Kenji Ide, who had been assigned to the Japanese Embassy's naval section in Washington, was aboard the USS *Holland VI*, commanded by Lieutenant Harry H. Caldwell, USN, during diving trials in the Potomac River. This included the successful firing of the dynamite gun whilst submerged.

With regard to the dynamite gun, the original idea was for the submarine to carry torpedoes and artillery weapons. One 18in (460mm) torpedo tube was installed in the bows of the boat with a slight downward inclination. The idea was to use it for shooting the new Whitehead torpedo, also known as a 'self-propelled mine'. Five torpedoes were carried mounted in racks above the torpedo tube in a specially-designed compartment. The breech of the dynamite gun was above the rear end of the torpedo tube. The dynamite gun had an 8.4in (213mm) calibre and had a smoothbore barrel rigidly mounted to the submarine's hull with a fixed angle of elevation. To protect the tube from water, a hinged cover was provided on the superstructure, controlled from the inside. Firing the torpedo was done by compressed air. When the valve was opened, the compressed air from the cylinders was forced into the barrel hurling the projectile out. A similar arrangement for a second gun involved the use of another barrelled weapon, in the stern of the boat. It was suggested using a small-calibre torpedo tube for the so-called. dynamite torpedoes. Although the trials were relatively successful, it is not known if either of the ideas were adopted.

USS *Holland S-1* in dry dock. (*USN*)

USS *Holland* showing her Dynamite Gun with the cover removed. (*USN*)

The results of the trials greatly impressed the Japanese and in 1904, with the outbreak of war between Japan and Russia, the Japanese Government ordered five Holland VI submarines to be built by the Electric Boat Company in Massachusetts. The submarines were built in sections and shipped to Japan aboard a merchant ship for reassembling at the Gokaska Dockyard in the Yokosuka Naval Arsenal (later renamed the Yokosuka Shipyard). It was whilst reassembling these boats that the Japanese decided that they could improve on the design and construction. One of the director of the Kawasaki Shipyard in Kobe was sent to the United States to discuss these proposals with John Holland and, after lengthy negotiations, acquired the rights to make modifications to the design of the submarine and build it. Within months of acquiring the rights, work started on two newly-designed experimental submarines given the designations No. 6 and No. 7. Lieutenant Commander. Kōzaburō Oguri, who had had some experience with the Royal Navy's submarine section, was appointed commander of the first Holland submarine and Commandant of the Japanese Submarine Force.

The two Holland VI submarines arrived in Japan together with Frank Cable, an electrical engineer from the Electric Boat Company, who had been sent with a team of engineers to assist in assembling the boats. The American team arrived in Yokohama on 30 May 1905 and proceeded to Yokosuka where the submarines were to be reassembled. By July 1905 the two submarines had been completed and

USS *Holland VI* on sea trials firing her 'dynamite gun'. (*USN*)

had finished their sea trials, but were too late to enter the naval war against Russia as Vice Admiral Heihachiro Togo had crushed the Russian fleet at the Battle of Tsushima, bringing the conflict to an end. Frank Cable later wrote:

> The Battle of the Sea of Japan had just been fought and won, but the disappearance of Rodjestvensky's fleet had not depleted Russia of war vessels. The Japanese saw immediate work for at least two submarines off Vladivostok, and were eager to have the boats ready for transport to the harbor there.
>
> Toward the close of June we made a surface run in Tokio Bay with one of these boats, which thus became the first submarine operated in the Japanese

John Holland emerging from one of his submarines. (*USN*)

USS *Holland* being launched. (*USN*)

navy. When a submerged run was later made we had a full crew of Japanese naval officers in addition to our own crew of six men. These officers were to be trained to operate the boat in actual service.

The boat was ready for official trials with its native crew by July 22nd and I so notified the commandant of the navy yard. Unlike our experience with the Russian Navy Department, to say nothing of our own, there was no delay. In war Japan's watchword was dispatch. My advice was sent on a Saturday afternoon, and that evening official word came from the commandant that the board of inspection had been appointed and the trials would begin the next morning. I demurred to running trials on a Sunday, and we agreed to hold them the following day.

The trials occupied two days and fulfilled requirements. The board of inspection immediately left for Tokio, and the following morning reported to me that the boat was accepted. When could she be delivered? At once, was my answer. The craft was ready except for checking up certain spare parts. In less than two hours all material had been delivered, the boat's flag hoisted, and lines cast off, and she put out to sea in commission with a full Japanese crew and no Americans.

The Japanese submarine stayed at sea four days, during which they navigated the boat several hundred miles under her own power and without convoy.

The first Japanese-built Holland submarine. (*Author*)

Japan's first submarine fleet. (*Author*)

Japanese Holland class No. 6 about to leave on a sea trial. She accidentally sank in Hiroshima Bay, killing all sixteen of her crew. (*JMSDF*)

On returning they hitched her at the end of a tow line attached to a steam vessel and were off again. They spent several days thus trying out her towing capabilities. Once more returning, they placed torpedoes aboard and all supplies necessary for a long cruise. This time she was to be on the warpath – and then peace was declared.

Although no submarines took part in Battle of Tsushima, the Russians themselves were aware of the existence of these secret underwater boats through agents. Rumours had been rife of these secret weapons and the Russian fleet were convinced that they were lying in wait for them during the battle. So paranoid were the Russian admirals, that they issued the most ridiculous instructions to the captains of their ships, such as in the event of them seeing a periscope, they were to batter it with hammers to prevent the crew seeing, or alternatively tie a rope around the periscope and tow it into the inner harbour of Port Arthur. The situation never arose.

Japanese interest in the submarine continued and for the next couple of years they examined designs from Britain, France and Italy. Then submarine No. 6

Captain Tsutomu Sakuma, commander of submarine No .6. (*JMSDF*)

was suddenly lost with all hands during a training exercise in the Seto Inland Sea. The accident happened when the snorkel tube, which fed air into the boat, became flooded as the submarine suddenly dipped into a large rolling wave. The sudden inrush of water into the boat flooded the engine, with the result that with no power the submarine sank and all fourteen men on board were lost. The following is a report written at the time of the accident by the submarine's commander, Lieutenant Tsutomu Sakuma and discovered after the boat had been raised the following day.

Words of apology fail me for having sunk His majesty's submarine No. 6. My subordinates are killed by my fault, but it is with pride that I inform you that the crew to a man have discharged their duties as sailors should with the utmost coolness until their dying moments.

We now sacrifice our lives for the sake of our country, but my fear is that the disaster will affect the future development of submarines. It is therefore my hope that nothing will daunt your determination to study the submarine until it is a perfect machine, absolutely reliable. We can then die without regret. It was while making a gasoline dive that the boat sank lower than was intended, and in our attempt to close the sluice the chain broke. We endeavoured to stop the inrush of water with our hands, but too late, the water entered at the rear and the boat sank at an incline of 25 degrees.

When it touched the bottom it was at an angle of 13 degrees. The current submerged the electric generator, put out the light, and the electric wires were burned. In a few minutes bad gas was generated, making it difficult for us to breathe. It was at 10 A. M. on the 15th inst. that the boat sank. Surrounded by poisonous gas, the crew strove to pump out the water. As soon as the boat sank the water in the main tank was being pumped out. The electric light was extinguished and the gauge was invisible, but it seems the water in the main tank was completely pumped out. The electric current has become useless, gas cannot be generated, and the hand pump is our only hope. The vessel is in darkness, and I note this down by the light through the conning tower at 11:45 A. M.

The crew are now wet and it is extremely cold. It is my opinion that men embarking in submarines must possess the qualities of coolness and nerve, and must be extremely painstaking; they must be brave and daring in their handling of the boat. People may laugh at the opinion in view of my failure, but the statement is true.

We have worked hard to pump out the water, but the boat is still in the same position. It is now twelve o'clock. The depth of water here is about ten fathoms.

The crew of a submarine should be selected from the bravest, the coolest, or they will be of little use in time of crisis – in such as we are now. My brave men are doing their best.

I always expect death when away from home. My will is therefore prepared and is in the locker. But this is of my private affairs. I hope Mr. Taguchi will send it to my father.

A word to His majesty the Emperor. It is my earnest hope that your majesty will supply the means of living to the poor families of the crew. This is my only desire, and I am so anxious to have it fulfilled.

My respect and best regard to the following: Admiral Saito, Minister of the Navy; Vice Admirals Shinamura and Fujii, Rear Admiral Nawa, Yamashita and Narita – the air pressure is so light that I feel as if my eardrums will be broken – Captain Oguri and Ide, Commander Matsumura, Lieutenant Commander Matsumura (this is my elder brother), Captain Funakoshi, Mr. Marita, and Mr. Ikuta – it is now 12:30 P.M. My breathing is so difficult and painful.

I thought I could blow out gasoline, but I am intoxicated with it – Captain. Makano – it is now 12:40 P. M.

Here the log ended. The crew had been suffocated by carbonic-acid gas.

This disaster highlighted the dangers faced by all submariners in the early years and indeed throughout the First and Second World Wars as well. When the story and the letter were published in Japan, to the Japanese people it was a perfect example of men fulfilling their duty to the Emperor to the end, but to the outside world of submariners

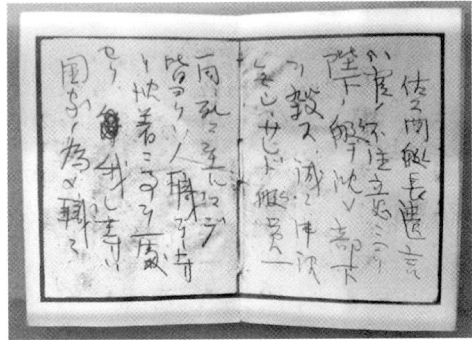

Captain Tsutomu Sakuma's journal. (*JMSDF*)

questions were raised. The submarine had sunk in only ten fathoms (60ft) and it should have been possible for some, if not all, of the crew to escape. But it appears that the commander made no effort to help his crew which should have been his first priority.

Work continued on the development of the submarine and when manufactured or acquired they were given sequential numbering. But some duplication of numbers caused a certain amount of confusion, so it was decided to establish three separate classes: 'I' for the large or first class submarines of more than 1,000 tons, 'Ro' for second class or medium-sized submarines between 500 and 1,000 tons and 'HA' for smaller third class or coastal submarines weighing less than 500 tons, this class also included the midget submarines. Problems still arose in the numbering system, so much so that in 1942 submarines I-52 to I-85 were renumbered I-152 to I-185.

Following negotiations with the British engineering firm Vickers, five Vickers-designed submarines were ordered. Nos 8 and 9 (HA-1 and 2) were built and assembled in Britain, No. 10, 11 and 12 (HA-3, 4, 5) being assembled in Japan. After acquiring the rights from Vickers to build their C3 Type submarines, three more were built based on the Vickers design No. 13, 16 and 17 (HA-6. 7 and 8).

In 1916 two submarines of the Schneider-Laubeuf design were ordered from the French and were given the designations No. 14 and No. 15. On completion No. 14 was immediately taken over by the French Navy and named *Armide* and put into war service. No. 15 was shipped to Japan and, using the French design of No. 15 (HA-10), the Japanese continued to build more submarines No. 14 (second version) (HA 9), 19, 20, 22, 23 and 24 (Japanese designations RO-11, 12, 14, 13 and 15 respectively) the latter were known as the K Type. They had also acquired the rights from the Italian company Fiat-Laurenti to build their F1 submarines using their design creating Nos 18 and 21 (Japanese designation RO-1 and RO-2) which were built in Kobe, Japan. These were the first of Japan's ocean-going submarines. The Japanese continued to build submarines mainly using the British Vickers 'L'-class design until the end of the First World War.

HA-202 on a high-speed test trial. (*JMSDF*)

With the end of the First World War came the confiscation of many of Germany's weapons including U-boats (*Unterseeboot*). Of the 176 U-boats captured, Britain obtained 106, France forty-five, Italy ten, Japan seven, USA six and Belgium two. Japan negotiated the release of a further seven from Britain on the understanding that they would be used specifically for research and experiments only. All weapons would be removed rendering the submarine useless as a military weapon. In addition to this agreement it was stated that all weapons and armament removed from the U-boats could not be re-installed into Japanese submarines. The Japanese agreed and the research obtained from the U-boats led to two different classes of submarines, the I-21 and I-121 class and the I-52 and I-152 class.

HA-201 transport submarine alongside the aircraft carrier *Junyo*. (*JMSDF*)

French submarine *Armide*. (*Author*)

French and German submarines in Japan after the First World War. (*Author*)

Chapter 3

Development

B y the end of the First World War the Japanese had expanded the development
of the submarine faster than anyone else, so much so that two additional
shipyards were turned solely over to the construction of submarines. The
arrival of the additional seven reparation U-boats gave the Japanese a new insight
into submarine design. The seven U-boats were redesignated; the U-125 became
O-1, U-46 the O-2, U-55 the O-3, UC-90 the O-4, UC-99 the O-5, UB-125
the O-6 and UB-143 the O-7. In June 1919, the American naval attaché in Tokyo
was given access to the ex-German U-boats and was seriously impressed with the
advanced technology of the Germans. In particular was the ability to raise or lower
the radio mast electrically from inside the submarine and the fitting of saw-like
torpedo-net cutters on the bows and beneath the boat. There was also a system
for purifying the air involving the use of chemicals and the fitting of rescue buoys
that would be released in the event of the submarine being stuck on the sea floor.
Incorporated into the cable attached to the buoy was a long rubber tube through
which air or liquid food could be fed into the submarine.

With the submarine firmly established within the Navy, training establishments
were set up with former submarine commanders as instructors. Discipline amongst
the junior officers and enlisted men was very strict and harsh, and punishments for
the slightest infringements could result in severe beatings without any chance of
appeal. Officers were all graduates from the Naval Academy of Etajima and were
kept strictly segregated from the enlisted men. The officers had to have spent at
least two years aboard surface ships before being considered for submarine duties
and no doubt the same rule applied to the enlisted men. The submarine force was

Submarine UC-90 in 1919. (*Author*)

regarded as an elite section of the Navy and as such the men were given preferential treatment in the way of food and cigarettes. One of the main training establishments was at Otake where there were two land-based submarine hulls fixed in concrete, which were used for attack and damage control training. Courses varied in length and lasted three to four months depending on which specialist course for which the men were being trained. Potential commanders were given much longer and more intense courses.

Once aboard an active submarine, however, the strict segregation of officers and enlisted men became very much relaxed, mainly because of the extremely cramped conditions to which the crews were now subjected. The lack of air-conditioning when in the South Pacific caused the crew to work in very hot, humid conditions and so the enlisted men wore just a *fundoshi* or loin cloth. As they were only able to wash or shower every four or five days, the atmosphere aboard soon became rather pungent. This, coupled with the fact there was almost no privacy and that there was only one toilet, which was frequently blocked up, led to a very insanitary environment.

Rations onboard for the first couple of weeks were quite good and consisted of boiled white rice, pickled vegetables, beef, pork, fish and eggs. But this soon ran out and the enlisted men and officers were reduced to eating tinned food and white rice. In fact every spare bit of space was filled with tinned food and bags of rice. Alcohol whilst at sea, in the shape of beer and sake, was available at the discretion of the boat's commanding officer and was usually only brought out on special occasions. Drunkenness was not tolerated either ashore or at sea and any infringements were dealt with severely. Segregation between officers and men in the crew mess, however, was still strictly adhered to. In the early years the recreation period, once ashore, provided the crews with extensive amenities, including female 'comfort' companionship, but in the later war years there was almost no time or places available for any rest or recuperation.

Rumours of collaboration between Germany and Japan started to circulate, and the American military attaché in Venezuela was told by his German counterpart that the rumours were true. At the beginning of summer 1919 German engineers who specialised in the design and construction of submarines arrived in Japan at the request of the Japanese government. Some of these engineers, who had helped build the U-boats in Kiel during the First World War, were sent to Kure to train officers and enlisted men in the complexities of operating the U-boat. All the German engineers were given five-year contracts with salaries of $12,000 (¥25,000) plus a yearly bonus between ¥5,000 and ¥10,000. In addition the Japanese government met all travelling expenses between Germany and Japan. American intelligence was immediately concerned as they realised that almost all the top German submarine engineers were in Japan and one of these was a man by the name of Kapitänleutnent Robert Bräutigam, a retired U-boat commander, who was recognised as the top specialist in his field. The Americans decided to try and recruit him, not only for his specialist knowledge, but also as a means of keeping track of Japanese progress. It is not known if they were successful or not.

Then in October 1919, the American military attaché in Tokyo informed the War Department in Washington that a Captain Takuo Godo of the Imperial Japanese Navy, together with a number of Japanese engineers, was in Berlin studying the design and construction of U-boats. By the end of 1920 it was rumoured that more than 800 German submarine engineers were working in Japan for the Kawasaki shipyard in Kobe, but later figures put this wildly exaggerated number at no more than 28. By the end of 1928 there were none as Japanese engineers had replaced them.

During the 1920s the manufacture of submarines from the shipyards was prolific; the K class (Ro type) was improved, as was the Vickers L class (Ro type). With the programme well underway the Japanese Navy realised the need for large I-class (KD (Kaidai) 1 Type) ocean-going submarines, the first of these being the I-51. This was the largest submarine ever built in Japan and was to be the prototype for future long-range submarines. Built in the Kure Navy Yard, the I-51 was 300ft (91.4m) long, had a 29ft (8.8m) beam, a draft of 15ft (4.57m) and was powered by four 5,200hp diesel engines for surface running and four 2,000hp electric motors for submerged running. It weighed 1,500 tons on the surface and 2,430 tons submerged. With a speed of 20 knots on the surface and 10 knots submerged and a 20,000nm range, the I-51 was well ahead of its time. It carried a crew of eighty officers and men, and was armed with eight 21in torpedo tubes mounted in the bow and carried twenty-four torpedoes. On deck two guns were mounted fore and aft: a 1.4in on the forward deck and a 1.3in gun on the aft deck.

It was around this time that one of Admiral Yamamoto's early idea of carrying a reconnaissance aircraft aboard a submarine came to fruition. This new innovation resulted in the I-51 initially having a crane installed to lower and raise the aircraft in and out of the water, then later having a compressed-air catapult fitted to her afterdeck, together with a hangar capable of taking two aircraft. The crane was retained for recovering the aircraft on its return. The aircraft chosen was the Yokosuka E6Y1 Type 91 reconnaissance seaplane, which was almost identical to the British Parnall Peto that was powered by the 130hp Armstrong Siddeley

The I-51 prior to being converted into an aircraft-carrying submarine. (*JMSDF*)

Mongoose engine. The Peto had been successfully tested aboard the ill-fated M-2 submarine which sank during trials in Weymouth Bay, Dorset, England in 1932 with the loss of the entire crew.

After a series of trials the I-51 was put into service and a second large I-class (KD2 Type) was to be constructed. The design of the I-52, as it was to be designated, was, like the I-51, based on the design of the German U-139. Construction started in the Kure Navy Yard, with a further five KD2 types ordered, but then production was dramatically reduced in 1922 with the signing of the Washington Naval Treaty and the orders were cancelled.

The Washington Naval Treaty, also known as the Five-Power Treaty, was a treaty among the major nations that had been the victors in the First World War, which, under the terms of the treaty, agreed to prevent an arms race by limiting naval construction. It was negotiated at the Washington Naval Conference held in Washington DC from November 1921 to February 1922, and was signed by the governments of the United Kingdom, the United States, Japan, France, and Italy. It limited the construction of battleships, battlecruisers and aircraft carriers by the signatories. However, the numbers of other categories of warships, that included cruisers, destroyers and submarines, were not limited by the treaty, but were limited to a displacement of 10,000 tons. Japan at this time had just one First Class, thirty-nine Second Class and ten Third Class operational submarines.

Present at the Washington Conference was Captain (later Rear Admiral) Nobumasa Suetsugu who was outraged at the limits placed on arms manufacturing.

The Conference on Limitations. (*Author*)

He quickly recognised, however, that the limits did not apply to the building of submarines, and the arrival of the seven German reparation U-boats had offered a chance to build a large fleet of submarines that could become a major part of the Japanese battle fleet.

One of the German U-boats, the minelayer UB-125, became the model of the *Kairi* type of submarine. Only four of these were built and were modified and fitted with aviation fuel tanks to serve as seaplane-refuelling submarines. This gave the reconnaissance seaplanes a much greater range and scope, which became important in the early part of the war. Given the numbering I-21 to I-24, these submarines still retained their minelaying capabilities and were slightly larger than their German counterpart.

The cancellation of the KD2 Type did not deter the Navy's progress so they switched to the development of a scouting or cruiser submarine designated the J1 (*Junsen* 1) type. Built by Kawasaki, four of this class of submarine were ordered and built over a four-year period. These submarines were developed from the best features of the German U-139 and the KD2 submarines. The first of the J1 Type, the I-1, was launched in October 1924, and during trials carried out over a period of 60 days and a range of 25,000 miles, the submarine dived to a depth of 250ft on a number of occasions, the deepest any Japanese submarine had ever gone. Powered by twin Maschinenfabrik Augsburg-Nürnberg AG (M.A.N) 6,000hp diesel engines that had been purchased from Germany, they gave the submarine a top surface speed of 10 knots. Two 2,600hp electric motors gave the I-1 a submerged speed of eight knots. The I-1 became the largest, fastest and most heavily armed submarine in the Japanese fleet and was to be the forerunner of the later *Kaidai* type.

The naval treaty had a profound effect on the Japanese. Cracks in the relationship between Japan and the West were starting to appear and with American and British superior industrial power, the Japanese realised that a long conflict, if it arose, would be very detrimental to them. Thus trying to gain parity on a strategic level was not economically possible. Many in the Japanese military considered the ratios of ships as another way of being snubbed by the West, although it can be argued that the Japanese, having a one-ocean navy (Pacific), were able to achieve a greater concentration of force than the two-ocean US Navy (Atlantic and Pacific) or the three-ocean Royal Navy (Atlantic, Pacific and Indian). It also contributed to the controversy within the higher ranks of the Japanese Imperial military, between the 'Treaty Faction' officers and those opposed to it, who were also allied with the ultra-nationalists of the Japanese Army and other sections of the Japanese government. For the 'Treaty Faction' opponents, the Treaty was one of the factors, amongst a number of others, that contributed to the deterioration of the relationship between the United States and Japanese governments. The perception of unfairness resulted in Japan's renunciation of the Naval Limitation Treaties during the 1936 Second London Naval Treaty conference. Admiral Isoroku Yamamoto, who later masterminded the attack on Pearl Harbor, argued that Japan should remain party to the treaty and was therefore regarded by many as a member of the 'Treaty Faction'. He believed the United States could out-produce Japan on all fronts because of its huge industrial advantage, on which he was somewhat of an expert having served with the Japanese Embassy in Washington for a number of years. 'Anyone who has seen the auto factories in Detroit and the oil-fields in Texas,' he commented after the signing of the treaty, 'knows that Japan lacks the power for a naval arms race with America', later adding, 'The ratio in the treaty works very well for Japan – it is a treaty to restrict the other parties'. He believed that other methods rather than a spree of construction would be needed to even the odds, which may have contributed to his advocacy of the plan to attack Pearl Harbor. It has to be remembered that Japan had to import almost all of her raw materials including oil, and if the other powers placed an embargo on Japan then the country would be in serious difficulties. However, Yamamoto did not have sufficient influence at Naval High Command, or in the government, to push through his concerns. On 29 December 1934, the Japanese government gave formal notice that it intended to terminate its part in the Naval Limitation Treaty. Its provisions, however, remained in force until the end of 1936, but were not renewed. Japan effectively ignored the treaty in 1936.

During the conference Kapitän Joachim Lietzmann, the German naval attaché in Tokyo, was approached by Admiral Inagaki Ayao, the Japanese Navy's delegate, and was told that if Germany were drawn into a conflict in Europe, they could be assured that the Japanese Navy would side with them and they would then take the opportunity to move against England. Lietzmann recognised the thinking behind this and was aware that if the British were tied up in a conflict in Europe, it would give the Japanese the opportunity to move against them in the Far East. He was also told that the Japanese Navy would give protection to German merchant ships and also supply Germany with intelligence information about British and American ship movements in the Pacific and Indian Oceans, specifically their warships.

Even at this early stage the US Navy realised that if their fleet were to move westward across the Pacific it would be long and arduous. It was decided to establish forward bases where ships could be replenished with supplies and repaired if necessary. The sites chosen included Pearl Harbor in the Hawaiian Islands (a naval base since 1908), Cavite (Sangley Point) in the Philippines and the island of Guam. The Japanese also realised the logistical problems

Admiral Isoroku Yamamoto. (*Author*)

facing the American fleet without forward bases and instituted a programme for the building of long-range submarines. If an attack were to happen, the vast distances the Americans would have to travel would stretch their supply routes and their movements would be easily monitored, so the use of long-range submarines would be a necessity.

Despite the ongoing rumblings within the Japanese§government and the Navy, submarine production continued to build. The early influence of the German, British and French submarine designs were now replaced with Japan's own. The navy yards were now in almost full production and in 1925 came the first of the KD3A/B (*Kaidai* 3A/B) long-range submarines, the I-53 (later changed to the I-153). The design of these boats differed greatly from the KD2 inasmuch as the bows of the KD3A were longer and more rounded, whilst the bows of the KD3B were much sharper like those of surface ships. The conning tower on both versions was much larger, enabling more lookouts to be used whilst running on the surface.

Relations with America had slowly been deteriorating for years. Hit hard by the Great Depression of the early 1930s, the Japanese people's disillusionment with the government grew and moderates gave way to militants. In 1931 Japan invaded and occupied Manchuria in northern China. Over the next few years the conflict intensified and in July 1937 war with China was declared. Such was the overwhelming force of the Japanese Army, that the Japanese Navy, with the exception of the Special Landing Force (Marines), was just assigned to patrol duties. In September 1937, six I-class submarines (I-1 to I-6) together with the submarine tenders *Taigei* and *Chôgei*, were tasked with patrolling and blockading the central and southern Chinese coastline. One year later they were all withdrawn from Chinese waters in an attempt by the Japanese government to defuse the growing tension within the international community. This had a detrimental effect on a submarine force that had had a very limited operational experience during the Sino-Japanese War. Just three years later they were to be thrown into the harsh

The I-53 on sea trials. (*Author*)

reality of a prolonged and demanding war against what was to be one of the most powerful adversaries in the world – the United States of America.

Occupying Manchuria was a practical necessity for Japan. Lacking in natural resources itself, it rapidly exploited Manchuria with the establishment of heavy and light industries, the search for alternative supplies underpinning foreign and military policy throughout the decade. The early military success and an inherent sense of racial superiority led Japan to believe that it deserved to dominate Asia. Higher birth rates and economic considerations required more land.

Up to this point the United States had looked upon Japanese ambitions with a level of sympathy, even indulgence, but with the occupation of Manchuria all that changed. Then the Japanese attack on the USS *Panay* and the Nanking Massacre (more than 200,000 killed in indiscriminate slaughter), caused public opinion in the West to swing sharply against Japan and increased Western fear of Japanese expansionism.

The *Panay* was hit and sunk by two 132lb (60kg) bombs dropped by Yokosuka B4Y Type 96 bombers and strafed by nine Nakajima A4N Type 95 fighters. In addition to the aerial attack, a Japanese launch sped up the Yangtze River and raked the *Panay* with machine-gun fire, seemingly oblivious to the large American flags on the ship. Three men were killed and forty-three sailors and five civilians were wounded. The Japanese claimed that they had not seen the American flags on the ship, which was helping to evacuate Standard Oil employees from Nanking. The Japanese government claimed the attack was unintentional, however US Naval cryptographers had intercepted and decrypted a message relating to the attacking planes, which clearly indicated that they were under orders to attack, and that it had not been a mistake of any kind, thus suggesting that it was the type of unauthorised action known by the classical Japanese term '*Gekokujō*'. This information was not released to the public at the time for reasons of secrecy. The Japanese later handed over a cheque for $2,214,007 in compensation.

This prompted the United States, the United Kingdom and France, under the umbrella of the League of Nations, to provide loan assistance for war supply contracts to the Republic of China. Historically, Japan had relied on America to supply many of its natural and industrial resources. As Japanese aggression increased, its relations with the Americans further deteriorated.

Alarmed by Japanese aggression, a commercial treaty dating from 1911 was allowed to lapse in January 1940. It was followed in the July by placing an embargo on scrap iron and aviation fuel. A statement in the US Congress said:

As evidence accumulated of the endangering of American lives, the destruction of American property, and the violation of American rights and interests by Japanese authorities or Japanese-sponsored agents in China, and after diplomatic representations had failed to effect a substantial alleviation of the

The USS *Panay* sinking after being attacked by Japanese aircraft. (*USN*)

situation, further consideration was given to the possibility of commercial retaliation against Japan. It was felt that the 1911 commercial treaty between the United States and Japan was not affording adequate protection to American commerce either in Japan or in Japanese-controlled portions of China, while at the same time the operation of the most-favoured-nation clause of the treaty was a bar to the adoption of retaliatory measures against Japanese commerce. Consequently, in July 1939 this government gave notice of termination of that treaty at the end of a six-month period prescribed by the treaty. That termination removed the legal obstacles to an embargo by the United States upon the shipment of materials to Japan.

In September 1940 Japan entered into a Tripartite Pact with Germany and Italy, making Japan a formal member of the Axis alliance that was fighting the war in Europe. This immediately posed real problems for the Americans. Although officially neutral, American sympathies lay with Britain and France and their struggle against Germany. President Franklin D. Roosevelt had already strained the terms of neutrality by supplying Britain with money and arms under the 'Lend-Lease' agreement. The Tripartite Pact meant that supplies to Japan would indirectly be helping Italy and Germany, so further embargoes followed. It is worth noting that a number of high-ranking naval officers, including Admiral Yamamoto, were strongly against the Axis alliance, saying that it was against Japan's interests. As a result Yamamoto received numerous death threats because of his opposition to the alliance, and so concerned were the Naval High Command, that they assigned him

Japanese embassy in Berlin showing the three flags of the Axis alliance. (*Author*)

to sea duties as the Commander-in-Chief of the Combined Fleet in a desperate effort to keep him safe from assassination.

In an effort to control supplies from America and Europe reaching China. the Japanese invaded French Indo-China, intending to take control of the Dutch East Indies oil fields. Almost immediately the United States halted all shipments of aircraft, aircraft parts, machine tools and aviation fuel to Japan, The Japanese regarded this as an unfriendly act. However, this did not stop oil exports to Japan at that time because it was thought in Washington that such an action, given Japan's almost total dependence on US oil, would likely to be considered a provocation by Japan. The Americans threatened to cut off all oil exports to Japan unless the Japanese Army withdrew from China. This placed the Japanese in a position where they either withdrew and lost face, or ignored the threat and pushed on to seize control of the European-controlled oil resources in South East Asia. Their decision is history.

When Rear Admiral Ugaki Matome – Chief of Staff to Admiral Yamamoto – wrote in his diary 'When we concluded the Tripartite Alliance and moved into Indo-China, we had already burnt the bridges behind us on our march to the anticipated war', he had realised that war was inevitable.

In 1936 Navy Minister Osami Nagano had said, that instead of making preparations for war against America and Britain, the Navy should be conducting itself towards friendly relations with those powers. In 1941 a senior Army staff officer wrote: 'The Navy's whole attitude and preparations to date have been directed towards the simple aim of expanding itself.' This was further endorsed by ex-prime minister Admiral Yonai who said: 'Whatever happens next, the Navy had only itself to thank.'

Despite the Army's control over the manufacturing programme the Navy managed to work on their own projects. One of these was the development of the mini or midget submarine. The idea of these small submarines came about after a submarine officer, who in 1936, when attached to the Naval Staff, saw a small one-man underwater craft being used during a commercial fishing operation. A proposal was submitted to the Admiralty and, after intensive trials had been carried out, the Navy accepted the idea and the first of the midget submarines, the A-1 and A-2 types, were built in 1938 at the Kure Naval Yard. The initial trials were very successful, resulting in the building of two other prototypes, the Ha-1 and Ha-2. These were two-man mini-submarines with an overall length of 78ft and a displacement of 46 tons. They had a range of 80 miles at a speed of 2 knots or 20 miles at 19 knots. Armament consisted of two 18in torpedoes mounted in the bows. The development continued and within four years the Japanese Navy had a fleet of forty-two midget submarines of the Ha-3 to Ha-44 types. This was to be the case when the Japanese launched their attack on Pearl Harbor in December 1941.

With the war in Europe erupting between Britain, France and Germany, the threat of the war spilling over into the Far East becoming more and more a reality, so the submarine force of the Sixth Fleet began training for the inevitable. The traditional tactics of the Japanese Navy was to meet the enemy in a head-on fleet versus fleet battle, the submarines' role was to try and intercept the enemy fleet and decrease their battle strength, thus giving the home fleet an advantage. On 7 December 1941 this role changed when Yamamoto decided to attack the American fleet in Pearl Harbor using aircraft.

Chapter 4

Pearl Harbor

Something that was to plague the Japanese military machine throughout the Second World War manifested itself on 7 December 1941, when aircraft from the Imperial Japanese fleet attacked Pearl Harbor. Communication between the Japanese Army, Navy and civilian hierarchy had never been good, in fact at times it was almost non-existent. The Army felt itself superior to the other branch of the military – the Navy, creating a rift between them, sometimes almost to the point of hostility, a situation that was to continue right until the end of the war. It was claimed that Prime Minister Prince Fumimaro Konoye and General Hideki Tojo, who was also the War Minister, did not know that the task force had sailed and was on its way to Pearl Harbor until word came back of the attack. Nor, it is said, did the Foreign Minister, Shigenori Togo. In fact the decision to attack Pearl Harbor was said to have taken solely by the Navy. It is hard to believe that not one of these people knew about the intended attack, the preparations for which alone would have alerted them to the fact that something was about to happen. The fact that all Japan's merchant ships had been ordered back to Japan, would have been enough to set alarm bells ringing. The movement of these ships did not go unnoticed by British Intelligence and they calculated that all the merchant ships would be home by the first week in December – a calculation that proved to be very accurate.

Early in October a plan was put forward for a midget submarine attack to take place on Pearl Harbor at the same time as the aerial attack. The plan was that five I-16 class submarines, each carrying a midget submarine on its deck, would take up station 10 miles outside the bay and release their midget submarines, which would then enter the bay and attack the warships that were either tied up alongside or anchored. The plan was submitted to Admiral Yamamoto for consideration who immediately responded by saying, that if the submarines were to go inside the bay they would not be able to return, and that was, in his opinion, unnecessary. The plan was then submitted to the crews of the midget submarines, who unanimously agreed that the plan should go ahead and were well aware of the risk involved to themselves. After some discussion Yamamoto agreed, providing that there was a plan for recovering the crews in place.

It is an accepted fact that Vice Admiral Nagumo's relationship with Yamamoto was not good, in fact they didn't like each other very much, and it is well documented that Nagumo, who was Commander-in-Chief of the First Air Fleet and to be the overall commander of the strike force, was against the attack on Pearl Harbor, saying that the priority should have been the American aircraft carriers. After a great deal of discussion with Yamamoto, Nagumo very reluctantly accepted the proposal of an attack on Pearl Harbor.

With plans having been formalised, Order No.1 was issued secretly to senior naval officers on 5 November by Yamamoto in the event that diplomats and politicians had not been able to reached a peace agreement. The order read: 'To the east, the American Fleet will be destroyed. The American lines of operation and supply lines to the Far East will be severed. Enemy forces will be intercepted and annihilated. Victories will be exploited to smash the enemy's will to fight.'

There followed a number of other orders, each laying out the plans for the attack. Then one week later Vice Admiral Nagumo, was on his flagship the aircraft carrier *Akagi*, when he received Order No. 9, his strike orders. What is interesting is that the detailed strike orders did not mention attacking the oil storage tanks or the machine shops, which should have been on the list of priority targets. The concentration seems to have been focussed on the ships in the harbour and the airfields.

On 22 November the strike force was ordered to assemble, under the utmost secrecy, in Tankan Bay, north of Hokkaido. In an effort to confuse American and British intelligence, Japanese warships patrolling the Inland Sea generated false radio traffic giving the impression that their aircraft carriers were still in home waters. The ruse worked, mainly because the Americans and the British had already lost track of the Japanese carriers and thought they were somewhere at sea.

Almost all the submarines rendezvoused at Kwajalein prior to heading toward Hawaii each with their own orders to dispatch the midget submarines mounted on their decks, then act as rescue boats for any downed airmen, pick up survivors from the midget submarine attacks or attack any American ships trying to escape from, or in the vicinity of, Pearl Harbor. On the morning of 25 November 1941, five Japanese submarines, the I-16, I-18, I-20, I-22 and I-24 of the 'Special Attack Force' from the 1st Submarine Group under the command of Captain Hanku Sasaki, each with a Type A midget submarine on the deck, slipped quietly away from the Kure Naval base and headed for the island of Oahu via Kwajalein. They were followed by three squadrons of submarines all of whom were to be involved in

The Japanese submarine I-1 carrying supplies to Guadalcanal. (*JMSDF*)

the attack on Pearl Harbor. Squadron One, under the command of Rear Admiral Tsutomu Satō, consisted of the I-9, I-15, I-17 and I-25. Squadron Two, I-1, I-2, I-3, I-4, I-5, I-6 and I-7 under the command of Rear Admiral Shigeaki Yamazaki, and Squadron Three under the command of Rear Admiral Shigeyoshi Miwa, consisted of the I-8, I-68, I-70, I-71, I-72, I-73, I-74 and I-75. A further two submarines, the I-10 and the I-26, were sent to reconnoitre the waters of the South Pacific and the Aleutian Islands.

Submarine I-3. (*Author*)

The submarine I-4 on patrol. (*Author*)

Japanese submarine I-5. (*Author*)

The Japanese aircraft carriers *Kaga* and *Zuikaku* in line abreast behind the *Akagi* on their way to attack Pearl Harbor. (*JMSDF*)

The light cruiser *Katori* was stationed off Kwajalein as the flagship for the submarines, which would relay the results of the attack back to the cruiser, who in turn would report the information back to the aircraft carriers. The submarines' part in the attack, however, was surprisingly very minimal considering there were over twenty of them stationed in the vicinity of Pearl Harbor at the time. The crews of the midget submarines understood that their missions were in fact almost suicide missions, and there was an underlying awareness that there was scant provision in place to pick them up after the attack had taken place.

The moment the submarines had arrived in Kwajalein they had come under the surveillance of American intelligence. The information was passed to US Naval Intelligence who estimated that one-third of Japan's submarine force was on the move. On 26 November, the day after the submarines had left for Pearl Harbor, the Japanese Task Force of six aircraft carriers, the *Akagi*, *Kaga*, *Soryū*, *Hiryū*, *Shokaku* and *Zuikaku*, the light cruiser *Abukuma*, destroyers *Isokaze*, *Urakaze*, *Tanikaze*, *Hamakaze*, *Arare*, *Kasumi*, *Ushio*, *Sazanami*, *Kagero*, *Shiranubi* and *Akigumo*, the battleships *Hiei* and *Kirishima*, heavy cruisers *Tone* and *Chikuma*, and the reconnaissance submarines I-19, I-21 and I-23, together with eight supply ships and tankers, departed northern Japan en route to a position north-west of Hawaii, with the intention of launching their 408 aircraft to attack the American Naval Base at Pearl Harbor. Two attack waves consisting of a total of 360 fighter-bombers were assigned to the attack, whilst 48 fighters set up combat air patrols (CAPs), which included nine aircraft from the first wave. The first wave, carrying torpedoes, was to be the primary attack force, whilst the second was to attack aircraft carriers as their first objective and cruisers

The I-26 on sea trials (*Author*)

as their second. A second wave was to attack the battleships. The first wave carried most of the weapons to attack the capital ships; mainly specially adapted Type 91 aerial torpedoes that were designed with an anti-roll mechanism and a rudder extension that allowed them to operate in shallow water. The aircrew were ordered to select the highest-value targets – aircraft carriers and battleships – or, if none of these were present, any other high-value ships – cruisers and destroyers. The first waves of dive-bombers were also to attack ground targets. Fighters were ordered to strafe and destroy as many parked aircraft as possible to ensure they did not get

SS *Cynthia Olsen* sunk by the I-26 on the day that Pearl Harbor was attacked. (*USN*)

SS *Cynthia Olsen*. (*Author*)

into the air to intercept the fighter-bombers, especially in the first wave. When the fighter's fuel got low they were to return to their carriers and refuel, rearm and return to the combat zone. They were also assigned to carry out CAP duties where needed especially over US airfields replacing the existing CAP aircraft .

Outside the perimeter zone set up by the midget-carrying submarines, other submarines were patrolling the Pacific looking for targets. Within hours the first of many merchant ships was spotted by the I-26 just north-west of Honolulu, the 2,140-ton cargo ship SS *Cynthia Olson*, that had been chartered by the US Army Transport Service to carry timber for the US Army in Honolulu. The I-26 had been given strict orders not to commence hostilities until 0330 (Tokyo time) on 8 December, the anticipated time of the attack on Pearl Harbor. The I-26, commanded by Commander Minoru Yokota, had found the *Cynthia Olson* before

The SS *Cynthia Olsen* sinking after being torpedoed and finally sunk by shellfire from the I-56's deck gun. The image was taken by one of the I-56's crew.

the attack time so remained submerged until surfacing near the steam schooner at 0330 (Tokyo time)/0800 7 December Hawaiian time. A warning shell was fired over the *Cynthia Olson* from the submarine's 14cm deck gun. The *Cynthia Olson* stopped, realising that they had no choice, and immediately sent out an SOS radio message that a submarine was attacking them and that they were taking to the lifeboats. The thirty-five members of the crew abandoned ship in lifeboats and watched in horror as the Japanese submarine's deck gun opened fire and sank the *Cynthia Olson*. Their SOS message was picked up by the steamship SS *Lurline*, but by the time they reached the area the crew of the sunken cargo boat were nowhere to be found and it was assumed that they had either all been lost at sea or killed by the crew of the Japanese submarine.

Prior to the attack, in Washington rumours were rife about the possibilities of war with Japan and the FBI were on full alert watching known suspects. It was noted that a large amount of smoke was emanating from the chimneys of the Japanese Embassy and it was obvious that large amounts of paper were being burnt. In Honolulu, a Japanese linguist by the name of Mrs Dorothy Edgers was translating an intercepted priority message from the Japanese Consul General Nago Kita to Tokyo that read; 'All Carriers and Heavy Cruisers Are At Sea. No Special Reports On The Fleet. Oahu Is Quiet.'

When she realised that the message contained information about the naval shipping movements in Pearl Harbor, she became concerned and brought the message to the attention to her senior officer. Already swamped with a number of translated diplomatic messages, he told Mrs Edgers to put it into his tray and he would deal with it on Monday. The rest is history. That is not to say that he was responsible, as there were many warning signs over the previous couple of months that something was about to happen. What is even more confusing is that messages about the naval shipping movements in Pearl Harbor, were being sent to Japan almost daily.

The final decision to carry out the attack on Pearl Harbor was made on 1 December. The following day Admiral Nagumo received a coded message that read: '*Niitaka yama nobore*' ('Climb Mount Niitaka'). The only thing that could prevent the attack from taking place now was if the fleet was spotted by the Allies. Admiral Nagumo, despite being kept informed about American warship movements in Pearl Harbor by Japanese intelligence in Honolulu,

Japanese spy Tadashi Morimura (Lieutenant Takeo Yoshikawa, IJN) stationed in Honolulu prior to Pearl Harbor. (*Author*)

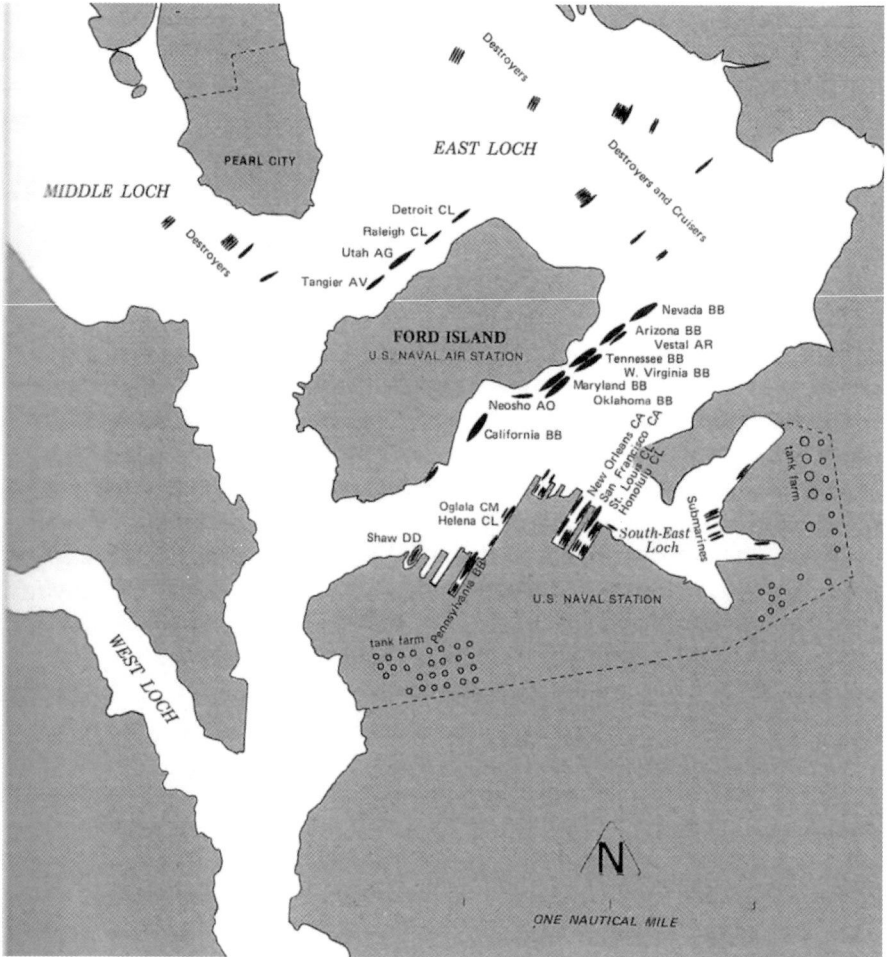

Plan of Pearl Harbor showing the positions of the American battle fleet prior to the attack. (*USN*)

was constantly worried about the fleet being detected. Prior to leaving Tankan Bay he had been led to believe that there could possibly up to six American aircraft carriers at anchor in the harbour, but within days he was informed that there were none. These would have been the main targets for the bombers when the attack started, because by sinking or disabling the carriers it would have put the United States Navy in a more desperate position than they found themselves in after the raid. This in itself was surprising and confusing considering Japanese Naval Intelligence had an agent in Hawaii by the cover name of Tadashi Morimura (Lieutenant Takeo Yoshikawa, IJN), who had been feeding information to Japanese Intelligence about US Naval activities and what ships were there since March 1941. In the early hours of 7 December, Vice Admiral Chuichi Nagumo received the following signal: 'Vessels moored in harbour: 9 battleships; 3 class B cruisers; 3 seaplane tenders, 17 destroyers. Entering harbour are 4 class B cruisers; 3 destroyers. All aircraft carriers and heavy cruisers have departed harbour … No indication of any changes in US Fleet or anything unusual.'

This raised the question as to whether or not Admiral Nagumo passed on the information to his flight commanders or just ignored it. What is even more puzzling is that it would have made more sense to attack Pearl Harbor when the aircraft carriers were there. But where were the aircraft carriers?

Task Force 8 (TF-8), under the overall command of Admiral Edward Kimmel, consisted of the aircraft carrier USS *Enterprise* (CV-6), cruisers USS *Northampton* (CA-26), USS *Chester* (CA-27), USS *Salt Lake City* (CA-24) and nine destroyers under Vice Admiral William F. Halsey, Jnr. They had been assigned to ferry twelve Grumman F4F-3 Wildcats of Marine Fighting Squadron (VMF) 211 to Wake Island and with the mission completed, TF-8 was to return to Pearl Harbor. At dawn on 7 December 1941, TF-8 was about 215 miles west of Oahu. The aircraft carrier USS *Lexington* (CV-2) was part of Task Force 12 under the command of Rear Admiral John H. Newton, and had sailed from Pearl Harbor to ferry eighteen Vought SB2U-3 Vindicators of Marine Scout Bombing Squadron (VMSB) 231 to Midway Island. The morning of 7 December found the *Lexington*, heavy cruisers USS *Chicago* (CA-29), USS *Portland* (CA-33) and USS *Astoria* (CA-34), and five destroyers about 500 miles south-east of Midway. The outbreak of hostilities resulted in cancellation of the mission and VMSB-231 remained on board. The aircraft carrier USS *Saratoga* (CV-3), having recently completed an overhaul at the Puget Sound Navy Yard, Bremerton, Washington, reached Naval Air Station (NAS) San Diego late in the morning of 7 December. She was to embark her air group, as well as Marine Fighting Squadron (VMF) 221, and ferry a cargo of miscellaneous aircraft to Pearl Harbor. The USS *Yorktown* (CV-5), USS *Ranger* (CV-4) and USS *Wasp* (CV-7), along with the aircraft escort vessel USS *Long Island* (AVG-1), were in the Atlantic Fleet, and the USS *Hornet* (CV-8), commissioned in late October 1941, had yet to carry out her shakedown cruise. The USS *Yorktown* would be the first Atlantic Fleet carrier to be transferred to the Pacific, sailing on 16 December 1941.

When the attack force left Tanaka Bay, they silently slipped away in dense fog, but the following day they were met with high winds and rolling seas, not the best of weather to launch strike aircraft. As they closed to within 400 miles of Pearl Harbor, still undetected, the weather worsened making it almost impossible to launch aircraft. In Washington, Ambassador Kichisaburo Nomura and Special Envoy Saburo Kurusu issued a formal declaration of war to US Secretary of State Cordell Hull at 0830 Hawaiian time. Admiral Nagumo had issued strict orders that the strikes were not to take place until after war had been declared – at 0800 Hawaiian time. Unfortunately amidst the confusion in the Japanese Embassy in Washington, coupled with unbelievable inefficiency of the staff, the declaration

Japanese mini-sub that was sunk by the USS *Monaghan* on 7 December 1941 at Pearl Harbor. (*USN*)

wasn't delivered on time. This then constituted an unprovoked attack which sent shockwaves throughout the world.

On 6 December 1941, the Japanese submarines came within 10 nautical miles of the mouth of Pearl Harbor and then, under the command of Commander Iwasa, the 'Special Attack Force' launched their midget submarines at about 0100. At 0342 local time, the minesweeper USS *Condor* (AMC-14), on a routine patrol, spotted one of the midget submarine's periscope south-west of the Pearl Harbor entrance buoy and alerted the destroyer USS *Ward* (DD-139). The *Ward* searched the area and at 0637 spotted the midget submarine and sank it, making the first American encounter of the war. A midget submarine on the north side of Ford Island had attacked and missed the seaplane tender USS *Curtiss* (AV-4) with her first torpedo and missed the attacking destroyer USS *Monaghan* (DD-354) with her second before being sunk by the destroyer at 0843.

A third midget submarine, manned by Ensign Kazuo Sakamaki and Chief Warrant Officer Kiyoshi Inagaki, grounded twice, once on the coral reef outside the

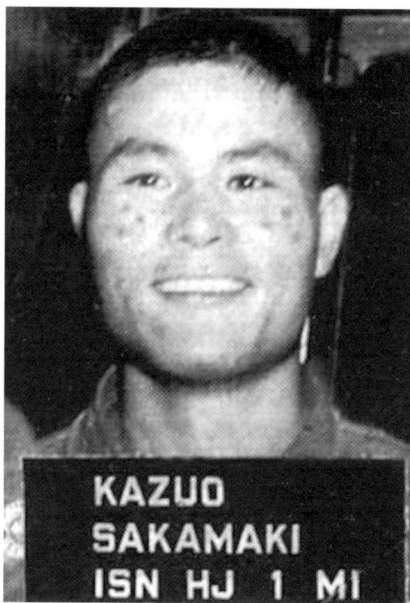

Photograph of a relieved-looking Ensign Kazuo Sakamaki as a PoW. He was the first Japanese prisoner of war and remained in custody throughout the war. (*USN*)

Aerial shot of a midget submarine aground on one of the Pacific islands. (*USN*)

Japanese midget submarine being raised from Pearl Harbor. (*USN*)

harbour entrance and again on the east side of Oahu, where it was captured on December 8. Ensign Kazuo Sakamaki had managed to get ashore and had been captured by Hawaiian National Guard Corporal David Akui, becoming the first Japanese prisoner of war. It is not known what happened to CWO Inagaki, one can only assume that he was either killed or drowned. A fourth midget submarine had been damaged by a depth-charge attack and abandoned by its crew before it could fire its torpedoes. (The fate of the crew is not known.) Japanese forces received a message from one of the midget submarines at 0041 on 8 December, claiming damage to one or more large warships inside Pearl Harbor. The fifth midget submarine was found in three parts in 1992, 2000 and 2001 by the Hawaiian Undersea Research Laboratory's submarines outside Pearl Harbor within the US amphibious warfare debris field. Both torpedoes were missing and their fate correlates to the reports of the firing of two torpedoes at the light cruiser USS *St. Louis* (CL-49) at 1004 at the entrance to Pearl Harbor and the possible firing at the destroyer USS *Helm* (DD-388) at 0821. This was probably the midget submarine spotted by the minesweeper USS *Condor* on 5 December. The fate of the two crewmembers is not known. The midget submarines were expected to cause havoc within Pearl Harbor, but in the end achieved absolutely nothing. The recovered midget submarines did, however, give the American Navy an insight into Japanese submarine development and technical ability.

Japanese midget submarine being hauled out of Taylor's Bay, Sydney Harbour. (*USN*)

On 7 December 1941, the six Japanese aircraft carriers turned into the wind and despite the heavy swell of the sea, launched their aircraft into the annals of history. The first wave of attacking aircraft were to drop their torpedoes from wave heigh on the primary targets, the battleships. The second wave of dive-bombers would attack the secondary targets, cruisers and destroyers, whilst fighter aircraft and dive-bombers would attack the airfields at Hickham, Wheeler, Kaneohe Bay, Ewa, Bellows Field and Ford Island. They were to strafe the airfields, destroying the parked aircraft, and intercept any fighter aircraft that managed to get airborne. This was the agreed order of battle as far as the Japanese commanders were concerned, but with the element of surprise on their side and meeting almost no resistance, for the next 15 minutes the air over Pearl Harbor suddenly became a mass of whirling dive-bombers and fighter aircraft. The raid was devastating to the Americans, nine battleships destroyed or damaged, two light cruisers damaged and three destroyers damaged, with total casualties of 2,403 killed and 1,178 wounded. On the airfields 188 aircraft were destroyed, 159 damaged, leaving just forty-three operational aircraft. Five Army Air Corps (AAC) pilots managed to get into the air in their P-40 Tomahawks and accounted for at least six enemy bombers and fighters for the loss of one of their own, flown by Lieutenant James Sterling.

There were three strategic targets that for some unknown reason were not attacked. These were the oil tanks where 4,500,000 barrels of oil were stored, the machine shops and nine submarines that were moored close together. Had the oil tanks been destroyed, this would have put Pearl Harbor out of commission as a naval base, so it is a mystery why they were not attacked.

The Japanese losses, comparatively, were minimal, fifteen dive- and high-level bombers, five torpedo-carrying aircraft and nine fighter aircraft were shot down by American fighter aircraft and groundfire. In addition all five midget submarines

USS *Wahoo* (SS238) on patrol. (*USN*)

USS *Wahoo* (SS 238) just having torpedoed a Japanese transport ship. (*USN*)

and their crews, with the exception of one who was captured, were lost. A second strike had been planned but Vice Admiral Nagumo had been informed that a large number of American bombers were within striking range and so it was decided to move the fleet out of the range of enemy bombers and back to the Inland Sea.

The attack on the US Battle Force at Pearl Harbor had put it out of action, leaving the west coast of America almost defenceless, with only fifty-one fleet class submarines as an operational naval defence. The American submarines had been designed and built primarily as advance scouts for the battle force, but fortunately they had the speed, endurance and weaponry to turn them into an attacking force. Orders came through from the Chief of Naval Operations (CNO) in Washington to carry out unrestricted attacks on all Japanese shipping especially merchant ships. The reasoning behind this was because Japan has very few natural resources, and had to rely heavily on its merchant ships to bring oil, coal, iron, medical and food supplies to its military garrisons scattered throughout the Pacific islands and to the Japanese mainland itself. The US submarine force went to work to strangle the Japanese lifeline, whilst back in America the shipyards went into overdrive to build new ships to replace the ones that had been lost.

As the attack on Pearl Harbor was taking place, word of it reached the 4,858-ton Norwegian freighter SS *Høegh Merchant*, carrying 80 tons of TNT and 20 tons of dynamite amongst other freight, and she was ordered to head for a British, Dutch or US port, so a course was set to return to San Francisco. The following day a radiogram was received by the *Høegh Merchant* via Vancouver radio, instructing them to go to Honolulu. In the late afternoon of 13 December they could see land straight ahead, but not knowing the situation they stopped about 20 miles from

SS *Hoegh Merchant*. (*Author*)

Makapuu Point to await further sailing instructions and daylight and were still lying up when the ship was torpedoed by the submarine I-4 in the early hours of 14 December. The torpedo struck on the starboard side close to the No. 3 hatch. The captain ordered the radio operator to contact the Naval station in Honolulu for assistance but the radio had been knocked out in the initial explosion. A fire started in the No. 3 hold followed by a violent explosion. Realising that if the fires spread to the other hold, which contained the explosives, the whole ship would explode, the captain ordered the crew to abandon ship and take to the lifeboats. All the members of the crew and the five passengers survived and were rescued soon afterwards by the destroyer USS *Trever* (DMS-16) and taken to Honolulu. A few hours later the *Hoegh Merchant* exploded and sank. The I-4 left the scene to join with other members of No. 2 Squadron and proceeded to shell Kahului, Maui and Hawaii, causing little damage.

The day after the attack on Pearl Harbor and despite the increased tightening of the defences, the I-7, under the command of Captain Kiichi Koizumi, managed to launch her aircraft on a dawn reconnaissance mission and was able to relay back a detailed description of the damage caused by the raid. Two days after the aerial attack had taken place Japanese submarines had some limited successes by sinking a number of merchant ships, but not one military vessel. The original idea was that after the aerial raid on Pearl Harbor the submarine squadrons would stay behind and patrol the waters off the Hawaiian Islands. They would attack enemy warships or merchant ships as the United States attempted to rebuild their fleet. Captain Kyūgorō Shimamoto, commander of Submarine Division Seven, complained

Torpedoes striking home on an unknown merchant ship. (*Author*)

bitterly that there was no basic or co-ordinated plan of action in place to carry this out. He pointed out that if one of his submarines sighted an enemy ship and was ordered to pursue and attack, its area of patrol was left open for other vessels to sail through unmolested. What was also very concerning was that invariably the top speed of Japanese submarines at the time was usually much less than that of the vessels they were pursuing and, more often than not, they were unable to make

Japanese submarine I-10 alongside a supply ship (*USN*)

Torpedoes striking home as seen through the periscope. (*Author*)

contact. Added to this was the increased activity of the enemy's rapidly improving ASW detection equipment on their aircraft and ships. On the face of it, the sinking of these merchant ships gave the impression that the Japanese submarines were in complete control of the seas in the Pacific, but amongst their victims there was not one warship or military vessel of any kind. The Japanese Army was quick to take advantage of the lack of success of the submarine force during the attack on Pearl Harbor, by pointing out the failure of the Japanese Navy to sink any of the US Navy's main warships i.e. aircraft carriers and heavy cruisers, insisting that they were now the driving force behind the war. The activities of the midget submarines was also analysed after the raid on Pearl Harbor and was found to have contributed absolutely nothing, but it did show that they had the ability to penetrate even the tightest of defences, something that would be re-kindled later in the war when the Japanese reverted to desperate kamikaze measures.

Two days later the I-10 sank the unarmed Panamanian motor vessel MV *Donerail* just 200 miles south-east of Hawaii. The ship, carrying thirty-three crew and seven passengers, was sunk by shellfire, leaving just eight survivors. On 10 December the I-9, under the command of Captain Akiyoshi Fujii, intercepted the 5,645-ton American freighter SS *Lahaina* and attacked it with shellfire. The crew abandoned ship and took to the lifeboats, although a number of them had been wounded in the attack. The ship somehow remained afloat and the following morning the crew re-boarded her, but the fires were out of control and the ship later exploded and sank. Two of the crew died in the explosion and two it is said committed suicide, but the remainder managed to reach Maui on 23 December.

At this early stage of the war the Japanese submarines were operating almost unopposed and any vessel within the vicinity of the Hawaiian Islands was considered to be fair game and would be attacked irrespective of nationally. December turned out to be almost a turkey shoot for the Japanese submarines, sinking the freighters SS *Manini*, *Pruse*, *Absaroka* and *Dorothy Phillips*, and the tankers SS *Emidio*, *Agwiworld*, *Montebello*, *Idaho*, *Larry Doheny* and *Connecticut*.

With the air assault against Pearl Harbor completed, the carrier strike force returned to Japan to re-supply and refuel, and prepare for the next phase, the attack against Colombo and Trincomalee in Ceylon (present-day Sri Lanka). In preparation for the attack, the Combined Fleet Headquarters needed to reconnoitre the waters around Ceylon, so Submarine Squadron 2, which consisted of the I-1 to I-7, was ordered into the area. With the exception of the I-1, the remaining six submarines set sail for the Indian Ocean. The I-7 was one of the few submarines that carried a scouting aircraft, which was to be used to overfly the coastal area looking for targets in preparation for air strikes, but because of a strong British air and naval presence the I-7 never managed to launch its aircraft and was unable to obtain any information, so was relegated to just patrolling the waters south-east of Ceylon.

The invasion of the Philippines on 8 December 1941 was approached by the submarine force in the same casual manner as they would later adopt during their patrols off the West Coast of America on 18 December 1941. Only two minelaying submarines from Submarine Squadron 6 were assigned to the invasion force, the I-23 and I-24. Their role in the invasion was to lay minefields, one at the entrance to Manila Bay by the I-23, which laid forty mines, the other by the I-24 in the Balabac Strait where thirty-nine mines were laid. Once this operation had been completed their role became to act as rescue boats for any downed aircrew and to intercept and sink any merchant ships in the area. The only success as far as this was concerned was said to be the sinking, by the I-24, of a small unknown cargo ship on 10 December.

With the Philippines now under the control of the Japanese Army, Vice Admiral Ibō Takahashi took command of a reorganised Philippine Invasion Force to support the invasion of the Dutch East Indies. Some of the submarines that were still in Hawaiian waters were ordered back to become part of the new offensive. The reducing of the submarine patrols in Hawaiian waters was once again a move that showed no strategic planning, because Pearl Harbor was continuing to be a hive of activity with US warships moving in and out unhindered. The rapid expansion of Japanese land forces throughout the Pacific was proving to be a problem for the Japanese Navy. Their submarine patrols were being stretched and weakened because of the vast oceans (Indian and Pacific) they were being asked to patrol and all the time the Americans were rebuilding their fleet.

Vice Admiral Ibō Takahashi split his submarine force into three groups, A, B and C: Group A was to patrol the Java Sea, B the Bay of Bengal and C to patrol between Java and Australia. Submarine Group A, under the command of Rear Admiral Setsuzō Yoshitomi, commander of Submarine Squadron 4, and Rear Admiral Chimaki Kōno commander of Submarine Squadron 5, made up the group. It consisted of six old I-class submarines, two coastal defence Ro type submarines and four I-class minelayer submarines. Submarine Group B, under the command of Rear Admiral Tadashige Daigo consisted of Submarine Squadron 3 and had six old I-class submarines. Submarine Group C, under the command of Rear Admiral Hisashi Ichioka, consisted of Submarine Squadron 2 and had seven I-class, I-1, I-2, I-3, I-4, I-5, I-6 and I-7.

The splitting of the force into three groups proved to be an effective one, as all three groups had considerable success with a total of forty merchant ships sunk and eight badly damaged, during the period of the invasion. However, two submarines however were lost when the I-24 was first depth-charged then rammed by the American sub-chaser the USS *Larchmount* (PC-487) after being forced to the surface, and the I-60 was depth-charged by the destroyer HMS *Jupiter*. This was the first sinking of a Japanese submarine by a British warship in the Second World War. There seemed to be no specific submarine operations other than those of the minelayers, the remainder of the submarine fleet, on the face of it, apparently did their own thing. This of course was not the case, but whatever their role was, there were no recorded torpedo attacks against any Allied warships during this period.

The Japanese attack on Pearl Harbor had been a severe blow to the US Navy and placed them in a defensive situation. The one weapon they had in the armoury that was immediately available and unaffected by the attack, was their submarine force. Even when there were rumblings of war, President Franklin D. Roosevelt had said that 'unrestricted submarine warfare would be undertaken in the event of a war with Japan'. Immediately the US submarine force was ordered to carry out attacks on Japanese merchant shipping as well as on their warships. Unknown to the Japanese the Allies had broken some of their codes and the intelligence obtained aided the Allied submarine force at the beginning and throughout the war. The Japanese Navy prepared for the war in a rather haphazardly way and were not really ready for what was to come when the Americans got back to full strength and joined forces with the Allies. By the time this happened it was too late, this was to become very apparent during the war in the Pacific, especially at Midway when the American Navy won a spectacular victory and irreversibly turned the tide of the war.

Prior to the attack on Pearl Harbor, the American Navy had been developing a programme of anti-submarine warfare (ASW). This programme was further honed by the development of ASDIC (Anti-Submarine Detection Investigation Committee), a sonar device, developed after the attack on Pearl Harbor, when

Japanese submarines were more easily detected from the noise they made whilst submerged. The Japanese had almost no knowledge and understanding of sound promulgation in relation to water temperature layers and noise reduction methods were not incorporated into the design of their submarines. For the Americans this meant that by careful manoeuvring and using their radar and sonar systems whilst submerged, they could dramatically reduce the chance of being detected before surfacing. The Japanese submarines, without ASW and ASDIC, would have to go to periscope depth for a rapid 360-degree visual reconnoitre before surfacing. This made them more vulnerable to attack because, although much faster on the surface and more heavily armed than their opponents, they had a much slower submerging speed and slower manoeuvrability. Towards the end of the war Japanese submarines were fitted with ASW equipment, but in comparison with the Americans it was extremely primitive and not terribly effective.

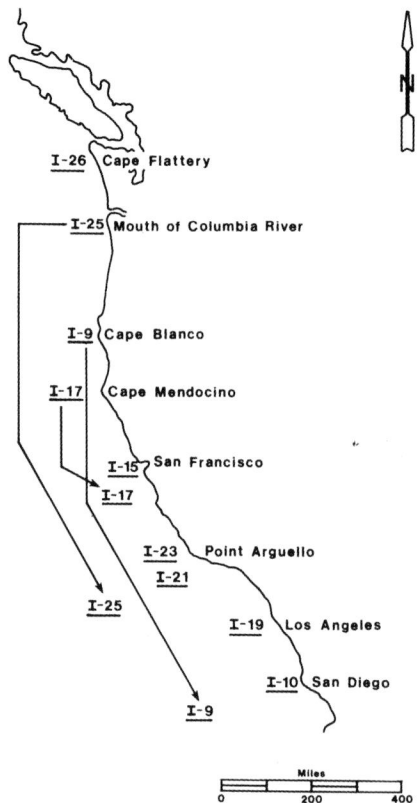

Map showing the location of the Japanese submarines that carried out shore bombardments.

One of the reasons why the Japanese submarines didn't have more success in sinking merchant ships around Hawaii at the time, was that Vice Admiral Mitsumi Shimizu, commander of the Sixth Fleet based at Kwajalein, was sending radio messages to the submarines informing them of impending air strikes. These radio messages were being monitored by the port authorities in Hawaii, who were able, to a large extent, to locate the position of the submarines that were receiving the messages. Armed with this information they were then able to re-route ships approaching the area where the submarines were thought to be operating.

The disappointment of not finding the aircraft carriers at Pearl Harbor caused the Japanese Naval High Command to completely re-think their strategy. Then information came through that the I-9 had sighted an American *Lexington*-type carrier accompanied by two cruisers east of Oahu making 20 knots and heading towards the West Coast of America. This was the first indication to Vice Admiral Shimizu that the American aircraft carriers had not been at Pearl Harbor. He

USS *Enterprise* about to launch her aircraft. (*USN*)

apparently had not known that they were not there, displaying a perfect example of the lack of communication within the Japanese military, even between senior officers of the Navy. Shimizu immediately ordered the I-10 and I-26 to give chase, to be followed by the I-9, I-15, I-17, I 21, I-23 and I-25. They were to set up a

I-70 damaged after a collision with the I-69. Later sunk by USN aircraft, it became the first loss of a submarine for Japan and the first victory for the USN. (*USN*)

picket line and patrol along the West Coast from Cape Flattery in the North to San Diego in the south. The I-9 was to go to Cape Blanco, I-10 to San Diego, the I-15 to San Francisco, I-17 to Cape Mendocino, I-19 to Los Angeles Harbour, I-21 to Estero Bay, I-23 to Monterey Bay, I-25 to the outlet of the Columbia River, Oregon and the I-26 to the Strait of Juan de Fuca on the border of America and Canada.

Amongst the three submarines ordered to intercept the USS *Enterprise* (CV-6), which according to intelligence reports was now heading towards the East Coast looking for a safe haven, was the I-70. The *Enterprise* was part of Task Force 8 which had left Pearl Harbor on 10 December after she and her escorts had re-fuelled and re-supplied. As they closed on the Task Force, Douglas SBD Dauntless dive-bombers from the *Enterprise* spotted the three submarines closing and went into the attack. The SBDs dived and bombed the I-70 submarine, causing enough damage as to prevent the submarine from diving. Some time later another SBD from the *Enterprise* found the I-70 still on the surface and sank her with a direct hit. There were no survivors. The remaining two submarines escaped and were recalled.

Information came through to submarine command at Kwajalein that the aircraft carrier USS *Saratoga* had been spotted in Hawaiian waters. The I-18, I-22 and I-24, which had just arrived at Kwajalein to re-supply, were ordered back to sea and on 4 January they left to find the USS *Saratoga*. On 9 January the I-18 sighted the aircraft carrier with her cruiser and destroyer escort near Johnson Island. Immediately the commander of Submarine Squadron 2 ordered all submarines in the area to form a picket line and to maintain reconnaissance operations on the area. Then word came through from Commander Michimune Inaba, commander of the I-6, that they had spotted the carrier and were closing in to fire her torpedoes. Three torpedoes were fired at the carrier and inside the submarine two explosions were heard. Within minutes of firing her torpedoes at the *Saratoga*, the I-6 came under

The USS *Camden* lies dead in the water after being torpedoed by the I-25 off Coos Bay, Oregon. (*US Coast Guard*)

an intense depth-charge attack from the escort destroyers, forcing the submarine to go deep to escape. A message was flashed to Kwajalein that the aircraft carrier had been sunk, but when the I-6 surfaced some hours later there was no sign of any enemy ships. The Japanese later discovered that although the *Saratoga* had been badly damaged in the attack, she had not sunk. The explosions had flooded three of her boiler rooms and killed six crewmen. Although listing quite badly, the *Saratoga* managed to reach Pearl Harbor where temporary repairs were made and her four twin 8in gun turrets removed and installed as part of the shore batteries. She then sailed for the Bremerton Navy Yard at Bangor, Maine for permanent repairs.

The temporary loss of the *Saratoga* was a bitter blow to the Navy so early into the Pacific war. It was fortunate that the Japanese submarines did not take advantage of this loss, because during the next couple of months Pearl Harbor became a hive of activity as warship after warship, including the aircraft carriers *Lexington*, *Enterprise* and *Yorktown*, steamed in and out, none of which were attacked by the submarines. In fact only a couple of merchant ships were sunk during this period, obviously considered the softer target. There were a number of reports of shellfire coming from the submarines but the damage they inflicted was considered to be minor. This highlighted the concerns voiced earlier by Captain Kyūgorō Shimamoto.

The failure of the submarine force to follow up on the aerial attack on Pearl Harbor set alarm bells ringing in the Japanese High Command, giving the Army more ammunition to criticise the Navy's failures and enabling it to become the more dominant power. It became obvious that Pearl Harbor's garrison was to be increased substantially thus giving the Americans a strong foothold in the Pacific, so a number of Japanese submarines were sent to patrol the West Coast. The submarines were on station for less than a month and during that period only sank five merchant ships and damaged five others, but the psychological impact it had on the residents of the West Coast was quite considerable. Stories of invasions were rampant and up and down the West Coast and residents prepared themselves for something which. as we all now know, never happened.

Four days after the Japanese attack on Pearl Harbor, Germany declared war against the United States. The Tripartite agreement between Japan, Italy and Germany only briefly covered naval cooperation, but with the declaration of war by Germany, Japan discussed their respective submarine operations in the Indian Ocean. The head of the U-boat arm of the German Kriegsmarine, Commodore (later Admiral) Karl Dönitz, immediately put forward a proposal to increase the building programme for the construction of Type X-B minelayers. His thoughts were to use the minelayer submarines around the Cape of Good Hope, off Colombo and Singapore, thus reducing the need for U-boats in the Indian Ocean.

The Allies had been monitoring Japanese radio traffic between Germany and Japan and realised that submarines were to be used for the transportation of vital goods and technology between the two powers. In a message to the American Naval High Command, the British Admiralty sent the following message:

> There are strong grounds for believing plans have been made by Germany and Japan for large scale exchange of vital commodities. If these plans succeed, German's principal deficiencies, in particular rubber, tin, wolfram, hemp, hides and vegetable oils will be largely made good by Japan. The latter will obtain in return chemicals, specialised machinery, prototypes of naval and military material blueprints and instructions for plant and processes and expert technicians. Similar exchanges are believed to be contemplated with Italy.

A number of these missions were undertaken by both Axis powers, but with little success as almost all the submarines that took part were either intercepted and sunk or, as in the case of the I-30, struck a mine and was destroyed. These missions are described in greater detail later in the book.

One of the major stumbling blocks for the Japanese forces was that the US Marine Corps were still holding Wake Island. This tiny atoll was an important site for an airfield and a submarine base, and was in the process of being completed when the Japanese bombed it the day before Pearl Harbor was attacked. This attack was a prelude for a bitter battle that lasted from 8 December to 23 December 1941. On 11 December the Japanese attempted an invasion of the island but were beaten back. During the battle they lost two destroyers, the *Hayate* and *Kisaragi*, and a third, the *Yubari*, was badly damaged by the 5in guns of the shore battery. Ten days later a second invasion was mounted and this time, after ferocious fighting, the garrison on Wake Island surrendered but the loss of life to the Japanese Army was estimated at between 700 and 900.

The Japanese submarine force suffered no better. On 12 December three submarines, consisting of the RO-60, RO-62 and RO-66 under the command of Captain Yoshiyasu Matsuo, had left Kwajalein to assist in the assault on Wake Island. Just 25 miles south-west of Wake Island, the RO-66 somehow collided with the RO-62 and sank. Only three of RO-62's crew, who were on watch at the time, survived after being thrown into the water by the impact. The RO-60, on returning

RO-66 having what appears to be a laundry day. (*Author*)

to Kwajalein, hit the reef outside the harbour during heavy weather and also sank. The crew were rescued by other craft in the area with no loss of life.

As the war progressed the Japanese expressed an increasing interest into taking over the 'Southern Important Territories' as they called Malaya, Burma, Philippines and the Dutch East Indies. On 8 December 1941 the Twenty-fifth Army Corps had landed on the Malay Peninsula supported by Submarine Squadron 4, under the command of Rear Admiral Setsuzo Yoshitomi, and Submarine Squadron 5 under the command of Rear Admiral Tadashige Daigo. Between them they had a total of fifteen submarines, twelve old fleet boats, the I-53, I-54, I-55, I-56, I-57, I-59, I-60, I-62, I-64, I-65 and I-66, two coastal defence submarines RO-33 and RO-34 and two minelayers I-21 and I-22. A picket line was thrown around the Malay Peninsula together with the laying of a mine field giving the Japanese total control of the seas in that area and were able to detect any British reinforcements that might come. It was during the positioning of the picket line that the battleship HMS *Prince of Wales* and the battlecruiser HMS *Repulse* were detected by the I-65 and pursued. Information was fed back giving the position and speed of the two warships until contact was lost during a rain squall. All available submarines were ordered into the area to search for the two warships.

The following day the I-58, commanded by Lieutenant Commander Sōshichi Kitamura, made contact with the two warships and closed in to attack. Once in position he fired five torpedoes but all missed. Determined to catch the two warships, he surfaced and continued to track them but lost them after both warships increased their speed. The information that was fed back gave rise to an air search for the

HMS *Prince of Wales* and HMS *Repulse* underway with a destroyer escort. (*Author*)

two warships that subsequently ended with them being sunk by Japanese bombers on 10 December 1941.

Word came through to the Japanese High Command that both the ships had been sunk by bombers, but this was not relayed to the two submarines forces searching for the ships. It was not until 27 December that word was finally passed to the searchers to call off the hunt for the two ships. Another example of the continuing lack of communication between the Army and the Navy. During this period only two of the submarines had any success and that was the I-56, which sank a small cargo ship, and the I-66 that sank a Dutch submarine, thought to have been either the O-16 or K-XVII. (Both Japanese submarines were later sunk as a result of hitting mines just off the Gulf of Siam.)

The success of the Malayan invasion force was solely down to the Army and its air force, the Navy's role being limited to patrolling the waters around the invasion area to warn of enemy activity in the shape of reinforcements. Such was the complacency after the success of Pearl Harbor, that a number of the submarines that were patrolling the Hawaiian waters, were recalled to patrol new areas. This was despite the increased traffic of American warships going in and out of Pearl Harbor.

The British counter-attack, which was intended to take place on 10 December, never happened after the sinking of *Prince of Wales* and *Repulse*, thus taking away their main naval threat. This gave the control of the seas around the area to the Japanese Navy who were able to move around almost unrestricted.

At the beginning of January 1942, with preparations underway for the offensive on Southeast Asia, two submarine squadrons, Nos 4 and 5, were assigned to the invasion force, under the command of Rear Admiral Setsuzō Yoshitomi (Squadron 4) and Rear Admiral Tadashige Daigo (Squadron 5). Squadron 4 consisted of the I-53, I-54, I-55, I-56, I-57 and I-58, and two minelayers I-21 and I-22. Squadron 5 consisted of the I-159, I-60, I-62, I-64, I-65 and I-66. Group A, consisting of

I-58 on sea trials. (*Author*)

I-9 getting ready for sea trials showing her hangar in front of the conning tower. (*Author*)

the submarines I-121, I-122, I-123 and I-124, was assigned to minelaying duties in Australian waters off Port Darwin and in the Torres Strait. On completing their task the group were in the process of returning to Davao in Philippines, when they were contacted by radio informing them that ships of the US Asiatic Fleet had been spotted in the Flores Sea just east of Java. Then the I-124, under the command of Lieutenant Commander Koichi Kichigami, reported spotting the heavy cruiser the USS *Houston* (CA-30) but was unable to close in to attack because of her heavy destroyer escort. The *Houston* was later torpedoed and sunk by Japanese warships in the Sunda Strait. The I-124 was later sunk with all hands by the destroyer USS *Edsall* (DD-219) and the Australian corvette HMAS *Deloraine*. It was later discovered that the submarine had sunk in just 40ft of water, so US Navy divers went inside the boat and were able to recover valuable charts and codebooks.

At the beginning of March 1942 another attack/reconnaissance on Pearl Harbor was being planned, this time using two Kawanishi H8K 'Emily' flying boats flown by Lieutenant Hisao Hashizume, who was in command of the mission and Ensign Shosuke Sasao flying the second aircraft. The submarine I-22 was tasked with preparing a fuel base en route for the flying boats on an area known as the French Frigate Shoal Atoll. She was also required to carry out a preliminary reconnaissance between Midway Island and Hawaii. The submarines I-15, I-16 and I-26 took on board supplies of aviation fuel and delivered them to the atoll. The I-9 was then sent to a position between Jaluit in the Marshal Islands and the French Frigate Shoal Atoll to act as a radio homing station. The two flying boats were sent to Wotje Atoll in the Marshal Islands, where each aircraft was re-fuelled and loaded with four 250kg (550lb) bombs. From there, they flew 3,100km (1,900 miles) to French Frigate Shoals. They touched down at the atoll on the evening of 4 March and refuelled again before taking off to carry out the

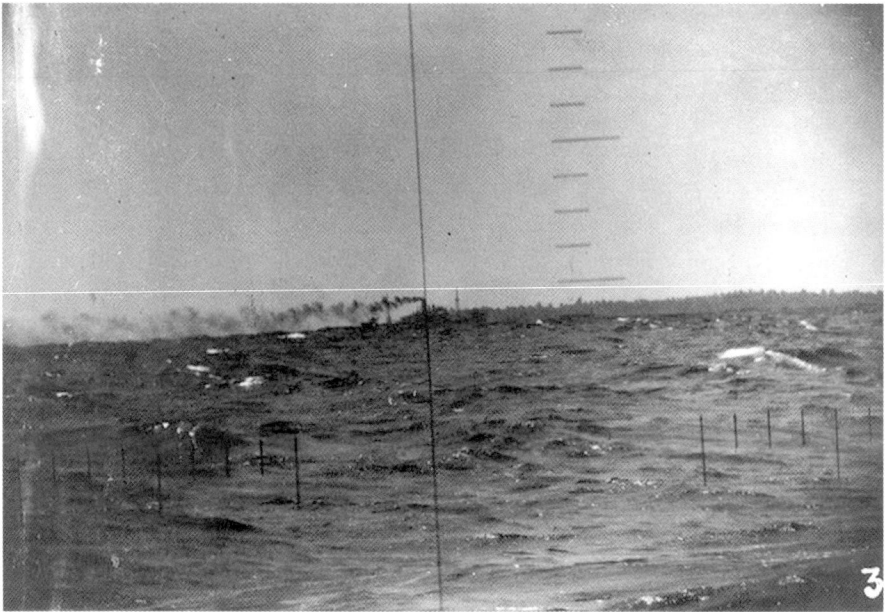

Japanese view through the periscope of ships in Wotje Atoll in the Marshall Islands. (*Author*)

attack on Pearl Harbor, a distance of 900km (560 miles). In addition to their reconnaissance mission, they were to bomb the 'Ten-Ten' dock – named for its length, 1,010ft (310m) – at the Pearl Harbor naval base to disrupt salvage and repair efforts. Thick cloud over Oahu confused the pilots so, using the Kaena Point Lighthouse as a reference, Lieutenant Hashizume, having lost sight of his wingman, decided to attack from the north. Ensign Sasao did not hear the order to attack and decided to go along the coast of Oahu. Thinking he was close to the naval base, Lieutenant Hashizume dropped his bombs, which landed on the slopes of the extinct volcano Tantalus Peak, shattering some windows at a local school. It is assumed that Ensign Sasao dropped his bombs in the sea, because there were no other reports of bombs being dropped. The two flying boats set a course for Wotje Atoll, but Lieutenant Hashizume's aircraft had suffered some hull damage when taking off from the French Frigate Shoals. He was concerned that the base there would not have the facilities to carry out the repairs so decided to fly non-stop to his home base at Jaluit Atoll, making it the longest bombing mission in history up to then. Japanese radio reported that the attack caused considerable damage to the Pearl Harbor Naval Facility with thirty deaths and seventy injured. This was typical of the misinformation and propaganda that was being fed back to the Japanese people. A second attack was planned for the following day, but whilst their 'attack' on Pearl Harbor was taking place, an American task force had attacked Wake Island. The submarines were ordered to leave the atoll and take-up positions to wait for the returning task force.

On 11 March 1942, some 60 miles south of Padang, west of Sumatra, the I-2 sighted the 4,360-ton armed British freighter the SS *Chilka* on a voyage from Calcutta to Padang. The I-2 surfaced on *Chilka*'s port quarter and opened fire with both deck guns. The *Chilka* returned fire, but after her only gun was disabled, the captain ordered the engines stopped and signalled his surrender. The I-2 ceased firing and allowed the survivors to abandon ship. The *Chilka* sank soon afterwards. The fate of the survivors is not known.

Early in the morning of 7 April 1942, 150 miles south-west of Colombo, the I-3 sighted five Allied merchant ships sailing eastward and one merchant and a tanker on westbound course. After a fruitless chase lasting several hours the I-3 surfaced on the 4,872-ton British armed steam merchant SS *Elmdale* en route from Karachi to Colombo. The I-3 fired a total of thirty-nine 5.5in shells and four torpedoes, scoring just fourteen shell hits, the torpedoes missed and she failed to finish off her target. The following day 300 miles off Colombo, the I-3 came across the British armed merchant ship the SS *Fultala* sailing from Calcutta to Karachi with 8,000 tons of coal. After receiving one Type 89 torpedo hit the 5,051-ton merchantman sank. Her entire crew were later rescued.

Whilst on patrol, the I-7 came across the MV *Glenshiel* and sank her with torpedoes and gunfire. The destroyer HMS *Fortune* rescued the entire crew. Despite these minimal successes on lightly-armed merchant ships that were easy prey to the well-armed submarines, the information that they accumulated during the reconnaissance patrols was of great assistance to Admiral Nagumo's air attacks when they sank the light aircraft carrier HMS *Hermes* and the two heavy cruisers HMS *Cornwall* and HMS *Dorsetshire*. The loss of these three warships was a bitter blow to the British as it weakened their naval strength in the Indian Ocean enormously. The British could not afford to send any more warships to the Indian Ocean because of their heavy commitment against Germany in the Atlantic and North Sea.

The relative ease with which the Japanese had taken the 'Southern Important Territories' heralded a rethinking of the strategic plan with which they had started out. The Imperial Army's thinking was to leave in place the existing plan, but Admiral Yamamoto, Commander-in-Chief of the Combined Fleet, argued that they should not become complacent and that the fleet should be on the offensive with the aim to take over the Hawaiian Islands, thus depriving the Americans of a very important forward base. The Naval Headquarters Staff advocated expanding toward the south-east, occupying the Samoan Islands and Fiji with the intention of cutting off the vital communication links between Australia and America. It also advocated exercising caution about expanding too rapidly because it would ultimately stretch the army to such an extent that it would be extremely difficult for the Navy to keep it supplied.

In March 1942 Vice Admiral Teruhisa Komatsu replaced Vice Admiral Mitusmi Shimizu as commander of the Sixth Fleet, giving him complete control over the submarine force. Both Komatsu and Shimizu were strong advocates for attacking merchant ships, totally ignoring the submarine commanders who said that the aircraft carriers, battleships and cruisers were more of a threat than unarmed merchantmen. The intransigence of Admiral Komatsu would eventually lead to the further weakening of the Japanese submarines effectiveness in the Pacific and Indian Oceans.

At the beginning of 1942 Japanese senior naval staff were looking at using the midget submarines for reconnaissance and attacks, in areas from which the Allies were actively deploying ships and men. They considered an area from Sydney, Australia to Madagascar. The I-10, I-16, I-18 and I-20, under the overall command of Captain Noboru Ishizaki and each carrying a small reconnaissance aircraft, set out to patrol the Indian Ocean in search of enemy ships. For over a month the submarines searched but without success, then a reconnaissance aircraft, a Yokosuka E14Y1 'Glen' from the I-10, spotted a Royal Navy group at Diégo Suarez, Madagascar. Swooping down and almost landing on the water between HMS *Ramillies* and the cruiser HMS *Frobisher*, they identified a '*Queen Elizabeth*' class battleship, a cruiser, a large tanker and a number of other smaller ships that were at anchor in the harbour. The '*Queen Elizabeth*' class battleship was in fact the *Royal Sovereign* class battleship HMS *Ramillies*. On their return to the I-10, Captain Ishizaki ordered the I-20 to launch a midget submarine attack on both *Ramillies* and *Frobisher*. Three submarines, the I-16, I-18 and I-20 carrying Ha-3 and Ha-4 midget submarines, were tasked with this mission and their target was the harbour at Diego Suarez, Madagascar. On the morning of 30 May 1942 the three midget-carrying submarines immediately headed for Madagascar and prepared to attack the group. The submarines would get as close as they could to the entrance of the harbour and then launch their midget submarines. Realising that the aircraft had been on a reconnaissance mission and had already reported its findings back, *Ramillies* and *Frobisher* weighed anchor. *Frobisher* put to sea, whilst *Ramillies* steamed

Japanese submarine HA-3 seen here in 1911 on trials. (*USN*)

around the harbour, finally anchoring in another position alongside the tanker MV *British Loyalty*. In the meantime an air search was carried out to try and find out where the aircraft had come from, but nothing was found. In this early part of the war aircraft-carrying submarines were still unknown to the Allies. The I-6, I-8, I-18 and I-20 were to release their Ha midget submarines when nine miles from the harbour. They were to negotiate the submarine nets and make their way into the harbour. The two-man crews were told than in the event of the mission not being completed they were to scuttle their submarine and to then swim back to the mother submarine where they would be picked up. To expect the two men to swim nine miles back to the mother submarine was complete nonsense and each mission was considered to be a one-way trip. The I-8 was the first to launch her midget submarine, but the engine failed to start, whilst the I-18's midget submarine failed to even reach the harbour entrance.

The I-20 launched her midget submarine and when within range, it fired a Type 98 'Long Lance' torpedo with its 350kg warhead hitting the *Ramillies* just forward of 'A' turret, opening up a 30ft by 30ft hole. The damage was considerable, knocking out all electrical power. The forward magazines and shell rooms were flooded and the 6in armour plate immediately above the point of the explosive contact was buckled. The midget submarine then fired a second torpedo at *Ramillies* but hit the *British Loyalty*, which had weighed anchor after the first attack and had inadvertently moved into the torpedo's path. The tanker was hit aft in the engine room and sank to the bottom close to the Antsirana lighthouse with the loss of five crew members and one gunner. In December 1942 she was refloated, repaired and towed to Addu Atoll where she was used as an oil storage hulk. After controlling the flood of water coming into the ship, the *Ramillies* immediately weighed anchor and moved to a narrower section of the harbour and moored in a position giving the narrowest angle to try and limit the possibility of another attack. In the meantime the crew of the midget submarine, Lieutenant Saburo Akieda and Petty Officer

An image from an escort ship of a B-25 Mitchell taking off from the USS *Hornet*. (USN)

Masami Takemoto, realising that they could not get back to the I-20, beached their submarine near to a pre-arranged pick-up point. After trying to buy food from a nearby village they were informed on and were shot dead by Royal Marines after refusing to surrender. The Japanese High Command later claimed to have sunk the *Queen Elizabeth* class battleship *Ramillies*, but the Admiralty counter-claimed by saying quite truthfully that there was no *Queen Elizabeth* class battleship at Diego Suarez and that there were no ships sunk.

After the relative success of the 'Southern Important Territories' campaign, discussions between the Imperial Army and the Navy took place about what to do next. The Army wanted to revert back to the pre-war National Defence Policy of the Empire by withdrawing some of the forces to strengthen Japan's defences. Admiral Yamamoto objected, saying that what was required was a more offensive action rather than a defensive one. If Japan was to go on the defensive it would give the Americans time to strengthen their naval fleet, and that would be a disaster for Japan. The Army opposed the suggestion, saying that the Navy had been so weakened as not to be a threat to the Americans, and that they would be better served supporting and supplying the army's invasion forces as they moved through Asia. This only went to show the ongoing festering hostility between the Army and the Navy and their inability to work together.

In April 1942, Japan suffered a shock when sixteen B-25B Mitchell bombers, led by Lieutenant Colonel (later General) James Doolittle, took off from the deck of the aircraft carrier USS *Hornet* (CV-8) and bombed mainland Japan. Some of the bombers attacked the centre of Tokyo, the city's docklands, outlying steel plants and oil refineries. The remaining bombers attacked industrial facilities at Osaka, Kobe, Nagoya and Yokohama and, although inflicting some serious structural damage to the Kawasaki aircraft factory at Yokohama, the raid had minimum effect with regard to material and production. But the war had been taken to the Japanese mainland and the effect on the morale of the Japanese people was devastating. All sixteen B-25B bombers crash-landed in China after running out of fuel and their crews rescued. Up to this point the Japanese people had been led to believe that their military were in complete control of the war and that their homeland was safe from attack. The raid raised serious doubts about the military's ability to defend against long-range strikes and the reliability of the information they were being given on how the war was progressing. Admiral Yamamoto took advantage of the incident and maintained that an offensive strategy was now required and not a defensive one, but not until a strong defensive perimeter could be established. The attack by the 'Doolittle Raiders' on the Japanese mainland should have had the effect of endorsing a defence strategy, but it did the opposite and, very reluctantly, the Army agreed with Yamamoto's recommendation that an offensive was needed. Immediately plans were drawn up for attacks on Midway, the Aleutian Islands and Port Moresby. Almost immediately ten submarines of the 1st and 3rd Submarine

Groups were sent to set up picket lines A and B in an effort to intercept any US naval ships on their way to Midway. Picket line A was to cover the area 700 miles south-east of Midway whilst picket line B covered the area 700 miles along the south-east-north-east sector. All submarines were due to be in place by 30 May, but because of a number of difficulties, including confusing communications and orders, they were deployed piecemeal with the result that the majority of the submarines arrived late.

One mission that brought the reality of war home to the American people was on the night of 19 February 1942, when the I-17 under the command of Commander Kozo Nishino, covertly surfaced off Point Loma, San Diego, to determine her position after arriving from the Kwajalein Atoll. The submarine then submerged and headed north along the coast of California. Two days later on the evening of 23 February, she surfaced a few hundred yards off a beach 10 miles (16km) west of Santa Barbara, California within the Ellwood Oil Field area. Over the next 20 minutes, the I-17 fired a salvo of seventeen shells from her 14cm gun at the giant

Soldiers examining one of the shell holes in the sand after the attack on the Richfield Oil Depot, Santa Barbara, California by the submarine I-21. (*USA*)

Richfield aviation fuel storage tanks on the bluff top behind the beach. The shots were wild and aimless, one of the shells landing more than a mile inland. The closest shell exploded in a field 30 yards (27m) from one of the tanks. The shelling only managed to inflict minor damage to a pier and a pump house, but the fact that the mainland had been attacked triggered an 'invasion' scare along the West Coast. The following night, the anti-aircraft defences around Los Angeles exploded into action in response to an imagined invasion (later to be known as 'The Battle of Los Angeles', against a supposed UFO attack). During a 30-minute fusillade, anti-aircraft guns hurled 1,440 rounds of 3in (76mm) and 37mm ammunition into the night sky, and about 10 tons of shrapnel and unexploded ammunition fell back on the city causing some damage and minor injuries to the inhabitants. The damage caused by the I-17 was miniscule compared to the psychological effects to the residents of California. Propaganda information being fed to the Japanese people, gave the impression that the shelling of installations in America was causing a tremendous amount of damage, and creating widespread panic amongst the American people.

As the war gathered momentum and Japanese forces made rapid advances, so their supply lines became more and more stretched. American submarines were now coming to the fore and were hitting the merchant ships loaded with medical supplies, food and ammunition, whilst the Japanese submarine force showed little, if any, decisive or assertive action.

Japanese Naval High Command planners, who were in the process of putting together an attack on Guadalcanal, were of the opinion that the element of surprise was on their side and that the American carriers were in the South Pacific. But in reality they had no idea where the American carrier forces were and were making their decisions blindly based solely on predictability. They calculated that if the Americans were alerted to an attack, their carriers would have to call in at Pearl Harbor to re-fuel, re-supply and re-provision before going on to Midway, but it was calculated that they would not arrive until after the Japanese attack and the two submarine picket lines, A and B, would be in place. Picket line A, was established by seven submarines from the 1st Submarine Group and stretched for 100 miles in a north-east-south-west direction just 200 miles east of Malaita and north-west of Guadalcanal. Picket line B was 30 miles long and about 150 miles from Guadalcanal and had just three attack submarines patrolling it. They were supported by three minelaying submarines from the 7th Submarine Group stationed east of Malaita and two coastal submarines that patrolled the waters between Guadalcanal and Malaita. What the Japanese High Command still didn't realise was that their radio traffic was constantly being monitored and that almost all their codes and cyphers had been broken. It was discovered later when their attack on Guadalcanal started, that the American carrier task force had actually passed through both A and B picket lines before the submarines had arrived to take up station, and it was this weakness in their deployment that was one of the contributing factor to the defeat of the Japanese Carrier Force.

Chapter 5

Coral Sea and Guadalcanal

With the advance of General McArthur's forces at Lea in New Guinea the need to rush more and more reinforcements and supplies to the area increased. The 7th Submarine Group, under the command of Rear Admiral Jiro Harada, was assigned to the task together with some destroyers. During the defence of Lae over 1,000 troops and 1,500 tons of supplies were transported by the submarines and surface ships of the Japanese Navy, but to no avail as within weeks the garrison there was overwhelmed by McArthur's forces.

The Aleutians campaign, which had started in April 1942, was also underway at the time with five submarines from the 1st Submarine Group patrolling the waters of North America and Canada. Although sending back information regarding the weather and some aircraft movements, they had no successes. They were relieved in June 1942 by seven of the old I-class submarines from the 2nd Submarine Group. They had some limited success when the I-7 and the I-25 each sank a small cargo ship.

At the beginning of April 1942, the Japanese Fourth Fleet, commanded by Vice Admiral Shigeyoshi Inoue, had attacked Port Moresby in an attempt to take control of New Guinea. The fleet, consisting of the large aircraft carriers *Shokaku* and *Zuikaku*, and the light aircraft carrier *Shoho*, together with destroyers and troop transports, were accompanied by submarines from the 21st Submarine Flotilla (RO-33 and RO-34), Submarine Squadron 8 (I-29), Submarine Squadron 11 (I-28) and the 3rd Submarine Flotilla (I-22 and I-24). This attack was to become known as the Battle of the Coral Sea.

The I-29. (*Author*)

At the beginning of May 1942 a decisive sea battle took place in the Coral Sea. The Japanese submarines' part in it, as far as attacking American warships was concerned, was almost negligible. Japanese forces had already landed on the island of Tulagi, which was adjacent to Guadalcanal, with the intention of establishing a seaplane base, which would support the planned invasion of Port Moresby. On 2 May the submarine I-21 was spotted by a reconnaissance SBD Dauntless aircraft from the aircraft carrier USS *Yorktown* (CV-10). The Dauntless attacked the submarine but it managed to crash-dive and escape. The I-21 had obviously not spotted the carrier group, because they failed to launch their Aichi E16A1 Zuiun spotter aircraft, which would most certainly have found the carriers, as they were only 30 miles away. What is more surprising is that the submarine commander must have realised that the aircraft had to have come from an aircraft carrier. So why he never followed up on the incident will never be known.

In an attempt to rush reinforcements to New Guinea, Japanese transport ships escorted by destroyers, were sent but were attacked by US Army Air Force (USAAF) aircraft in the Bismark Sea. Once again the coded radio traffic between the Japanese Navy and Army had been intercepted and decoded, giving the Americans almost two weeks' notice of the intended movement of the troops. Eight transport ships and four destroyers were sunk by USAAF bombers, with the loss of over 3,000 men. A number of submarines, including the I-17 and I-26, were immediately dispatched to the area to look for survivors, but only 200 were rescued. This was disastrous for the Japanese Army as they could ill afford troop losses of that magnitude, but also from the Navy perspective, the loss of the transport ships and destroyers, together with their crews, was also devastating.

The Japanese Navy, with their light carrier *Shoho* accompanied by the two large carriers the *Shokaku* and *Zuikaku*, were surprised to encounter the USS *Enterprise* and *Yorktown*. There followed the first carrier-versus-carrier battle in naval history and it is interesting to note that neither ships ever saw each other as the Battle of the Coral Sea was a battle fought in the air. The Japanese claimed a tactical victory as they had sunk the *Lexington* and badly damaged the *Yorktown*. However the Japanese suffered serious losses of aircraft and their crews from the aircraft carriers *Zuikaku* and *Shoho*. The *Shoho* was also badly damaged as was the *Shokaku*. All three carriers were withdrawn and returned to Japan for repairs and refurbishment. Repairing the aircraft carriers was comparatively easy, but replacing the lost aircraft and their crews was a different matter altogether, as aircraft manufacturing and pilot training was not a programme that could be rushed, although in the last few months of the war such was the demand for pilots that a large number of aircrew were thrown into the war with barely a couple of hours of flight training. The absence of both aircraft carriers and their aircraft during the Port Moresby campaign was instrumental in giving the Americans a strategic victory in the Coral Sea engagement. With regard to the Battle of the Coral Sea, none of the Japanese submarines were in a position to engage with the enemy during the battle, the nearest one was the newly-built I-28, which was suffering engine trouble.

Vice Admiral Komatsu's headquarters ordered the I-28 to return to Truk with I-22 and I-24. The I-28 gave her position and reported that she was still having trouble with her diesel engines, this was the last message received from her. The message was picked up by American code-breakers and relayed to US Naval Headquarters. The submarine USS *Tautog* (SS-199) was ordered to intercept the Japanese ships returning from the Battle of the Coral Sea, including the damaged aircraft carrier *Shokaku*. Soon after receiving the message the *Tautog* sighted two I-class submarines (probably I-22 and I-24) separately heading towards Truk. Then the *Tautog* sighted a third Japanese submarine with I-28 clearly marked on its conning tower, making 12 knots, on the same northerly track. The *Tautog* fired two Mark XIV torpedoes and one hit, halting the I-28 and leaving her dead in the water. With both her engines stopped and taking on water, the Japanese submarine took on a heavy list to starboard. At least fifteen officers and sailors appeared on the bridge. The *Tautog* closed to 800 yards and fired another torpedo, hitting the submarine right under the conning tower. Within minutes the I-28 had sunk with all hands. Around the same time, the I-21, which was still operating in the area, reported that she had sunk two merchant ships, the freighters SS *John Adams* and the SS *Chloe*.

The Japanese submarines were now all in desperate need of fuel and maintenance and a number had to return to their base at Kwajalein. One of these was the I-64 who was on her way back when the USS *Triton* (SS-201) caught her cruising on the surface. The *Triton* fired a single torpedo from a range of over 6,000 yards hitting her amidships. The I-64 exploded and sank with all hands south of Shikoku off the coast of Japan.

On 30 May 1942, the Japanese submarine I-31 was sunk in a surface action with the destroyer USS *Edwards* (DD-950) north-east of Chichagof Harbour. After an intense battle the Japanese surface ships that were attempting to supply their troops abandoned the idea of re-supplying the Japanese garrisons on the Aleutian Islands using surface ships. Such was the problem of getting food supplies and ammunition to the Japanese troops that had secured the island of Attu, that the submarine's role was now reduced to delivering supplies to the beleaguered troops and they were finding that increasingly difficult. The rapid deterioration of Japanese troops through malnutrition and disease on Guadalcanal and other islands was mainly due to supply boats being intercepted and sunk. On the Aleutian island of Attu, food, medical supplies and ammunition were not being delivered and so the decision was made to withdraw the troops from the island at the end of February. The Japanese had already lost the I-1, I-3, I-18, I-31, I-178, I-182, RO-34, RO-102 and RO-107 that month, most of which were attempting to deliver supplies or troops to the beleaguered garrison. With the loss of the troops and surface ships, the Japanese High Command decided that troop and supply movements using surface vessels

Japanese midget submarine beached on Guadalcanal alongside the Japanese transport *Yamazuki Maru*. (*USA*)

was too risky and so experiments were carried out using submarines. Trials with a small 55ft landing craft barge (Daihatsu) attached to the deck of the submarines carrying supplies were started, but amounted to nothing. Also trialled was a 155ft torpedo-shaped container (*Unkatō*) that was towed behind the submarine, but this proved to be fraught with control problems and the idea was abandoned.

Japanese supply submarine with two landing craft on her deck. (*Author*)

Daihatsu landing barge on the deck of an I-class submarine. (*Author*)

At the end of May plans were drawn up for Operation Aleutians, Operation Port Moresby and Operation Midway. Word came through that American forces were on the move, so ten submarines from the 1st and 3rd Submarine Groups were assigned to set up two picket lines: line A stretched 200 miles and 700 miles south-east of Midway, line B stretched 200 miles and 700 miles east of Midway along a north-north-east line, to intercept the American fleet. The Japanese Naval High Command were convinced that the American aircraft carriers were still operating in the South Pacific which meant that they would have to put into Pearl Harbor to refuel and re-provision. This meant that all the submarines would be in position in plenty of time to intercept them. They also thought that the American fleet would leave Pearl Harbor after the Japanese assault on Midway had begun. One again this '*laissez faire*' attitude of the Japanese High Command would cause problems between the Army and the Navy. One of the most decisive battles of the war was about to begin.

In the meantime a second strike force consisting of the I-21, I-22, I-24, I-27 and I-29 was making its way towards Australia and Sydney Harbour. Stored in a hangar aboard the I-21 was an Aichi E16A1 floatplane (Allied code name 'Paul') and this was launched to carry out a reconnaissance of Sydney Harbour. On its return the pilot reported that there were a number of large warships at anchor in the harbour. On 1 June 1942 when just seven miles off the entrance to the harbour, the remaining four submarines launched their midget submarines. As

I-15 surfacing with two *Kaiten* submarines on her deck about to be launched. (*Author*)

they approached the entrance the lead submarine noticed that the submarine net was open and proceeded to lead the others through. The last midget submarine, however, somehow got itself inextricably entangled in the net and was lost. The remaining three proceeded into the harbour and spotted two heavy cruisers, the USS *Chicago* (CA-29), which had just returned from the Battle of the Coral Sea, and HMAS *Canberra*. One of the midget submarines fired its torpedo but it got stuck in the launch tube and exploded. This immediately alerted the crews of the two cruisers who immediately opened fire with a barrage of 8in shells, forcing

Supply container that was towed behind a submarine. (*JMSDF*)

Side view of a supply container. (*Author*)

the two remaining midget submarines to the surface. In a panic the crews of the submarines launched their torpedoes, one ran ashore and failed to explode, the second hit HMAS *Kattabul*, a converted ferry, killing nineteen sailors. Seconds later the two midget submarines were blown out of the water. The whole mission was a disaster and the five mother submarines were recalled. The bodies of the Japanese midget submarine crewmembers, Lieutenants Kein Matsuo and Katsuhisa Ban, Petty Officers Masao Tsuzuki and Mamoru Ashibe, were recovered and buried in a military funeral by the Australian Navy.

In June 1942 whilst patrolling off the coast of British Columbia, Canada, the I-26 shelled the Estevan lighthouse. It is thought that the intended target was the Royal Canadian Navy's radio/radar-detection finding station near the village of Hequiat just inland from the lighthouse. No damage was reported. In the meantime

The I-401 aircraft-carrying submarine with a suicide boat being prepared to be lowered into the water. (*Author*)

no sooner had the I-9 and the I-10 got into position than they were rerouted, the I-10 ordered back to Kwajalein and the I-9 to Panama. The reason for moving both these submarines is unknown.

There was one uncorroborated incident reported to a local newspaper in June 1942, when a man by the name of Herbert Lester, who lived with his wife and children on a remote island called San Miguel situated 40 miles south of Port Arguello, Santa Barbara County, California. He claimed to have seen a small inflatable rubber dinghy with Asian-looking men carrying weapons land on a small beach on the far corner of the island. He watched as they walked along the shoreline as if looking for a landing spot for a larger vessel before returning to the dinghy. Why this was not reported to the authorities at the time is not known, but it was to be four months before the military visited the island by which time Herbert Lester's wife and two daughters had left. Herbert Lester committed suicide not long after the incident.

Chapter 6

The Battle of Midway

The Battle of Midway on 3 June 1942 has gone down in history as one of the most intense naval battles of the Second World War. Admiral Yamamoto had chosen Midway because he calculated that it was outside the effective range of American land-based aircraft. However, typical of Japanese naval planning, Yamamoto's battle plan was very complicated and required the careful coordination of multiple battle groups over hundreds of miles of open sea. His plan was based on intelligence suggesting that the USS *Enterprise* (CV-6) and USS *Hornet* (CV-8) that formed Task Force 16 were the only carriers available to the US Pacific Fleet. He was also told that during the Battle of the Coral Sea one month earlier, the USS *Lexington* (CV-2) had been sunk and the USS *Yorktown* damaged so severely that she too had almost been lost. In fact the *Yorktown* had been damaged but had been hastily repaired at Pearl Harbor and was still operational. She later played a critical role in the discovery and eventual destruction of the Japanese fleet carriers at Midway. In an effort to try and confuse the US fleet Yamamoto dispersed his fleet in such a way that his battleships would trail Nagumo's carrier force by several hundred miles. It was considered unlikely that the Americans would discover them and they would intercept any support vessels that came to the American carriers' aid.

What Yamamoto did not know was that the Americans, having broken his codes. were well aware of his plan of strategically dispersing his fleet, and they also knew that none of his formations would be in a position to support each other. When Nagumo's carriers carried out their strikes against Midway, they bore the brunt of American counter-attacks, the only warships in his fleet larger than the screening force of twelve destroyers being two battleships, two heavy cruisers, and one light cruiser. On the other hand Yamamoto and Admiral Nobutake Kondo had between them two light carriers, five battleships, four heavy cruisers, and two light cruisers, none of which saw action at Midway. The battleships, and the small carriers, of the trailing force were unable to keep pace with the larger carriers. Because the distance between Yamamoto and Kondo's forces and Nagumo's carriers was so great, the information accrued by the scout planes carried on the cruisers and carriers in the trailing force was denied to Nagumo. The Battle of Midway that started on 3 June was to be a major turning point in the war and almost devastated Japan's fleet.

The Japanese submarines' participation in the Battle of Midway was negligible. Twelve of the submarines, the I-168, I-169, I-171, I-174, I-175, I-156, I-157, I-158,

I-159, I-162, I-165 and I-166, were all positioned between Pearl Harbor and Midway Island in an attempt to prevent reinforcements reaching Midway. The original plan was that the submarines would arrive collectively five days before the assault on Midway began and take up their positions, but misplaced deployment, maintenance and repair delays caused the submarines to leave independently, which meant that they arrived on station not knowing where the others were. In fact the American carrier fleet had already passed through the picket line areas before the submarines arrived, which meant that no reports of sightings were sent back. Some sources state that the failure of the submarines to intercept the US fleet at Midway was a major factor in the defeat of the Japanese fleet. In addition to this, American and British cryptographers had made major breakthroughs in the reading of Japanese ciphers and codes and were constantly monitoring the signal traffic between the various military factions. One of the failings of the Japanese submarine force was, that unlike the German U-boats that hunted in 'Wolfpacks', they tended to act like 'lone wolves'. There was no attempt to co-ordinate attacks overall, although individual commanders would try and co-ordinate attacks with other submarines that were operating in the large areas they were patrolling if the situation arose.

The absence of the *Shokaku* and her sister carrier *Zuikaku*, together with the loss of the four aircraft carriers, *Hiryū*, *Soryū*, *Akagi* and *Kaga*, their aircraft and crews in one afternoon, was a devastating blow to the Japanese Navy, causing the high command to abandon their attack on Midway. In addition the loss of the heavy cruisers *Mikuma* and *Mogami* and over 3,000 men further compounded this. With the American fleet still in the area, Vice Admiral Teruhisa Komatsu, the new commander of the Sixth Fleet, ordered all fleet-type submarines to form a new picket line 200 miles and 500 miles east of Midway in an effort to still try and strike a devastating blow on the Americans. However, this was countermanded by Admiral Yamamoto, who, concerned that the main US carrier force was pursuing him, ordered that all submarines around Midway set up new positions west of Midway. Submarine Squadrons 3 and 5 (I-169, I-171, I-174, I-175 and I-156, I-157,

The I-56 being readied for sea. (*JMSDF*)

I-158, I-159, I-162, I-165 and I-166) and the 13th Submarine Division, all under the command of Vice Admiral Komatsu, were ordered to protect the Japanese fleet. The minelaying submarines I-121, I-122 and I-123, made their way westward to patrol Laysan Island and the French Frigate Shoal. The I-168 was ordered to patrol off Midway Island bringing the number of Japanese submarines at the Battle of Midway to fifteen. Admiral Yamamoto ordered the commander of the I-168, Lieutenant Commander Yahachi Tanabe, to carry out a surface bombardment on the Midway Island shore batteries that evening. The submarine would be joined by four heavy cruisers later that night, but after firing just six rounds from their 3.9in deck gun, all of which fell way short, they

Lieutenant Commander Yahachi Tanabe, captain of the I-168. (*Author*)

had to submerge after coming under intense fire from the shore batteries under searchlights. The attack by the cruisers was cancelled and the ships were withdrawn.

The problem now facing the submarine fleet was that they were all running desperately short of fuel and supplies and their losses were mounting. Then word came down from the Naval High Command that the American fleet was still east of Midway and so all the submarines were ordered back east. By this time two of the American aircraft carriers, the USS *Hornet* (CV-8) and the USS *Enterprise* (CV-6), were already on their way back to Pearl Harbor. Once again the Japanese Naval High Command were victims of their own failure to make decisions, coupled with the lack of reliable intelligence information and confusing communication.

There was just the one major success for the Japanese at Midway and that was the sinking of the USS *Yorktown* (CV-5). A Japanese reconnaissance aircraft reported seeing an enemy aircraft carrier listing heavily to starboard and apparently drifting. The *Yorktown* had been bombed by aircraft from the carrier *Hiryū* during the Battle of Midway, and badly damaged. She had been under tow by a minesweeper, with an escort of six destroyers, whilst a repair crew attempted to carry out temporary repairs, but the carrier had taken on water causing considerable damage to her engines and so the tow was abandoned. The destroyer USS *Hammann* had gone alongside to help by coupling up her electrical generator to the carrier's submersible pumps in an effort to pump out the water. The nearest submarine, the I-168, was ordered to the area where she found the *Yorktown* drifting helplessly almost dead in the water. Manoeuvring into a perfect firing position from about 1,000 yards, the I-168 fired four torpedoes and heard three explosions before coming under an intense depth-charge attack from the carrier's escort destroyers. Two of the torpedoes had hit the *Yorktown*, the third hit the *Hammann*, breaking the destroyer's back and sinking her almost immediately, and the fourth missed completely. Some of the depth charges aboard the *Hammann* exploded on the impact of the torpedo and caused fatal damage to the hull of the *Yorktown*. On 7 June 1942 the *Yorktown* rolled over on her port side then turned upside down and sank in 5,500ft of water. For more than seven hours escort destroyers subjected the I-168 to an intense depth-charge bombardment, which is said to have consisted of almost sixty near misses. Three of the depth charges exploded close to the submarine, shaking her violently and causing severe damage to the batteries. The lights in the submarine went out plunging the boat into pitch-black darkness and poisonous chlorine gas started to filter through the boat. With no power the pumps stopped working, leaving the boat crippled. The crew worked frantically to get power restored and get the pumps working again. This meant isolating the damaged batteries and reconnecting the good ones, all this had to be done using hand-held torches and the atmosphere slowly becoming toxic with chlorine gas. With temporary repairs made the captain, Lieutenant Commander Tanabe, made the decision to surface and engage the destroyers with his deck gun, knowing full well that it would be a hopeless cause. Upon breaking surface he discovered the destroyers to be some distance away steaming away from him, enabling him to make good his escape. It

Aerial shot of the USS *Hamman* taking off crewmembers from the USS *Yorktown*. (*USN*)

Aerial shot of the moment the *Hamman* exploded after being torpedoed by the I-168. (*USN*)

was revealed later that he was unable to stay submerged because with water coming in through the rear torpedo tube and, having no compressed air to pump it out, surfacing was the only option.

On 7 August 1942 news came back to Japan that the Allies had carried out an amphibious landing on Tulagi, Florida Island and on Guadalcanal. This came as a shock to the Japanese because they had had no warnings of any activity that would have led them to believe that such an attack was imminent. The Runga Point airfield on Guadalcanal was under construction at the time and capturing it gave the Allies a base from which to strike. It was renamed Henderson Field after Marine Major Lofton R. Henderson who had been killed at Midway. This tiny strip of land became one of the bitterest and bloodiest battlegrounds of the Pacific War and took six months of continuous fighting to secure it.

What is curious is that both I-169 and I-171 had been patrolling the waters around the Solomon Islands at the beginning of August and had reported nothing. I-174 and I-175 were also patrolling the waters around New Caledonia, whilst I-121, I-122, I-123, RO-33 and RO-34 were also patrolling the waters around Guadalcanal and not one incident or movement was reported from any of them. The Japanese immediately set about launching a counter-attack from the land, sea and air, but initially the submarine force was not included in the planning. Then Admiral Yamamoto ordered all available submarines to concentrate in the area around

Guadalcanal. Once again submarines from the 3rd and 7th Submarine Group that had been operating in the area were ordered to respond, but most of them needed to re-supply and put in for repairs. It was two weeks before Vice Admiral Teruhisa Komatsu, Commander of the Sixth Fleet, was able to launch a full submarine offensive. The intention was to establish two submarine picket lines, the first line 'A' consisting of seven submarines, was to take up a position 200 miles east of Malaita Island and north-east of Guadalcanal, line 'B' consisting of three submarines, was to take up a position 50 miles south-west of Rennell Island and 150 miles south of Guadalcanal. Three minelaying submarines from the 7th Submarine Group were deployed off Malaita Island whilst two coastal submarines maintained a continuous reconnaissance patrol off Malaita and Port Moresby. This plan was identical to the one used previously and once again it failed to intercept any of the American ships.

As the Japanese army under the command of Major General Kiyotake Kawaguchi prepared to launch a counter-attack to try and re-take Guadalcanal, unknown to them US naval intelligence had intercepted their coded radio traffic and knew all about the impending attack. This had come about because the Japanese port director at Truk continued to use the outdated codes to report shipping movements in and out of Truk. So when the build-up of makeshift troop carriers and other vessels started off from Truk and Rabaul, he reported all this information back to his superiors, completely unaware that it was being monitored by US naval intelligence. In addition to this, information was being relayed back to Pearl Harbor by 'coastwatchers' who were continually monitoring all sea traffic. Coastwatchers were part of Australian naval intelligence and, together with local natives, kept watch on Japanese troop movements throughout the war. This was a very important and extremely dangerous job fraught with difficulties, often having to move from island to island in order to evade capture by the Japanese when their islands came under threat.

It soon became obvious that the major Japanese offensive was slowing rapidly, and although there were still battles raging, the Japanese were now being put on a defensive footing. The submarine picket lines had failed to pick up any movement of US aircraft carriers, and when the Japanese light aircraft carrier *Ryūjō* was sunk by SBD Dauntless dive-bombers and Grumman F4F Wildcat fighters from the USS *Saratoga*, orders were made to shift the picket lines. Sighting of an American aircraft carrier by the I-15 and I-17 brought renewed movement of picket lines, and orders for all submarines to pursue the aircraft carrier were made, but to no avail. Within a couple of days of fruitless searching, all the submarines were ordered to return to their original positions and maintain the picket lines. Then information came that a US carrier group was steaming just 200 miles east of Guadalcanal and once again submarines were ordered to try and intercept. All the time the Americans were landing men, supplies and equipment on Guadalcanal and within weeks the first of the big bomber and long-range reconnaissance aircraft were landing on Henderson Field.

So desperate was the situation becoming for the Japanese army that almost all the submarines were now engaged in transporting food, medical supplies, ammunition and personnel, and if not involved in that, were assigned to attacking enemy transports, refuelling aircraft (flying boats) and watching for additional enemy forces. With the exception of just a handful of I-class submarines, the vast majority were not assigned to hunting down enemy warships for which they had been originally developed.

One of the major problems that affected both sides was the fact that most of the islands were in very badly charted waters and there were a number of cases of ships and submarines grounding on uncharted shoals and coral reefs. But the ever-improving radar technology of the Americans was beginning to pay dividends, especially at night. The Japanese still relied heavily on binoculars and lookouts, which in bad weather and at night were mostly ineffective.

I-121 and I-123 were ordered to bombard the enemy landing operations on Guadalcanal, whilst I-122 was sent to search the Santa Cruz Islands for enemy transport ships. As well as not coming into contact with the US carrier fleets, the submaries suffered a number of casualties. On 28 August 1942 lookouts on the destroyer-minelayer USS *Gamble* (DM-15), which was headed towards Guadalcanal, spotted the conning tower of a diving submarine. Using her magnetic anomaly detection system, the *Gamble* tracked the I-123 and then conducted several depth charge attacks. The submarine RO-34, which was patrolling to the west of that location, registered a number of explosions coming from I-123's location. After the last attack, the *Gamble* ran through a large oil slick. Her crew saw a large air bubble break the surface and later recovered broken deck planking. The I-123 was presumed sunk about 60 miles east of Savo Island with the loss of all hands.

The following day the RO-33 attacked the 3,310-ton cargo ship MV *Malaita*, which was being escorted by the destroyer HMAS *Arunta*. The *Malaita*, although hit by a torpedo and listing badly, was taken under tow to Port Moresby. *Arunta* then went on the hunt for the submarine. Then, 10 miles south-east of Port Moresby, the destroyer made sonar contact on the RO-33 and proceeded to make four attacks with Mark VII depth charges. Some time later a large oil slick appeared on the surface together with a large amount of debris. The RO-33 was presumed sunk with all seventy officers and men. Two more of the picket line submarines were attacked by ASW aircraft and had to return to Truk for major repairs, leaving the picket line in tatters. One success on 31 August was the attack on the aircraft carrier *Saratoga* by the submarine I-26. The *Saratoga* had only just come from Bremerton, Washington after being repaired from another submarine attack (I-6) in January 1942 when 400 miles south-west of Pearl Harbor. The I-26 fired two torpedoes at the *Saratoga*, but only one made contact, hitting the carrier amidships. This time the damage was not so severe, but enough to cause the aircraft carrier to head for Tongatapu where the hole in her side was temporarily filled with concrete enabling her to return to Pearl Harbor for permanent repairs. From the Japanese point of view this put the *Saratoga* out of commission for some time. At the time of the attack the I-26 immediately went deep because of the heavy depth-charge attack that followed from the carrier's destroyer escort, so was unable to confirm what damage had been caused. Once again Japanese propaganda claimed the sinking of the *Saratoga* in an effort to bolster the sagging morale of the Japanese people.

A major victory on 13 September 1942 came when the I-19, commanded by Lieutenant Commander Takakazu Kinashi, carrying out a patrol on the picket line 140 miles south-east of Cristobal Island, sighted a carrier force on the horizon. Closing silently, the I-19 saw an aircraft carrier, the USS *Wasp* (CV-7) accompanied by a cruiser and a number of escort destroyers. After manoeuvring into a good firing position and at a range of 1,000 yards, the captain fired a salvo of six torpedoes at the giant aircraft carrier. He immediately dived knowing that in the next few minutes the sea around him would be saturated with depth charges. Three of the torpedoes hit the *Wasp*, a fourth missed, but hit the battleship USS *North Carolina*, leaving a 32ft by 18ft hole in her hull below the waterline. It was enough to put her out of action and force her to return to Pearl Harbor for repairs. The fifth torpedo hit the destroyer USS *O'Brien* (DD-415), which later broke in two and sank. The sixth torpedo disappeared into the depths of the ocean without hitting anything. Although there was a tremendous amount of luck in the result of firing the six torpedoes, it showed that the quality of the torpedoes were far superior to those of the Allies because there were less dud ones. Later that day, the I-15 radioed back

The destroyer USS *O'Brien* being hit by a torpedo fired from the Japanese submarine I-19. In the background can be seen the aircraft carrier USS *Wasp* also hit by torpedoes from the I-19. (*USN*)

The I-15 on speed trials. (*Author*)

the message that the *Wasp* had sunk within hours of being hit by the torpedoes from the I-19.

Despite the initial success of the sinking of the *Wasp*, results coming back from the submarine operations were very disappointing. Apart from the sinking of the odd cargo ship and the shelling of a couple of Allied-occupied islands and a flying-boat base on Cristobal Island, the flow of American reinforcements and supplies to Guadalcanal was largely unaffected. The second attempt to try and retake Guadalcanal was a complete failure, so a third attempt was planned, this time using the Japanese Army's 2nd Division.

But what was so important about this little island that made both sides to commit overwhelming forces in an attempt to have control of it? Guadalcanal is part of the Solomon Islands, which lie to the northeastern approaches of Australia. Though it is a humid and jungle-covered tropical island, its position made it strategically important for both sides in the Pacific War. If the Japanese captured the island, they could cut off the sea route between Australia and America. If the Americans controlled the island, they would be better able to protect Australia from Japanese invasion and they could also protect the Allied build-up in Australia that would act as a springboard for a major assault on the Japanese. All these factors added together showed the importance of the island.

In November 1942, one 'Wolf Pack' of four Type IXD U-boats (*Gruppe Monsun*), entered the Mozambique Channel and, operating from the Japanese base at Penang (Malaysia), sank twenty-four merchant ships, but for some unknown reason they were withdrawn back to the Atlantic. Later it was discovered that one of the main problems of sending U-boats into South East Asia was a logistical one, the problem of refuelling the submarines was a major stumbling block. Two of the Type XIV *Milchkühe* (Milkcows) submarine tankers (U-487 and U-155) had been sunk and had the U-boats been supported and had consolidated their positions, they would have become a very serious threat to Allied shipping in the area. There were only a couple of other forays by U-boats into the Indian Ocean, mainly because they were starting to have a torrid time in the Atlantic as improved ASW technology started to make its presence felt. One of these 'forays', consisting of nine German submarines and two support/supply ships, was detected shortly after they had left their respective ports and attacked. The breaking of the Enigma Code in July 1941 had changed the face of the war to a large extent, especially where the U-boats were concerned. Six of the submarines and one support ship were sunk as they made their way across the Atlantic after their courses had been decoded. The remaining three submarines and supply ship entered the Indian Ocean where they were refuelled by Japanese tankers before arriving in Penang.

The Japanese gave part of the harbour in Penang over to the Germans where they established a U-boat base. But with limited manpower the Germans, made up mainly from crews of other submarines, found it increasingly difficult to maintain the U-boats because of the shortage of parts and other materials. Of all the U-boats that served in the Pacific and Indian Oceans, only two, the U-188 and the U-532, ever returned to Europe. Later the Germans established their own submarine base at Surabaja in Java where they could replenish their U-boats with fuel, torpedoes and supplies. There were problems in communication with the lower order of Japanese officialdom, as most of the lower-level officers had come from peasant or working-class backgrounds and had no concept of the Western way of life. They were also not very well educated and were still entrenched in the old customs and ideals of the Japanese feudal system. However, the senior officers, most of whom were descended from the Samurai nobility, had had a good education and were able to understand and bridge the gap between them, but these officers were few and far between. Such was the gulf between the two nationalities that the Germans acquired

Army submarine YU-1 made by the Japanese Steel Works seen here on trials. (*USN*)

Army submarine YU-1 underway in Tokyo Harbour. (*USN*)

a 4,400-acre plantation at Tjikopoe, Java and grew vegetables and other foods. This included baking their own bread, making themselves almost self-sufficient. Their recreation facilities were also better than those of the Japanese with beaches, a good supply of food, spirits and Japanese beer and included a regular supply of Japanese 'comfort' women.

The relationship between the Japanese Army and the Navy reached an all-time low at the end of 1942, when the Army initiated the building of twelve transport

Army supply submarine seen here in the Steel Works shipyard after a bombing raid. (*JMSDF*)

submarines known as *YUso-tei* (YU), YU-1 to YU-12, capable of carrying 40 tons of supplies. They did this without consulting the Navy or asking for their help. When confronted by senior naval officers asking why, they replied that the Navy's submarines had more important things to do, and that the submarines they were building were purely for transport purposes, with the intention of supplying beleaguered garrisons on some of the remote islands with food, ammunition and medical supplies. When the Navy offered their expertise in helping to build the submarines, the Army refused the offer saying they didn't require any help from the Navy. One wonders where they managed to get the Navy crews to man these submarines – but they did. The only armament the Army submarines carried was a single 37mm anti-aircraft gun. This aggressive, antagonistic attitude between these two military services was to play its part in the defeat of Japan.

With the battle on Guadalcanal still raging, getting food and medical supplies to the remaining Japanese soldiers on the islands highlighted the need for transport submarines. So desperate was the situation, that extreme measures were tried to get food to them including the firing of bags of rice (unsuccessfully) through the torpedo tubes of submarines. It was far too dangerous for submarines to surface and deliver food because the time on the surface would make them vulnerable to air attack from the constant American air patrols around the island. The fact that the airfield on Guadalcanal was now in the control of the Americans with little or no possibility of getting it back and any ship trying to supply the beleaguered garrison was likely to be sunk, caused the submarine commanders to discuss an alternative. They all agreed that any submarine delivering supplies could be going to its demise, but then an order from the Imperial Command announced that the troops on Guadalcanal would have to be supplied at all costs. There were no more dissenting voices. This of course meant that most of the submarine fleet was recalled from patrolling the Pacific and Indian Oceans and relegated to becoming supply boats, much to the anger and resentment of their commanders and crews. Over twenty submarines were recalled and all those involved had one of their deck guns removed and had just two operational torpedo tubes. This gave more room for carrying stores; in fact some reports said that there was barely enough room for the crew to move around. In addition to using submarines to deliver supplies, the

I-32 at sea. (*Author*)

Japanese used fishing boats and barges. This of course gave the Americans almost free rein to move supplies and reinforcements to their own men who were now making rapid advances through the islands.

The Japanese Navy's plan was to deliver the supplies from Rabaul to the port of Buin on Bougainville Island, then transfer them to the submarines who would then take them to Kamimbo Bay off Guadalcanal where they would be unloaded at night. One submarine was scheduled to make this trip every day. Initially rice was packed into rubber bags that were secured to the deck and released from inside the submarine. They would then float to the surface and be picked up by motorboats. But then it was discovered that seawater somehow managed to get inside the rubber bags so the rice was packed into drums. Although this was relatively successful, the majority of the packages were passed hand-to-hand from inside the submarine to the motorboats. Another method was a 'tanker-like' submarine that was towed behind and was able to submerge with the submarine. The tanker was capable of carrying 50 tons of supplies, but was rarely used because it was fraught with technical problems.

The first submarine to make the supply run to Guadalcanal was the I-1 under the command of Lieutenant Commander Eiichi Sakamoto. The round trip from Bougainville to Guadalcanal took four days and was carried out mostly submerged because of the increasing presence of American ASW ships and aircraft. The submarine carried enough supplies to last the garrison for two days, which meant that there was going to have to be a continuous shuttle service to the island every two or three days. On 29 January 1943 an American PT boat and the 607-ton New Zealand minesweepers, HMNZS *Kiwi* (T102, Lieutenant Commander C. G. Bridson) and *Moa* (T233, Lieutenant Commander Peter Phipps), encountered the I-1 just as she was about to enter the reef. After a frantic gun battle, in which the I-1's captain, Lieutenant Commander Eiichi Sakamoto, was killed, the two New Zealand minesweepers, unable to penetrate the I-1's hull with their deck guns, rammed it. With the captain mortally wounded and the submarine taking on water, the first officer, Lieutenant Sadayoshi Koreeda, took command and made the decision to attempt to beach the submarine in the shallow water of Kamimbo Bay, Guadalcanal. Giving the engines full power, the I-1 headed towards the beach and then grounded with the bows of the submarine partially protruding from the water and the stern sinking down into the lagoon. Of the eighty members of the crew aboard the submarine, thirty were left entombed inside the submarine, unable to get out because of the supplies that had shifted during the battle, trapping them in their compartment. The remaining members of the crew manage to get out and scramble ashore, their only weapons two swords and three rifles. After a few hours they joined up with members of the army garrison. Three days later Japanese soldiers and five members of the crew returned to the wreck of the submarine with the intention of blowing it up, in an attempt to destroy all the codebooks, charts and

The bows of the I-1 submarine projecting from the water after being sunk by the New Zealand corvettes *Moa* and *Kiwi*. (*USN*)

documents still aboard, but failed. One week later eight Japanese dive-bombers, escorted by over twenty fighters, were sent to the wreck site in an attempt to bomb the wreck, but of all the bombs dropped only one hit the submarine. Three days later the I-2 was sent to locate and sink the wreck but failed to find it. The Japanese

Crew of *PT-65* inspecting the wreckage of the I-1. (*USN*)

High Command tried unsuccessfully to destroy the boat with air and submarine attacks. The US Navy later salvaged a large amount of intelligence: code books, charts, manuals and the boat's log. This mission highlighted the dangers facing the submarine crews as they tried to re-supply the garrison on the island.

It wasn't only Guadalcanal that was facing desperate supply problems; a number of other Japanese garrisons on other islands were reporting desperate shortages of food, supplies and ammunition. Most of the supplies were coming from Rabaul, but now Rabaul itself was coming under very heavy aerial bombardment from American B-17 and B-25 bombers from Henderson Field on Guadalcanal. The supply submarines that were waiting to be loaded were being forced to submerge to depths of over 120ft to escape the bombs and for long periods of time. This made the loading of the submarines extremely hazardous. The American bombers were enjoying the freedom of almost unopposed day and night bombing and were being escorted by P-38 Lightning fighters which quickly dealt with the odd fighter sent up to intercept. It was becoming increasingly clear that the tide of war had turned dramatically in favour of the Allies and that the Japanese submarine force was no longer the force it had intended to be, but was just a collection of supply boats running errands for the Army.

Not all the Japanese submarines were concentrated in the Guadalcanal area. At the beginning of 1943, eight ocean-going submarines of the 8th Submarine Group, under the command of Rear Admiral Nobuo Ishizaki, were assigned to patrol the Indian Ocean. Their directive was to hunt down Allied merchant ships and sink them so as to prevent supplies reaching the American forces who were now making major strides across the Pacific. The problem that the submarine commanders faced was that all these ocean-going submarines and their crews were in dire need of repair and overhaul. This in effect left only three of the eight submarines serviceable at any one time and at the beginning of 1943 only the I-27, I-29 and I-37 were operational. Over a period of three months they managed to sink or damage just eight ships, the I-27 accounted for the sinking of five merchant ships and the damage of one cargo ship and the I-37 sank two cargo ships.

The I-29 leaving to go on patrol. Note the *Hinomaru* lashed to the conning tower.

On 20 March 1943 Rear Admiral Takero Kouta, Commander of the First Submarine Force, had issued an order to all submarine commanders: 'Do not stop at the sinking of enemy ships and cargoes. At the same time carry out the complete destruction of the crews of the enemy ship.' Most of the cases where this order was carried out was in the Indian Ocean but was not adhered to by all submarine commanders. The treatment of Allied POWs by the Japanese is well documented, and the reason for this harsh treatment was the Japanese code of honour, *Gyokusai* (Honourable Death), which forbade a soldier to surrender and to treat those that did as having no honour or value.

I-29, under the command of Captain Masao Teraoka, was given an unusual assignment in April 1943 and ordered to rendezvous with the German submarine U-180, commanded by Fregattenkapitän Werner Musenberg, south-east of Madagascar. They were to take on board the Indian Nationalist leader Subhas Chandra Bose and his adjutant Dr Habid Hassan, both of whom had been guests of Adolf Hitler in Berlin, and take them to Sabang on Weh Island off the coast of northern Sumatra. On board the I-29 were two Japanese engineers, Commander Tetsushiro Emi and Lieutenant Commander Hideo Tomonaha, who were to be transferred to the U-180 and taken to Germany to study U-boat construction. The mid-ocean meeting of the two submarines took ten hours, mainly because of rough weather, during which the exchange of passengers and confidential documents and cargoes took place. After delivering her passengers to Singapore the I-29 returned

U-189 meeting the I-29 in the Indian Ocean and transferring the Indian nationalist leader Subhas Chandra Bose. (*JMSDF*)

Crew of the I-29 with Indian nationalist Chandra Bose after their submarine had rendezvoused with the German submarine U-180. (*Author*)

to Penang and was then ordered to go to Germany. On 17 December 1943 the I-29 went to Singapore to load up with 80 tons of raw rubber, 50 tons of tungsten, two tons of zinc and a quantity of opium and coffee, She followed the same course as the I-8 and the I-30, successfully arriving at Lorient in France on 11 March 1944. On her return trip in April 1944, she was carrying some eighteen military personnel, blueprints for a Messerschmitt Me 262 and Me 163, a Walter HWK 509A rocket engine and twenty Enigma coding machines. Once again, unknown to the Japanese, their radio traffic was being monitored and decoded and one of these messages between Berlin and Tokyo gave a detailed manifest of the I-29's cargo. The submarine was tracked all the way from Lorient, but because of the delay in deciphering the messages the tracking was always slightly behind. After unloading her passengers at Singapore the I-29 was on her way to Penang, oblivious to the fact that her radio messages to Tokyo giving her position and the detailed itinerary of her trip, were being monitored. Three American submarines, the USS *Tilefish* (SS-307), USS *Sawfish* (SS-276) and USS *Rock* (SS-274) were sent the following message from COMSUBPAC (Commander Submarine Pacific):

The I-29 arriving in Lorient, France. (*Author*)

> The I-29 has recently arrived in Singapore from Europe carrying samples of plans of many recent German developments in fields of radar, communications, gunnery, aeronautics and medicine. Left Singapore 29 July en route to Kure, Believe the above is a very important cargo and very likely still aboard. Will pass through posit 15N., 117E., at 251400. and through Balintang Channel at 262100, speed 17 [knots], arriving western channel of Bungo Channel at 291000.

The I-29 at the German submarine base in Lorient. (*Author*)

The three submarines were lying in wait as the I-29 entered Bungo Channel, where she was intercepted and torpedoed by *Sawfish* with the loss of her crew and her cargo.

In April 1943, the Japanese Navy suffered a major setback when Admiral Yamamoto's plane was shot down whilst on an inspection tour of the Solomon Islands. Coded signals of his itinerary had been sent out and had been intercepted and decoded by the Allies. His aircraft was intercepted by P-38 Lightnings from the 339th Squadron USAAF and shot down. The death of Yamamoto was such a blow that it was over a month before the Japanese Military High Command even told the Navy of his death. With his death and his influence gone, the number of aircraft-carrying submarines to be built was reduced from eighteen to nine, then to five and finally three. Only the I-400 and I-401 actually entered service; the I-402 was completed on 24 July 1945 five weeks before the end of the war, but never made it into service.

The lack of communication and strategy within the Japanese High Command was causing major problems in the submarine force, mainly because people who had no concept of the submarines capability were controlling it. Up to this point there was no independent submarine section of the Japanese Navy, it was only when a Sixth Fleet was created that this happened. Prior to this there were two squadrons that were part of the overall fleet, Submarine Squadron 1 was part of the First Fleet, Submarine Squadron 2 part of the Second Fleet and then there was the Submarine School. All three squadrons were commanded by a Rear Admiral together with staff officers whose rank was no higher than that of a commander. Almost all of the submarine staff officers were assigned to different sections of the Navy, the General Headquarters, Combined Fleet Headquarters, Bureau of Naval Affairs, the Navy Ministry and the Operations Section of the Operations Department.

I-401 with a Daihatsu barge in front of the hangar. (*Author*)

These positions were regarded as no more that liaison posts, and because of their relatively low rank amongst the more senior officers, these staff officers had very little, if any, influence on decisions affecting the submarine service. Then in May 1943, the Bureau of Submarines was created under the command of Vice Admiral Shigeyoshi Miwa, his place later being taken by Rear Admiral Shigeaki Yamazaki. The bureau's responsibility was the planning of submarine readiness, research and technological development and liaising with senior commanders. Even after the bureau had been created, the senior officer in overall command discovered that not all the submarines were under his command, which hampered submarine development throughout.

The Naval Technical Bureau, which was responsible for all submarine technological development, contained three departments all with separate responsibilities. The Third Department was responsible for weapon development and testing, the Fifth Department for machinery and the Seventh Department was initially given responsibility for overall submarine technology, but in fact was only concerned with the hull and hull fittings. There was a further department, the Bureau of Naval Aviation that was concerned with plans for aircraft-carrying submarines. The problem was that these departments had to work with other departments that were also concerned with the same projects, but with no overall command structure. This confusing situation inevitably led to poor communication, with some department refusing to cooperate with others. This situation was to plague the submarine service throughout the war and instead of improving and upgrading the tried and tested existing submarines, emphasis was put on developing different types. As the war progressed and war materials became scarcer, the quality of production started to suffer. The Japanese submarine service found itself as the 'poor relation' of the Navy as the emphasis was given to the bigger surface vessels like aircraft carriers, battleships and cruisers.

On Guadalcanal the battle for the island was all but lost and the main priority was to evacuate what was left of the Army. This became a logistical nightmare, mainly because the Japanese Navy's presence in the Pacific and Indian Oceans was declining by the day, and rescues were almost impossible. In an attempt to try and regain some semblance of control, the Navy now had to consider desperate measures.

The main reasons given for the lack of success during these missions was that the area was very well protected by American ASW patrol aircraft and constant poor weather and visibility prevented them from delivering supplies or engaging or spotting enemy ships during this time. In addition what they still didn't realise was that the Allies had broken almost all of their codes and were constantly monitoring their radio communications. The original idea of expanding toward the south-east in an attempt to try and interrupt the interaction between Australia and America started to take shape with the deployment of a special attack force using midget submarines. The deployment was a two-part operation, Unit B and Unit C, B in the Indian Ocean and C in Australian waters. Unit B consisted of three submarines, the I-27, I-28 and I-29. The I-27 carried a midget submarine on deck, whilst the I-29 had a small reconnaissance floatplane in a hangar on the deck forward of the conning tower. Unit C consisted of the I-21, I-22 and I-24, all carrying a midget submarine. The assignment was simple; Unit B was to destroy all enemy shipping off the southern coast of Australia, whilst Unit C was to destroy all enemy shipping off the eastern coast of Australia and in the waters around New Zealand. Initially they were to have supported the Port Moresby invasion, but this was put on hold after Japan's major setback in the Battle of the Coral Sea and Midway.

At the beginning of September 1943, the island of Lae had become a cause for serious concern for the Japanese as it was becoming increasingly difficult to deliver supplies to the beleaguered garrison there. The I-177 (which, under the command of Lieutenant Commander Orita Zenji, was later to commit the infamous act of torpedoing HMAHS *Centaur*), was en route to deliver supplies to Lae when they received a message that the island would have to be abandoned. On arriving two lighters came out to meet the submarine and the supplies loaded on to them. They then took on board eighteen seriously wounded men who would be unable to make the withdrawal. As they were embarking the men, she came under fire from the land. Minutes later the I-177 was underway and was on her way out of the lagoon when she was spotted by a torpedo boat and fired upon. The I-177 dived, but then resurfaced 10 minutes later only to find two more torpedo boats bearing down on her. She immediately crash-dived and slipped away. The I-177 was then ordered to proceed to Finschhafen, Papua, New Guinea to pick up some more seriously wounded soldiers, but ASW aircraft were so active in the area that the pick-up became impossible.

Despite the overall disappointing failures of the midget submarine of the special attack force, there were some successes by the fleet submarines, the main one being the I-10 of Unit 'A' under the command of Captain Yasuchika Makihara. Throughout June and July 1942 the I-10 sank eight cargo ships, the *Atlantic Gulf* (2,639 tons), *Melvin H. Baker* (4,999 tons), *King Lud* (5,224 tons), *Queen Victoria* (4,937 tons), *Express* (6,736 tons), *Nymphe* (4,504 tons), *Hartismere* (5,498 tons) and USS *Alchiba* (4,427 tons). The I-16 sank four cargo ships, the *Susak* (3,889 tons), *Agios Georgios IV* (4,847 tons), *Supetar* (3,748 tons) and *Eknaren* (5,243 tons). The I-18 sank four cargo ships, the *Mundra* (7,341 tons), *Wilford* (2,158 tons) and *De Weert* (1,805 tons). The I-20 sank seven cargo ships, *Johnstown* (5,086 tons), *Christos Markettos* (5,209 tons), *Mahronda* (7,926 tons), *Hellenic Trader* (2,052 tons), *Clifton Hall* (5,063 tons), *Goviken* (4,854 tons) and *Steaua Romana* (5,311 tons). Throughout the Indian Ocean the Japanese submarine presence was being felt, but their successes were limited to cargo ships and no warships. Despite these successes and the problems they brought the Allies, the Japanese Naval High Command were being put under increasing pressure by the Army to utilise the submarines as supply boats for their campaigns.

Japanese submarine I-18. (*Author*)

As the war progressed it became clear that because of the intense rivalry between the Army and the Navy, the Army's power in Japan enabled them to persuade the government to use the submarine force for other duties. This meant that instead of patrolling and hunting for American and British warships and merchant ships, they were being used to transport ammunition, food and supplies to beleaguered troops on remote islands and indeed at times to transport troops. In short they were being used for general duties much to the disappointment of the Navy. Even in Japan the Army had control over the civilian workforce, which greatly reduced the shipbuilding programme, as workers were being assigned to factories to build more tanks, bombers and fighters for the army.

On 6 July 1943 the I-8, under the command of Commander Shinji Uchino and accompanied by the I-10 serving as a refuelling tanker, left Penang carrying a cargo of quinine for the Germans. Also on board was skeleton crew of forty-eight officers and men, who were expected to bring back a German U-boat, the U-1224, that Hitler had promised the Japanese. On about 20 July reaching just south of the Azores, the I-8 rendezvoused with the German submarine U-161, commanded by Kapitänleutnant Albrecht Achilles, upon which a German officer was transferred to the Japanese submarine to guide it into Brest safely. On entering Brest, escorted by German surface ships and aircraft, the I-8 unloaded her cargo of quinine and took on board special weapons and equipment desperately needed by Japan. The German specialists fitted radar-warning equipment to the I-8, enabling the submarine to detect Allied search radars whilst she was surfaced. After spending almost three months in the U-boat bunkers in Brest, during which time extensive modifications were made to the I-8, including a new radar and hydrophone system, the submarine left for Singapore on 5 October. On board were eighteen Germans including three naval officers, one Wehrmacht major, four radar and hydrophone technicians and ten civilian advisors who were to install the new equipment into other Japanese

The Japanese submarine I-8 arriving at Brest, France. (*Author*)

Admiral Kranke welcoming the crew of the I-8 to Brest. (*Author*)

Some of the crew of the I-8 with German officers at Brest. (*Author*)

submarines. Two months later I-8 safely arrived in Singapore where it discharged its cargo. The I-8 returned safely to Japan after completing 64 days at sea and a round trip of about 30,000 miles, the only one of the five missions to Europe by Japanese submarines to successfully to do so. A remarkable feat of seamanship.

The U-1224, renamed the RO-501 leaving Brest with a Japanese crew. (*Author*)

The I-8. (*Author*)

The skeleton crew that had accompanied the I-8 to collect the U-1224 spent three months in training before the submarine, redesignated the RO-501, was handed over. Loaded with war materials, models and blueprints for the Messerschmitt Me 163 rocket fighter, the RO-501 left France. Unknown to the Japanese, their radio transmissions were being monitored and, off the Cape Verde Islands, a US hunter-killer group were waiting. The RO-501 was tracked and depth-charged by the USS *Francis M Robinson* (DE-220) with the loss of the entire crew which included a German naval radar officer and a Luftwaffe pilot.

The I-8 wasn't the only Japanese submarine to make the hazardous journey to France, the I-30 had been the first to do so in 1942, but had been sunk by a mine whilst en route back to Japan with vital war material. The I-34 left for Germany, but was intercepted near Penang by the British submarine HMS *Taurus* and sunk. The

The I-14 aircraft-carrying submarine. (*Author*)

The I-52 on patrol. (*Author*)

I-52 was the last to make the trip to Germany, but she was caught by aircraft from the escort carrier USS *Bogue* (CVE-9) in the Atlantic and was sunk as described later in this book.

Towards the middle of 1943 the Japanese High Command became aware of the disturbing news that a large number of their submarines had been sunk. Two new submarines, the I-177 and I-180, were assigned to patrol the waters around the Solomon Islands. For the first month they recorded no contacts with enemy shipping and their only contact was when they rescued survivors from the light cruiser *Jintsu*. Together with other cruisers, the *Jintsu* had been escorting transport ships carrying troops and supplies between Truk, Roi and Kwajalein, when they were attacked by American cruisers and destroyers. During what became known as the Battle of Kolombangara, the *Jintsu* was subjected to heavy shelling from the American cruisers and was sunk. There were only a handful of survivors.

Things improved for the Japanese submarine fleet in the Indian Ocean, Bay of Bengal and the Arabian Sea, when a number of submarines, including the I-10, I-26, I-27 and I-37, in the space of just four months managed to sink over twenty merchant ships and damaged a number of others – but once again no warships. Some of this was down to the fact that Allied ASW ships were not as numerous as those in the Pacific Ocean. The German Navy wanted the Japanese Navy to adopt

The I-26 on speed trials. (*Author*)

The I-10 leaving to go on patrol. (*Author*)

a defensive approach in the Pacific and try to contain the American advance, whilst in the Indian Ocean to take offensive action against the British. But such was the momentum of the American advance that the Japanese felt that they had to take the offensive, which meant that they had to deploy their submarines where they felt they were most needed. Then in late 1943 the Allied advance gained momentum causing the Japanese submarine force to be stretched even wider.

After hearing intelligence reports that large American forces were building up in Hawaii and encouraged by the so-called 'success' of the flying boat mission, the Combined Fleet Staff decided to send one of their aircraft-carrying submarines, the I-36, on a reconnaissance mission. The I-36 left Yokosuka early in September 1943 and on arriving off the coast of Hawaii launched her aircraft, a Yokosuka E14Y-1 floatplane, the same type of aircraft that in August 1942 had dropped six incendiary bombs on a forest near Brooking, Oregon. After an abortive attempt to carry out a reconnaissance, thwarted because of increased CAP and improved American radar, it was decided to abandon the idea. The only other solution was to launch the aircraft from a distance of 300 miles south-west of Hawaii, knowing full well it would be a one-way flight for the pilot and his observer. In mid-October the aircraft was launched and later reported back that there were four battleships, four aircraft carriers, five cruisers and seventeen destroyers in Pearl Harbor. That was the last contact the submarine had with its reconnaissance aircraft.

The surrender to the Allies by Italy on 8 September came as a shock to the Japanese as the Tripartite agreement now became the Bipartate agreement.

Chapter 7

Kamikaze (Divine Wind)

At the beginning of 1943 the Japanese Navy's submarine force (*Sensui Butai*), having suffered a number of severe setbacks, had realised that the war at sea for the Japanese was deteriorating faster than other branch of the armed forces. The initial control of the seas was slipping away from Japan as the Americans continued to move forwards at a relentless pace, gaining ground all the time. It was decided to implement a series of what were called 'Kamikaze' (Divine Wind) attacks. (The word 'Kamikaze' was given to a typhoon that wrecked the Mongol fleet of ships in the thirteenth century that was preparing to invade Japan. The survivors were quickly dispatched giving the Japanese victory over the Mongol Horde.) One of the Navy's weapons was a newly-designed manned torpedo, based on the Long Lance. The 'Long Lance', or Type 93 torpedo, could travel three times the distance of any of the Allied torpedoes and carried a 1,000lb warhead, twice that of the British and American torpedoes. It was fuelled by a mixture of oxygen and petroleum, which meant that it left little or no wake in its trail and so was not easily spotted.

Japanese Type 93 Long Lance torpedo having run aground after missing its target. (*USN*)

Designed primarily for submarines, it was soon realised that destroyers and cruisers could be equipped with the Type 93 torpedo, together with the large oxygen-producing equipment required to fuel it. Under the guise of installing air-conditioning, by the end of 1942 all destroyers and cruisers of the Japanese Imperial Navy had the Type 93 torpedo installed. Unfortunately the Navy suffered so many losses of these ships during the early part of the war, that a vast number of the Type 93 torpedoes remained stockpiled at the Imperial Navy Ordnance Depots. Then the idea of using the Long Lance as a manned torpedo was put forward.

At first the idea of a manned torpedo was rejected by the General Staff as an expensive fantasy project, but as the Americans continued to make progress almost unabated, the losses continued to mount despite the lateness of radar being fitted into the submarines. In January 1943 the 'human torpedo' project was now being reconsidered. The first proposal meant certain death to the operator; this however was not acceptable to the Navy. The next proposal added a device that enabled the operator to eject from the torpedo when it was 150ft from the target. It is interesting to note that no mention was ever made of picking up the operator after he had ejected. Given the name 'Kaiten', which roughly translated meant 'The turn towards heaven', production started at the Kure Dockyard.

The first prototype appeared at the beginning of 1944 and was fitted with an escape hatch mounted beneath the tiny conning tower, because even at this stage of the war the idea of suicide vessels were not popular. At first the Kaiten was intended to be used solely for coastal defence, but as the war situation deteriorated it was decided that the situation required desperate measures, and production of the human torpedoes was increased. The first four to be built, known as the Type 1, were based on the Type 93 torpedo. It was 48ft 5in (14.75m) long with a 3ft 3in(1m) beam and had a range of 14 miles at 30 knots or 48 miles at 12 knots and weighed 8.3 tons. A small cockpit and conning tower, which was surmounted by a short periscope, replaced the usual automatic directional equipment. Some of the I-class submarines were modified to carry between three and five human torpedoes, and a tube was fitted between the entry hatch and the mother submarine so that the pilot could enter his submarine whilst both craft were submerged. This of course made for a rapid deployment of the human torpedo when within range of its target and the chance of being detected minimised. There were later improved versions of the Type 1 but they only came into production just as the war was coming to an end.

Production of the Type 1 was initially very slow, but as it became increasingly obvious that the battle for the Marianas had been lost, the Japanese General Staff ordered production to be speeded up. The call went out for 'volunteers' to become pilots of the new Kyukoko Heiki (National Salvation Weapon) and even though it was quite obvious that the missions were only going to be one-way, there was no shortage of volunteers. The criteria was that volunteers had to be unmarried, have

Lieutenant Hiroshi Kuroki and Lieutenant Sekjo Nishina, the two naval officers responsible for the invention of the *Kaiten* torpedoes. (*USN*)

a strong spirit of patriotism, not to be the only son or be the sole family provider, and be physically and psychologically well.

A top-secret training base was set up on the island of Otsushima, south-west of Honshu under the supervision of Lieutenants Hiroshi Kuroki and Sekio Nishina, who, together with naval architect Hiroshi Suzukawa, had designed the Type 1 human torpedo. The volunteers were not allowed to leave the island until their training was completed. The training was intense and covered the construction and function of the Type 93 torpedo and its propulsion system. All the volunteers had to be of a small stature as the inside of the midget submarines was extremely cramped. One trainee pilot, Lieutenant Miroru Warda, gave a detailed description in his diary of what it was like when seated in the submarine. He described how the 'simple' controls required all his experience and training to enable him to operate and maintain control of the craft. When sat in his seat, directly in front of him was the small, chunky viewing glass of the periscope, which he was able to lower and raise by means of a crank lever situated to the right of his seat. On a panel behind the periscope was fitted a gyro compass, a depth and fuel gauge and a clock. Above his head and slightly to the right, was a valve that controlled the oxygen flow to the submarine's engine, which was fitted directly behind the pilot's seat. In an overhead position, but slightly to the left, was a lever that controlled the *Kaiten*'s diving planes when the submarine was diving or rising when underwater. Below this was a valve

Kaiten pilot in his midget submarine during training. (*Author*)

that would allow sea water to come inside the boat in order to stabilise it if, and when, the oxygen to the engine ran out. The only other control was a lever that operated the rudder which allowed the *Kaiten* to move left or right. This became known to the pilots of the *Kaiten* as the 'Dead Man's Handle' as it was the last

Kaiten pilots about to go on a suicide mission. (*Author*)

lever they would operate before aiming for their target. The close proximity of the valves and levers to the pilot's head in the cramped space caused many of the pilots to suffer minor head injuries as the boat rocked and moved when it was underway. Bandaged heads became the norm for many of the trainee *Kaiten* pilots.

After the initial training was completed, it was followed by a series of programmes covering the use of the *Kaiten* culminating in an operational dummy run. There were of course a number of incidents including a fatality when one of the training *Kaiten*s, piloted by Lieutenant Hiroshi Kuroki, got stuck in the mud at the bottom of the lagoon and was lost.

Preparing a midget submarine for a mission. (*Author*)

Kaiten pilot graduation ceremony. (*Author*)

After completing all their training the *Kaiten* pilots, now members of the *Kairyu*, the nautical members of the *Kamikaze* fraternity, were given leave to essentially say goodbye to their parents and loved ones, before returning to their respective bases. There they waited for a mission, but during this time they were given extra rations and were entertained by what were euphemistically called 'comfort women'. On the eve of the mission the crews were given a farewell party in the presence of senior Imperial Submarine Fleet officers. The following morning they would parade in their Number One uniform, whilst their belongings were packed up and returned to their families. After the parade and just prior to departure, they would all take part in the ritual drinking of sake (rice wine) and then put on the traditional *Hachimaki* (headband) with the name of their *Kaiten* group and their own slogan emblazoned on it.

Initially the midget submarine was destined to be used for coastal defence, as they could operate from shore bases or be transported aboard I-class submarines to wherever they were needed. This resulted in some of the submarines being used during the Philippines campaign (1944–5) where they were used around the Surigao Strait. Development continued and by the end of 1942, a three-man midget submarine had been produced that had a range of 350 miles at 6 knots on the surface, or a range of 120 miles at 4 knots submerged. The production models were given the designation Type C Ha-62 to Ha-76 and had been designed to be carried on the deck of modified I-class submarines. As the war progressed and

Japanese submarines HA-105, HA-106 and HA-109 tied up alongside an American aircraft carrier in 1945. The number of the fourth submarine is obscured by smoke. (*USN*)

Japan's forces were forced back to their homeland desperation started to creep in, calling for desperate measures. The midget submarines were now being converted into human torpedoes, in an effort to stem the ever increasing tide of supply ships that were accompanying the Allied forces as their relentless push continued towards Japan. But once again the results were disappointing and almost all the missions using the midget submarines ended in failure. The human torpedoes did have one result and that was it had an continuing effect on the morale of Allied ships' crews, who couldn't understand the fanaticism that drove the Japanese to blow themselves up in the name of the Emperor.

On 2 January 1944 submarine commanders were told that the Eighteenth Army and Eighteenth Naval Base at Rabaul were surrounded and that the whole force was to be evacuated by sea in submarines. Two submarines were to head for Sio, New Guinea, where they were to rendezvous with two launches carrying all the HQ Staff. As the submarines surfaced and prepared to take the staff on board, two American PT (Patrol Torpedo) boats appeared coming toward them at high speed. The submarines immediately crash-dived and went deep whilst the two PT boats made their escape. The following day they tried again and once again the PT boats appeared, then on the third day they managed to get the HQ Staff aboard just as the PT boats appeared on the horizon. The submarines then headed for Truk. It had been over a year since they had left and now they were badly in need of repairs and a refit. This was a major problem facing almost all the Japanese submarine commanders. Their boats and crews desperately needed to be refitted, rested or replaced. Repairs that had been temporary were now regarded as permanent, crews were exhausted and in need of rest and medical attention. But there was to be no respite as the Americans continued their relentless advance and forced the Japanese military from the occupied islands back towards Japan.

Entering Truk harbour was becoming increasingly difficult for the submarines because of the number of sunken ships with their masts just poking through the surface, that now littered the bottom of the lagoon. Within days of the submarines arrival, aircraft from American carriers that had approached Truk under cover of a storm that had grounded all Japanese reconnaissance aircraft carried out a massive raid on the airfield at Takeshima, destroying over 180 aircraft both in the air and on the ground. The remaining Japanese aircraft were ordered to withdraw to bases in the Philippines. Within days battleships appeared and started shelling the oil depots, setting them ablaze. The Solomon Islands were taken back by the Americans altering the battle front from Saipan-Guam to Philippines-Okinawa. The war was now almost on Japan's own doorstep.

The RO-39 was ordered to take urgent supplies to the starving garrison on Mille Island in the Marshall Island Group. Now relegated to a supply ship, an opportunity arose for the RO-39 when close to Mille Island with information about two enemy aircraft carriers accompanied by a battleship in the area. Under normal circumstances this would have been an ample opportunity to attack, as there were no destroyer escorts to be seen. However, their orders were defined for supply and reconnaissance missions only, so reluctantly the crew allowed the huge targets to slip by. On the submarine's return, the captain was reprimanded for not attacking the aircraft carriers when he had the opportunity. A perfect example of the expression, 'You'll be damned if you do and you'll be damned if you don't'.

On 29 February 1944 the Americans launched their attack on the islands of Iwo Jima. The massive US fleet that accompanied the landings caused another human torpedo unit, the *Chibaya*, to be hurriedly put together. Three parent submarines; the I-44, I-368 and I-370, were readied and immediately set sail for Iwo Jima. The mission was a complete disaster. The I-370 was running on the surface preparing to launch her *Kaiten*s when she was picked up on the radar of the USS *Finnegan* (DE-307). The I-370 crash-dived before releasing her human torpedoes and was subjected to an intense depth-charge attack. Five minutes later there was a massive explosion followed by a large oil slick and debris. The I-370 was lost with her crew of 79 and five *Kaiten* pilots.

On the same day the I-368, just 35 miles off Iwo Jima, was on the surface about to launch her human torpedoes when she was picked up on the radar of a Grumman TBM Avenger from the escort carrier USS *Anzio* (CVE-57). The I-368 crash-dived but the Avenger had dropped a Mark 24 acoustic homing torpedo. Minutes later a second Avenger from the *Anzio* arrived and dropped another acoustic homing torpedo, both found their target and the I-368 sank with her crew of eighty-six and five *Kaiten* pilots. There were no survivors. The I-44 was spotted on the surface and crash-dived and was subjected to an intense depth-charge attack. So intense was the attack that the I-44 had to stay submerged for more than 48 hours with the result that the air inside the submarine became so bad that the crew were almost on the point of suffocating. The captain, Lieutenant Commander Genbi Kawaguchia, abandoned the mission and returned to base and was later relieved of

潜水艦に搭載された特潜

Type A midget submarine on the deck of its mother submarine during rough weather. (*Author*)

his command for failing to obey his original orders. After a bitter fight Iwo Jima fell to the overwhelming American forces. Japan was now really on the back foot.

A second unit, the *Kongo*, was formed and again three parent submarines, the I-36, I-53 and I-58, carried a total of six human torpedoes. The I-58 had been fitted with anti-aircraft radar, but from the word go it never functioned properly and again lookouts became the eyes of the submarine. So-called intelligence information about

Kaiten suicide 'pilots' welcoming aboard the captain of the I-368. (*Author*)

Guam indicated that there was at least one aircraft carrier and about seventy other vessels at anchor, but an air reconnaissance report never mentioned any ships. The entire unit of midget submarines were launched but none were ever heard from again. Of the fourteen successful launches, there were ten failures due to technical problems, the remaining four managed to enter the area where the ships were supposed to be anchored but were lost. The only recorded success was the sinking of an oil tanker that was hit by a torpedo from one of the midget submarines.

The Japanese Naval High Command deemed the *Kaiten* missions to be a great success, but in truth they were not and, although other missions were planned, none ever really came to fruition. The vast majority of the *Kaiten* volunteers died before they ever reached their objectives and the results from those who did, were very disappointing.

On 26 March 1944, the I-8, under the command of Captain Tatsunosuke Ariizumi, was involved in some of the worst atrocities committed by a Japanese submarine crew during the Second World War. It concerned a Dutch-registered merchant ship the SS *Tijsalak*, which was torpedoed by the I-8 whilst sailing from Melbourne to Ceylon with 103 passengers and crew. The survivors, who took to the lifeboats, were ordered out of them and assembled on the stern of the I-8. One of the survivors, James Blears, recalled seeing the prisoners being attacked systematically by members of the crew with hammers, swords, bayonets and a sledgehammer before being thrown into the sea and into the churning propellers. A number were beheaded and thrown into the sea. James Blears managed to escape by diving overboard amidst a hail of machine-gun fire and after swimming for a number of hours managed to get to a lifeboat. He was later joined by an Indian crewman, who told him that twenty-two of his fellow crewmembers had been tied to a rope and towed behind the I-8 as it dived. Of the 103 passengers and crew only five managed to escape the slaughter. Two days later the five were lucky to escape once again, as the Liberty ship SS *James A. Wilder* approached, on seeing what they thought was the conning tower of a partially submerged submarine, opened fire before realising that it was in fact a lifeboat. Fortunately their aim was as bad as their eyesight.

Two months later, I-8 was involved in another atrocity when she torpedoed the 7,176-ton American Liberty ship SS *Jean Nicolet*. The 100 crewmen abandoned their

Captain Tatsunosuka Arizumi. (*Author*)

Koryu Type D midget submarines in the dry dock at Kure after the war. (*USN*)

Oil tanker ablaze and sinking after being torpedoed. (*Author*)

burning ship and took to the life rafts. Again, the survivors were gathered on the submarine's deck. The massacre took several hours, as they were made to walk one at a time past the conning tower, where they were slashed with swords, bayoneted and beaten with clubs before being thrown overboard. When an aircraft approached, the submarine dived, plunging the remaining bound prisoners into the ocean, where most drowned. It is believed twenty-three men made it to a life raft, from which they were rescued by the trawler HMS *Hoxa* 30 hours later. The captain of the I-8, Captain Ariizumi, is said to have committed suicide, but some sources say he faked his own death to avoid standing trial for war crimes.

On 27 April 1944 the I-36 was at sea with six *Kaitens* aboard and came across a 36-ship convoy headed for Okinawa. Closing to 8,000 yards, the captain ordered the launch of all six *Kaitens*, but two of the *Kaitens* remained, jammed in their racks, while the other four headed for the convoy. Five minutes later four explosions were heard and a message was flashed to Tokyo claiming that four US transports or cargo ships had been sunk. In reality only one cargo ship, the SS *Canada Victory*, was hit and sunk. It is strongly believed that all four *Kaitens* aimed for the same ship, as there were no other reports of ships in the same convoy being attacked.

In May 1944, the 7th Submarine Group, under the command of Rear Admiral Noboru Ōwada, was supplied with a new type of submarine – the *Tei-gata/Sen-tei-gata* Type D1. This was a purpose-built transport submarine designed specifically for carrying supplies (mostly ammunition and troops) to beleaguered islands. These submarines were vulnerable as they did not carry the same amount of armament as the other submarines and as such suffered serious losses. The first three built were not fitted with torpedo tubes but after bitter complaints from the submarine commanders they were.

The Type Ds, as they were known, were split into three classes, the I-361 class, the I-372 class and the I-373 class. The I-361 class consisted of the I-361, I-362, I-363, I-364, I-365, I-366, I-367, I-368, I-369, I-370 and I-371. The I-372 was converted to a tanker as were the I-373, I-374 and I-375. Within six months almost all these submarines had been sunk. The I-364 was sunk by the USS *Sea Devil* (SS-400) on her maiden voyage shortly after leaving Honshu, the I-365 was caught returning from a supply run to Truk by the USS *Scabardfish* (SS-397) six weeks later and one month later the I-362 was caught by the USS *Fleming* (DE-32) whilst on a mission to Woleai. These and subsequent successes were down to the Allied 'Ultra' and MAGIC interception of Japanese secret radio traffic. Messages at this time were usually of a desperate nature and were reduced, as in one message in May 1944 from the beleaguered Japanese Eighteenth Army in Wewak, New Guinea that read: 'Please rush to Wewak as absolute necessary supplies by the end of June the allotment of two submarines (30 tons).'

In May 1944 the Japanese Naval General Staff became aware of heavy radio traffic and a large number of reconnaissance flights being carried out over the Carolinas.

The Allied interest appeared to be centred around Palau in the Caroline Islands and the high command realised that if the Americans were to successfully invade and take the islands, it would then extend their control to the Philippines. With this in mind it was decided to concentrate on the area between the western Carolinas, western New Guinea and Mindanao, an area that became known as The Great Triangle. Admiral Takeo Takagi ordered the I-41, I-43, I-53 and RO-47 to patrol between Wewak and the Admiralty Islands, whilst the RO-44 searched the area around the Eniwetok Atoll and the RO-42, the Kwajalein area. In the meantime the Japanese Combined Fleet was patrolling the area of The Great Triangle with submarines from the 7th Submarine Group forming a warning picket line, when word came through from the I-10 and the RO-44 that the American battle fleet was nowhere to be seen.

The assault on Saipan came first from the air by aircraft from the US carriers and then from the sea, catching the Japanese completely by surprise. Before they could react, US Marines had stormed ashore and had established a beachhead. On hearing of the first attack from the air, the Japanese High Command were unsure as to whether or not it was the start of an assault or just a probing attack. On hearing of the assault taking place, Admiral Takagi had ordered the I-10, I-38, I-184, RO-41, RO-42 and RO-44 to leave their patrol areas and head at full speed to try and intercept the US assault force. The hesitation cost the Japanese dear as four days after the assault the town of Garpan, the command HQ of the Submarine Advanced Expeditionary Force, under the command of Vice Admiral Takeo Takagi, was put out of action. Control was then passed to Rear Admiral Noboru Ōwada stationed on Truk. The recalled submarines now had to run the gauntlet of heavily-armed ASW ships and aircraft who were now supporting the invasion force. The submarines were ordered to set up three picket lines, one 500 miles east of Guam along a 100-mile north-south line, a second 300 miles east of Guam along a 200-mile north-south line and a third 200 miles east of Guam along a 300-mile north-south line. Because the Allies were able to monitor and decipher the messages between the submarines and their command HQ, it became extremely difficult to maintain the picket lines as they were constantly being hunted, forcing them to take almost constant evading action. Between May and June more than fourteen Japanese submarines were detected and sunk.

With the Americans now in control of Saipan, the Japanese High Command considered a counter-attack, but although they had sufficient aircraft for it, they were not deployed effectively. In addition to this there were problems regarding a shortage of battle-experienced pilots, and of those who were considered to be operational, a large number were suffering from illnesses that were linked to the lack of food and the conditions they forced to live and work under. On 19 June 1944, Vice Admiral Jisaburō Ozawa launched an attack on the American carrier force which was 350 miles away. His thinking was, that after the first attack of the carriers his aircraft would land at Guam, refuel and re-arm, then carry out a second strike accompanied by land-based bombers. What he did not know was that Guam had been attacked and almost destroyed by aircraft from the American carriers earlier. Once again a perfect example of the lack of communications that plagued the Japanese. The result was that the first attack on the American carriers was ineffective inasmuch as Japanese search planes had difficulty in locating the fleet, causing the incoming attack force to jettison their bombs to conserve fuel. Some of those who did not jettison their bomb loads ran out of fuel and were lost. Japanese carriers were also under attack from American submarines, causing problems for returning aircraft. The end

Vice Admiral Jisaburo Ozawa. (*JMSDF*)

result was that the whole attack ended in what was to be called 'The Marianas Turkey Shoot'. In the first day of the attack the Japanese lost 273 aircraft, a devastating blow by any standards and by the end of the battle a total of 350 carrier aircraft and over 200 land-based fighter and bombers had also been lost. The losses increased when some of the Japanese aircraft found that their carriers *Taiho* and *Shōkaku* had been sunk and other carriers were unable to take them aboard. Japan lost nine aircraft carriers compared to just three American – the Battle of the Philippine Sea was starting and the tide of war was about to turn.

Japanese submarines were assigned to rescue Vice Admiral Takagi and his staff together with over 100 pilots and other crewmembers from Saipan. Other submarines were tasked to patrol the islands around the Marianas to search for survivors who might have made their way on to some of the more remote islands, but none were found. The I-10 was sent to Saipan to collect Admiral Takagi and his staff but was intercepted by the USS *Riddle* (DE-185) and USS *David W. Taylor* (DD-551) and sunk with depth charges. The I-6 was then tasked with the mission but that too was intercepted and sunk by the USS *William C. Miller* (DE-259) and the USS *Gilmer* (DD-233). In desperation the I-41 was sent to Guam and this time successfully rescued over 100 pilots and other crewmembers, the only submarine to carry out its task. Admiral Takagi and his staff were killed by American Marines on Saipan later in the month.

The toll on the Japanese submarine force was mounting almost daily and of the forty submarines that had been deployed in the Marianas, over half had been sunk

The I-53. (*Author*)

and several others badly damaged. In addition to this all the surviving submarines and crews were in desperate need of repair, servicing and rest. In the Japanese High Command recriminations and questions as to why the submarine force was almost at breaking point were abound. Amongst the submariners the blame lay squarely at the feet of the Naval High Command, who had spent more time and money on the development of the battleships, aircraft and aircraft carriers, leaving the submarine force a poor relation, but expecting it to produce the same performance figures and results as the other naval departments. When setting a picket line, submarines were ordered to retain a fixed position in a straight line, but as one commander commented, staying in a fixed position anywhere near an enemy base was a recipe for disaster, especially with the advanced ASW technology carried aboard enemy aircraft and ships. Detection rates became high and submarines were constantly on the move to avoid the hunter/killer groups that scoured the seas for them. This in itself was enough to displace any picket line being set up. The lack of communication was another contributing factor as submarine commanders rarely talked to each other and this, coupled with the lack of intelligence and misinformation that was being handed out, caused confusion.

As the Japanese lost more and more submarines, so the German U-boats were required to do more and more patrols and found themselves being pushed farther and farther east. One of these was the U-862 which left Germany in May 1944 to assist other U-boats in the area. The arrival of an additional U-boat caused serious refuelling and re-supplying problems for the Japanese, mainly because the Germans had to rely on their surface supply ships. This meant that servicing and repairs to the submarines were taking longer and longer and the port of Penang, which had become the principal operating base, was overwhelmed with the repair work. At one point the Germans only had two serviceable U-boats available and, because of the mistrust that was developing between the U-boat crews and the Japanese, the U-862, commanded by Korvettenkapitän zur See Heinrich Timm, had the Japanese flag painted on his submarine's conning tower, so that Japanese forces could identify her after a couple of close calls. These longer patrols also meant that the crews when they returned, needed longer periods of rest and more often than not, medical treatment, the main one being for malaria. Despite having access to quinine, malaria caused serious logistical problems in the shape of depleted manpower. By the end of the war it was estimated that a total of fifty-seven German U-boats had at one time operated in the Indian Ocean. Two Italian submarines, that had been taken over by the Germans and converted into transport submarines, had also been assigned to operate in that theatre of operations, but there is almost no information about their activities – if any. Later in the war, with the threat over the Atlantic convoys reduced dramatically, Admiral Dönitz sent a number of his remaining U-boats into the Indian Ocean to search for Allied cargo and supply ships in an attempt to stem the Allied advance.

In a report by Vice Admiral Tadashige Daigo, commander of the Sixth Fleet, he said that the methods used by the American Navy's ASW force was not only aggressive, but thorough. Group submarine methods did not work as they were easily detectable and spiritual valour was commendable, but – in a war that was increasingly being reliant on technology – pointless.

While the battle in the Pacific raged on, the Japanese Naval High Command still clung on to the hope that the Germans would come to their aid with their improved technology. So in June 1944 the I-52 was assigned a top secret mission to the German submarine base at Lorient, carrying 9.8 tons of molybdenum (piston grease), 11 tons of tungsten, two tons of gold in 146 bars packed into forty-nine metal boxes and three tons of opium and some caffeine. The gold was to be used to purchase German optical technologies. The I-52 also carried fourteen passengers including engineers and technicians from Nihon Kogaku K.K. who were to study German anti-aircraft gun sights, and scientists/engineers from the Denki K. K. and the Mitsubishi Instrument Company who were to study German anti-aircraft directors. Another engineer aboard was to study Daimler Benz's techniques for building engines for torpedo boats. The mission was doomed from the start as the Allies were monitoring and deciphering almost all of the Japanese radio traffic between the submarine commanders and their bases.

The I-52 arrived in Singapore and loaded 120 tons of tin ingots, 59 tons of 'caoutchouc' (raw rubber) in bales and 3⅓ tons of quinine. From Singapore the submarine went via the Sunda Strait into the Indian Ocean, to attempt a passage around Cape of Good Hope, Africa, en-route to the German U-boat base at Lorient, France. The I-52, code-named 'Momi' (Evergreen), was the fifth IJN submarine to attempt such a passage to France. The submarine travelled submerged during the day and surfaced at night to charge her batteries and replenish her air supply.

After passing around the Cape of Good Hope and entering the Atlantic, the captain, Commander Uno Kameo, sent his first message to the Germans. However,

The U-862 arriving in Penang Harbour. (*Author*)

by this time in the war, British and American Intelligence had broken both Germany and Japan's military codes. The code-breakers picked up her transmission and relayed her position and predicted route to an American ASW group patrolling in the Atlantic. The Japanese naval attaché in Berlin signalled Tokyo and the I-52 telling them that the Allies had landed in Normandy, stating that the arrival of the I-52 at Lorient would be dangerous and, depending on the situation, they might have to proceed to Norway. He also instructed the captain of the I-52 to rendezvous with a U-boat giving them the coordinates. The radio transmission was intercepted, decoded and passed via special intelligence 'Ultra' signals to an American ASW group operating near the Azores. The I-52 rendezvoused with Kapitänleutnant Kurt Lange's U-530, 850 miles west of the Cape Verde Islands. One of the U-boat's crew, Leutnant Schafer, was taken aboard the I-52 to help navigate the last leg of the journey. They also took on board two German radio operators and a Naxos FuMB 7 radar detector. The Naxos was to be installed and be operational by the time I-52 reached European waters. After the U-530 left, the I-52 once again ran on the surface at night, but then a Grumman TBF Avenger torpedo bomber of VC-69 from the escort carrier USS *Bogue* (CVE-9), picked up the I-52 on her radar. The pilot, Lieutenant Commander Jesse Taylor, dropped flares illuminating the huge 2,564-ton Type C3 submarine on the surface making about 12 knots. He then dropped two 354lb Mark 54 depth bombs, but the I-52 dived and evaded the attack. The crew of the Avenger then laid sonobuoys over a square mile of sea and tracked the submarine. Minutes later, the Avenger's radar operator, Ed Whitlock, heard the I-52's propellers in his headset. Jesse Taylor manoeuvred his aircraft into

Japanese submarine I-52. (*Author*)

position and dropped a new top-secret Mark 24 'Fido' acoustic homing torpedo. After a long wait, Taylor's crew heard a loud explosion. By this time another TBF Avenger, flown by Lieutenant jg. William Gordon, with a civilian underwater sound expert Price Fish aboard, arrived and dropped more sonobuoys. Minutes later they picked up the sounds of the damaged submarine's propellers. The second Avenger then dropped another 'Fido' torpedo that found the submarine and seconds later Gordon and Fish heard the explosion and then the sounds of the submarine breaking up underwater. The I-52 sank with all ninety-five crewmen, fourteen passengers and the three German sailors. The following day the USS *Janssen* (DE-396), one of the *Bogue*'s escorts, found a large oil slick at the site of the sinking and salvaged over a ton of raw rubber bales and other debris floating on the surface.

Had the Allies not been able to decipher the Japanese codes things may have turned out very differently. Despite the loss of the submarines and their cargoes that ran the blockade, a substantial amount of important technological material did manage to get to Japan from Germany and more was destined to be sent. This was highlighted when, just after the D-Day landings, a number of factories and warehouses in Bordeaux and in some other manufacturing towns were discovered to have large amounts of technical equipment ready for shipment to Japan. Also the Japanese had developed their version of the Messerschmitt Me 262 jet fighter (Nakajima 9JY) and the rocket-propelled fighter the Messerschmitt Me 163B Komet (Mitsubishi J8M), neither of which were used in combat. It would be interesting to know how the Japanese did obtain this technology as it wasn't until much later in the war that the Germans developed these types of aircraft.

As the war progressed, and after making initial gains against the enemy, the submarine force never became a major weapon in the Japanese armoury and towards the end of the war was relegated to delivering supplies and reinforcements to beleaguered islands. The US Navy recognised that as they made major gains in the Pacific and their supply lines became stretched as they closed in on Japan, the Japanese submarine force would become a formidable defence weapon. But because the submarines' role as an attack weapon had been greatly reduced it lost its effectiveness and subsequently gave the Americans almost a free rein in the Pacific and Indian Oceans.

Front three-quarter view of the Mitsubishi J8M, a copy of the German Messerschmitt Me 163 Komet. (*Author*)

With the Marianas lost and Japanese forces now in retreat, new defence lines had to be drawn up, only this time they included the Japanese homeland. The Japanese High Command decided that there were four areas of attack that the Allied forces might take. It was thought that the Philippines would most likely be the target for the next invasion, The four areas were given the name Shō-Gō (Victory Operation); Shō-Gō 1 covered the Philippines, Shō-Gō 2 Formosa, Shō-Gō 3 Honshu and Shō-Gō 4 Hokkaido and the Kirile Islands. Whilst the remnants of the air force were reorganised into new Air Fleets, the Navy's submarines were recalled to bases in Japan for refitting, repairs and servicing. Inexperienced crews replaced some of the battle-hardened crewmembers who were undergoing long-overdue medical treatment. The loss of so many aircraft and crews during the 'Marianas Turkey Shoot' was of major concern.

Admiral Soemu Toyoda, Chief of the Combined Fleet, after receiving intelligence information, decided that 1 August 1944 would most likely be the day that the

Japanese version of the Messerschmitt Me 262, the Nakajima J9N1. (*Author*)

Americans would launch their attack to attempt to retake the Philippines and Shō-Gō 1 would be the area that would take the brunt of the attack. Admiral Toyoda placed the Sixth Submarine Force, which consisted of the I-12, I-26, I-35, I-37, I-38, I-41, I-44, I-45, I-53, I-54, I-177, RO-41, RO-43, RO-46 and RO-47 under his direct control. These submarines would be used to ambush the American ships and assist in the attacks by surface ships. The Seventh Submarine Force, under the command of Rear Admiral Noburu Ōwada, had just three submarines, the RO-112, RO-113 and RO-115, and these would remain in a state of readiness to be used for transportation purposes.

During the summer of 1944, the Americans, under the command of Admiral William F. Halsey, carried out a number of successful hit-and-run attacks on the Philippines, just to test the strength and readiness of the Japanese force. Halsey figured that the Japanese were suffering from a lack of men and supplies, as resistance during these 'skirmishes' was found to be sadly lacking. With this in mind the Americans decided to cut Japan's supply lines to south-east Asia by depriving them of fuel and supplies. There were two schools of thought regarding this, Admiral Chester Nimitz favoured blockade, whilst General Douglas McArthur favoured a more direct approach by invading the Philippines. After lengthy discussion it was decided to take a direct approach and invade the central island of Leyte. When the army attacked, the Seventh Fleet, accompanied by ships of the Australian navy, would give close naval support.

In July all the submarines that had survived the Marianas battle were recalled to various island bases for servicing, repairs and supplies. This was just the start of the retreat of the Japanese forces in preparation for what they realised was to become the decisive battle. August 1st 1944 was the date set as the day of readiness by the commander-in-chief, Admiral Soemu Toyoda. The plan, on paper, was a relatively simple one. The land-based air forces based in the Philippines would attack the enemy fleet, whilst the surface fleet would leave their base in Brunei and attack the American invasion force as they approached the landing beaches of the Philippines.

Shō-Gō 1 was initially set up around surface ships, including the giant battleships *Yamato* and *Musashi*, and, because the carrier-based aircraft groups had been decimated in the 'Marianas Turkey Shoot', the land-based air groups. The remnants of the carrier-based aircraft of the First Air Fleet were placed under the command of Vice Admiral Kimpei Yeraoka and based in the Philippines, whilst a new Second Air Fleet, under the command of Vice Admiral Shigeru Fukudome, was formed and based on the island of Formosa and southern Japan.

The battle for the Philippines as far as the Japanese were concerned, consisted of four main separate engagements: the Battle of the Sibuyan Sea, the Battle of Surigao, the Battle off Cape Engano and the Battle of Samar plus a number of comparatively minor skirmishes. It began in earnest on 12 October 1944 with a series of raids by US carrier aircraft on the Japanese airfields on Formosa and the

Ryukyu Islands. The intention was to destroy as many enemy aircraft as possible in order to reduce the aerial threat to the invading forces. The air battle between the American carrier-based aircraft and the Japanese land-based aircraft was intense, with the end result that the Japanese lost over 600 aircraft, which was almost their entire air strength in that area. This was a devastating blow to the Japanese. At sea, Admiral Shigeyoshi Miwa instructed the 1st Submarine Group, consisting of the I-12, I-26, I-36, I-37, I-41, I-44, I-45, I-53 I-54, I-177, RO-41, RO-43 and RO-47, to operate within the Shō-Gō 1 area, co-ordinating their attack with surface ships and to try and ambush the American Fleet.

The deployment of Japanese submarines during the Leyte Gulf battle. Three of the submarines, I-45, I-46 and I-54, were lost on the first day, 27 October 1944.

The 7th Submarine Group, under the command of Rear Admiral Noburu Ōwada, consisting of just three submarines, the RO-12, RO-13 and RO-15, remained in Truk ready to be used as transports or for attacking any American ships that may have managed to slip through the Shō-Gō 1 cordon.

The first major *Kaiten* attack had been scheduled to take place at the end of September 1944, but was delayed after the Americans had captured Ulithi Atoll in the Carolinas. Twelve Type 1 *Kaiten*s were readied for the mission led by Lieutenant

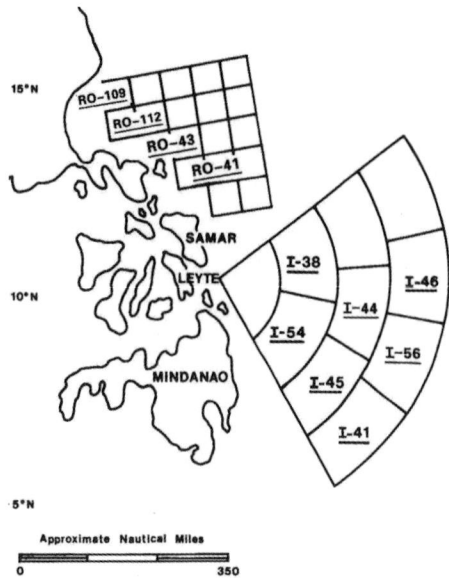

The I-47 submarine with *Kaiten*s on her deck rendezvousing at sea with a supply ship. (*Author*)

Seiko Nishina, the co-inventor of the *Kaiten*. At his feet in his submarine were the ashes of his friend and co-inventor of the *Kaiten*, Lieutenant Hiroshi Kuroki, who had died during a training exercise. Three I-class submarines, the I-36, I-37 and I-47, were assigned to be the mother submarines and on 8 November left Otsushima with their charges aboard. Once in the open sea the I-37 headed for Kossol Passage whilst the I-36 and I-47 headed for Ulithi Atoll. On 19 November the I-37 was preparing to launch her *Kaiten*s when she was attacked and sunk by depth charges from the destroyers USS *McCoy Reynolds* (DE-440) and the USS *Conklin* (DE-439), after being picked up on the radar of the destroyer USS *Nicholas* (DD-449).

The I-36 and I-47 headed towards Ulithi Atoll, keeping in constant touch with a Mitsubishi Ki-46 reconnaissance aircraft (one of the few times the Army co-operated with the Navy), the messages being relayed via Tokyo. As they approached the atoll they were told that there were three groups consisting of battleships and aircraft carriers at anchor. The four *Kaiten*s aboard the I-47 were launched successfully as it approached the lagoon, the pilots ordered to penetrate as far as they could before attacking their targets. One hour later the I-47, now submerged south-east of Ulithi Atoll, heard explosions and immediately set a course for Japan. The I-36, however, was having major problems. Two of her *Kaiten*s were stuck fast and could not be launched, whilst a third was starting to leak rapidly. The fourth managed to be launched and headed for the lagoon. As soon as the three *Kaiten* pilots were back inside the I-36, the submarine set a course for home. Three days after arriving back at base a debrief was held using aerial photographs taken by reconnaissance aircraft and reports from the crews of the I-47 and I-36. It was claimed that an aircraft carrier had been sunk along with two battleships, but in truth it was a propaganda exercise because the only ship sunk was the auxiliary oil tanker USS *Mississinewa* (*AO*-59) with the loss of sixty-three of her crew.

The situation as far as the Japanese High Command was concerned was that the war had reached a critical stage, so much so that they were desperately looking for any signs of victory at any cost. Then on 13 October Air Wing T of the Second Air Fleet became embroiled in the battle for Formosa when they intercepted the American landing force. The battle lasted three days and at first it appeared that the US task force had retreated, with the Japanese Navy Headquarters claiming that their aircraft had sunk eleven aircraft carriers, two battleships, three cruisers with serious damage to a further eight aircraft carriers and four cruisers. In Japan the news was greeted with great excitement, but in reality the only casualties suffered by the American task force were serious damage to the heavy cruiser USS *Canberra* (CA-70) and the light cruiser USS *Houston* (CL-8), both of which were later repaired and returned to active service. On 17 October 1944 over 700 American ships appeared off Leyte Gulf and over the following three days discharged more than 100,000 troops. The Battle of Leyte Gulf had begun.

USS *Mississinewa* burning after being hit by a *Kaiten* suicide torpedo. (*USN*)

The Japanese submarines which had been assigned to Shō-Gō 1 were told to patrol designated sectors rather that set up picket lines. The setting of staggered picket lines had proved to be ineffective in the past, patrolling sectors was deemed to be the best way of intercepting the American battle fleet, but by the time the submarines were in position the decisive sea battle was over. The submarines were ordered to go after any ships in the area and over the following month has some success. During the latter part of October 1944 the I-56 carried out an unsuccessful torpedo attack on the escort carrier USS *Santee* (CVE-29) whilst two days later the I-41 attacked the USS *Reno* (CL-96). Both aircraft carriers were damaged, but nor serious enough to put them out of action. The I-45 also has a success when it torpedoed and sank the destroyer USS *Eversole* (DE-404) before she was sunk by the destroyer USS *Whitehurst* (DE-634). The Japanese also suffered the loss of six of their fleet submarines during the same period.

American and Allied losses during the Battle of Leyte Gulf:

The United States lost seven warships:
One light aircraft carrier, the USS *Princeton* (CVL-23).
Two escort carriers, the USS *Gambier Bay* (CVE-73) and USS *St. Lo* (CVE-63) (*St. Lo* was the first major warship to be sunk by a kamikaze attack).
Two destroyers, the USS *Hoel* (DD-533) and the USS *Johnstone* (DD-557).
Two escort destroyers, the USS *Samuel S. Roberts* (DE-413) and the USS *Eversole* (DE-404).

The Australian cruiser HMAS *Australia* (D84).

Japanese losses during the Battle of Leyte Gulf:
One fleet aircraft carrier, the *Zuikaku*.
Three light aircraft carriers, the *Zuiho, Chiyoda* and *Chitose*.
Three battleships, the *Musashi, Yamashiro* and *Fuso*.
Six heavy cruisers, the *Atago, Maya, Suzuya, Chokai, Chikuma* and *Mogami*.
Four light cruisers, the *Noshiro, Abukuma, Tama* and *Kiru*.
Nine destroyers, the *Nowaki, Hayashima, Yamagumo, Asagumo, Michishio, Akizuki, Hatsuzuki, Wakaba* and *Uranami*.

This was a devastating blow for the Japanese Navy: their air force had also been crushed in terms of aircraft and, more importantly, air crews. During the battles the Japanese submarine force contributed almost nothing as they were deployed in the wrong places and for the wrong reasons and so were unable to close on the American fleet. Once again the lack of communication, the mixed messages and the wrong deployment of the submarines, highlighted the problems between the submarine commanders and their command headquarters. This inevitably gave the Army more ammunition, in the way of criticism, to further their control over the armed forces and decide strategy and policy.

Despite early setbacks the *Kikumizu* Unit, as it was called, was ready for operational duties by the end of November 1944. Three parent submarines, the I-36, I-37 and I-47, were readied to take the *Kaiten*s, the I-36 and I-47 were sent to Ulithi and the I-37 to the Kossol Passage close to Palau island, south-east of the Philippines. Reports had come back that there were over 100 American ships, including six aircraft carriers and a battleship, at anchor in Ulithi Atoll. This of course provided an opportunity not to be missed, but with only two submarines and eight human torpedoes the targets had to be selected with care. All the human torpedoes were launched but no results ever came back and the fate of the crews is not known, one can only assume that the mission was a failure and all the crews lost. There were no reports of attacks by the Americans, so it was assumed that none of the *Kaiten*s reached their targets and were lost. Two of the three submarines, the I-36 and I-47, returned to Kure without incident, but just hours before the attack the I-37 was spotted, and two American destroyers, USS *Conklin* (DE 439) and USS *McCoy Reynolds* (DE-440), immediately started a search and within hours had picked up a sonar signal. The two destroyers attacked with a pattern of Mark 10 Hedgehog projector charges. A series of violent underwater explosions followed and minute's later debris and oil came to the surface. There were no further contacts and no survivors were found.

By the end of 1944 the Japanese submarine force was in disarray and struggling to remain operational. They had suffered disastrous losses and the submarines that remained were in dire need of repairs and servicing. The strain and stress on the crews was also creating problems and sickness was rampant throughout. As the American drew nearer and nearer to the Japanese mainland the Japanese Navy was now reverting to a defensive position.

What was becoming more and more apparent was that, unlike the Allied and the German submarine commands, the Japanese appeared to have almost no strategy. At the beginning of the war the Japanese submarines roamed the Indian and Pacific Oceans almost unopposed, but once the Americans had recovered from Pearl Harbor, and had created an operational strategy, things started to change. The Japanese on the other hand still had a tendency to operate as 'lone wolves', unlike their German counterparts who operated in 'wolfpacks', and only appeared to have some sort of strategy when deployed on picket lines. A lot of the problems the Japanese suffered from was the lack of leadership, intelligence information, communication and the sometimes almost vitriolic infighting between the Army and the Navy.

Chapter 8

Aircraft-Carrying Submarines

The Japanese use of aircraft-carrying submarines was without doubt one of the most innovative developments of the war, and had these giant submarines been put into action very much earlier, then they might have caused the Americans and the Allies a great deal of concern. Japan was the only country to ever use this innovation successfully under battle conditions and I feel it deserves a chapter on its own.

The use of aircraft on submarines was not a new concept; the Germans had trialled it during the First World War by putting a Friedrichshafen FF29a seaplane across the bows of the U-12 submarine and floating it off. It then flew along the coast of Britain before returning to Zeebrugge. The British attempt was to convert the M-2 submarine by removing its 12in gun and replacing it with an aircraft hangar and then used a catapult to launch the aircraft, a Parnall Peto. After some initial success, in 1932 a disaster happened when the submarine sank during a rapid surfacing trial, resulting in the death of the entire crew, causing plans to continue the experiment to be scrapped. The Americans with their S-1 submarine and MS-1 aircraft attempted it with limited success, as did the French with their giant submarine *Surcouf* and its Marcel-Besson MB-35 aircraft. The *Surcouf* disappeared off the island of Martinique in the Caribbean during the Second World War under mysterious circumstances. No trace was ever found, although a number of bodies were found washed ashore at San Blas, Panama.

Two years after Japan had acquired seven war-prize U-boats at the end of the First World War, they purchased two Heinkel-Caspar U-1 aircraft, with the intention of placing them on a submarine, but it was 1927 before trials had been completed. By this time the Japanese had developed their own aircraft, the Yokosho 1-go, based on the U-1, but with one or two modifications and a more powerful rotary engine. This aircraft was operated from their submarine the I-5 for 18 months, but the submarine was deemed to be too slow and so the aircraft was transferred to one of the I-51 class submarines at the beginning of 1928. Using the knowledge gained from I-go, the Yokosuka E6Y1 was developed. The first successful testing of the Yokosuka E6Y1 was in May 1928, from the submarine I-51. Subsequent tests in 1930 and 1931 were successful and the aircraft was officially adopted as a reconnaissance seaplane for the submarine fleet.

The Germans had experimented with another type of aircraft on a submarine operating in the Atlantic and the North Sea, but such was the unpredictable weather

Friedrichshafen FF.29a across the bows of the German submarine U-1. (*Author*)

in both these waters that the idea was scrapped. But with the Japanese coming into the war, the German long-range Type IXD2 submarines of the Monsoon Group, were ordered to co-operate with the Japanese and by doing so started to patrol the Indian Ocean. They developed the radically simple single-seater Focke-Achgelis Fa 330 *Bachstelze* (Water Wagtail) gyrocopter. The parts were housed in waterproof cylinders on the aft section of the deck, where they were assembled and the craft attached to a tethered cable on a specially constructed platform. The submarine then increased speed and the little rotorcraft would lift off its platform to an operating height of between 200 and 500ft. The craft had no engine and was much

Parnall Peto being launched from the submarine M-2 in Weymouth Bay. (*Author*)

The French submarine *Surcouf* with her Marcel-Besson MB-35 scout aircraft on her aft deck. (*Author*)

like a kite, but with rotor blades. In the event of an emergency the observer would release the tethering cable whilst the submarine crash-dived, with the intention of picking up the luckless observer later. This was not always successful. Admiral Yamamoto had been looking at this concept for some time, realising the need for good reconnaissance, as they knew that observation was the most reliable way of finding out the enemy's activities.

Early trials with the I-6 submarine were very encouraging, resulting in the adoption of a new submarine design that allowed for a catapult to be mounted on the deck. Eleven more aircraft-carrying submarines were built, the I-5, I-7, I-8, I-10, I-15, I-17, I-19, I-21, I-23 and I-26. Initially the aircraft used were small single-seaters with a maximum speed of 90 knots and endurance of just three hours. The aircraft carried a simple W/T set and were unarmed, making them extremely vulnerable if spotted and attacked by enemy fighters. The one main stumbling block was the launch and recovery procedure that took one hour for each to complete.

Japanese E6Y1, designed for use on a submarine, in flight. (*Author*)

Focke Achgelis Fa 330 being launched from a German U-boat. (*Author*)

This meant that the submarine had to be on the surface for these periods of time and extremely vulnerable to attack, so the usual launch times were just before dawn and recovery carried out just after sunrise. However there were a number of occasions when the submarine had to abandon the aircraft and dive after being spotted on the surface. The I-25 and I-26 left Yokosuka in May 1942, to carry out an air reconnaissance of Kodiak in the Aleutian archipelago. Submarine-borne air reconnaissance was becoming more and more hazardous and on two occasions both the I-26 and I-25 had to crash-dive, only just managing to get their aircraft aboard and into its hangar. Later, off the Solomon Islands, the I-9 lost her aircraft when she had to crash-dive leaving it still on deck. There is no record of what happened to the pilot in these circumstances. Another problem that faced the crews was the weather. If the seas were too rough it became extremely difficult to launch and recover the aircraft, but despite these dangers a number of successful missions were carried out, none more so than the mission carried out by the I-25 submarine.

Warrant Flying Officer Nobuo Fujita had put forward the idea that if he were able to take-off from the I-25, he may be able to inflict substantial damage on the American ships. The I-25's Executive Officer, Lieutenant Tatsuo Tsukudo, was impressed by the suggestion and discussed with Fujita in detail how he thought the Panama Canal Locks, aircraft factories and naval bases around the San Diego and San Francisco areas could be attacked.

'Put your ideas in writing to the Admirals in Tokyo,' said Tsukudo. Fujita laughed, 'Why would superior graduates who had studied at Etajima Naval Academy listen to a mere farm boy?' But at the insistence of Tsukudo he wrote a letter outlining his plans and gave it to the Executive Officer. In the months that followed, Fujita and his crewman Petty Officer Shoji Okuda carried out a number of reconnaissance

Series of images showing the assembling and launching of a Fa 330 rototcopter from a German 'Monsoon' group submarine in the Indian Ocean. (*Author*)

flights over Australia and New Zealand. These were hazardous, because had they been spotted by Allied fighters they would most certainly been shot down. Because of this risk, Nobuo and Okuda agreed that they would lead the enemy aircraft away from the I-25 and crash the aircraft into the sea. If they survived the crash they would commit suicide.

The I-25 was involved briefly in the Battle of Midway and was off Vancouver Island, having just attacked the US Naval Wireless Navigational station with her deck gun, causing little damage, when she was ordered to attack the US Naval base at Fort Stevens, Astoria, Oregon. After managing to get off seventeen rapid rounds of 5.5in shells, causing only very slight damage, the I-25 set sail for Yokosuka. Nobuo Fujita had forgotten all about the letter he had sent to the Japanese Imperial Naval Headquarters, until on 10 July 1942, Lieutenant Commander Tagami handed him a message: 'WARRANT OFFICER FUJITA IS INSTRUCTED TO REPORT TO IMPERIAL NAVAL HEADQUARTERS AT ONCE'.

A nervous Fujita reported the following morning to the Japanese Imperial Naval Headquarters at Yokosuka. Entering the office of Commander Iura, he was told that

Warrant Flying Officer Nobuo Fujita in flight gear. (*Author*)

Shoji Okuda, who was Fujita's observer on his two bombing missions. (*Author*)

his idea had been accepted, but he was going to bomb the American mainland, not warships. Minutes later the door opened and in walked another naval commander who Fujita immediately recognised as Prince Takamatsu, the Emperor's younger brother. Totally bowled over to be in such distinguished company, Warrant Officer Fujita could only vaguely remember what the meeting was about. He was shown a map of the West Coast and a point 75 miles north of the Californian border. He was to bomb the Oregon forests with four 76kg incendiary bombs. These bombs were of an especially powerful type which generated a temperature of around 1,500 degrees within a radius of 300 yards. At first Fujita was not too happy about bombing forests, preferring to hit the cities of Seattle, Portland, Los Angeles and San Francisco, but he was told that the forests would burn, causing great devastation.

Admiral Yamamoto had long been an advocate of attacking America and it came to fruition on the morning of 9 September 1942, when a plan was formulated to bomb the vast forests of Oregon using incendiary bombs with the intention of setting fire to them. If successful, it would be the first time the United States of America had been subjected to mainland aerial bombing. Fujita and his observer Petty Officer Shoji Okuda made their final preparations by placing some strands of their hair, fingernail cuttings and a will in a special box made of paulownia wood. In the event of the aircraft not returning from the mission, these remains would be sent to their families. Their Yokosuka E14Y1 'Glen' aircraft was catapulted from the deck of the I-25 and headed towards Cape Blanco lighthouse off the coast of Oregon. They were to carry out one of the most audacious missions of the war by carrying out an aerial attack on the American mainland, something no country had ever done or since, and setting fire to one of the forests of Oregon. Crossing the coast, the aircraft swung north-east heading for the forests, close to the town of

Fujita and Okuda with their Yokosuka E14Y1 floatplane. (*Author*)

Brookings, and after flying for about 50 miles, Fujita ordered his observer Okuda to drop the first of the 76kg incendiary bombs. The first one struck the ground and burst with a brilliant white light, causing a fire to start. Continuing in an easterly direction for a few more miles he ordered the second bomb to be dropped. Both bomb attacks caused short-lived fires mainly because in the preceding weeks heavy rain had soaked the forests thus preventing the fires from spreading. The aircraft returned to its pre-arranged rendezvous and was picked up by the submarine. It was while disassembling the aircraft that the submarine was spotted by a patrolling Lockheed A-29 Hudson bomber. Fortunately the crew had just closed the hangar door and with minutes the I-25 had crash-dived. The Hudson dropped a couple of depth charges that caused some minor leaks, but nothing serious.

The following day a second attack was planned, this time just before dawn. Once again the two 76kg incendiary bombs caused a couple of minor fires, but nothing serious. On returning to the rendezvous point the aircraft's crew discovered that the submarine was not there. After flying around in ever-increasing circles for what must have felt like an eternity, Fujita spotted some oil on the surface of the sea glinting in the dawn light and by following it came across the submarine on the surface. By sheer luck, coupled with an oil leak from the submarine's engines, he had managed to find the proverbial needle in a haystack. The aircraft was quickly hoisted aboard and stowed away in its hangar. To recover the aircraft after a mission a collapsible crane was used. The crane had an electrically-operated hoist and was capable of lifting approximately 4½ tons (5 short tons). It was raised mechanically to a height of 26ft (8m) via a motor operated from inside the boat. The boom extended out to a length of 39ft (11.8m). The crane would lift the aircraft from the water, swing it inboard and place it on its launching cradle. The aircraft landed close to the submarine and taxied to where it could be recovered by the crane. The wings would be folded back against the fuselage, the tail folded down and the floats removed and stowed in their containers. The aircraft was then pushed back easily into its hangar. The crane would then be collapsed and stowed in an open recessed compartment on the

An E14Y1 about to be launched from the I-29 submarine. Note the laced Japanese flag (*Hinomaru*) on the side of the conning tower. (*Author*)

An E14Y1 being launched from the I-29. (*Author*)

forward port side just below the top deck. This whole process took less than 30 minutes. Civilian observers on land had spotted the Japanese aircraft flying away from the forest and had alerted the authorities. Fighter aircraft were scrambled to intercept but were sent in the wrong direction.

The second mission had highlighted one of the major problems facing the use of aircraft operating from submarines and that was locating the submarine after the mission. So to help the crew of the aircraft a special temporary trim system was fitted to the submarine, allowing it to loiter submerged and stationary whilst awaiting the return of the aircraft. However, the operation of this system was noisy and its usefulness was in doubt as it left the submarine vulnerable to attack if spotted.

An E14Y1 climbing away after being launched from the I-29. (*Author*)

Cape Blanco lighthouse just north of Brookings.

It was not adopted. The missions were not the success that had been hoped for, mainly because the incendiary bombs had been dropped on rain-soaked forests and subsequently did not cause any serious fires. A third raid was planned, but the weather had turned rough so the submarine's captain, Lieutenant Commander Meiji Tagami, called it off. Launching the aircraft would have not been such a problem, but recovering it would have been almost impossible. However, it did show that America was vulnerable to attack, heightening the country's awareness. On his return to Japan, Warrant Flying Officer Fujita was hailed as a hero and spent the rest of the war as a flying instructor. In 1962 Fujita was invited to Brooking. After being given assurances that he would not be accused of being a war criminal, he presented his family's 400-year-old *katana* (sword) in a gesture of atonement. Shortly before his death he was made an honorary citizen of Brooking.

Admiral Yamamoto's proposal to Fleet Headquarters on 13 January 1942 had come about shortly after the attack on Pearl Harbor. He conceived the idea of taking the war to the United States mainland by making aerial attacks against cities along the US western and eastern seaboards using submarine-launched naval aircraft. He commissioned Captain Kameto Kuroshima to make a feasibility study. Trials, and indeed some successful missions, had been carried out with single reconnaissance aircraft being used aboard submarines as in the case of the I-25 and stated that the success of this mission called for the concept of submarine design to be taken to a new level. From these initial successful experiments Yamamoto proposed the building of much larger submarines capable of carrying three fighter-bomber aircraft. The I-400 class submarines, as they were called, were to be the flagships of the submarine

An E14Y1 about to be recovered by crane after a reconnaissance flight. (*Author*)

fleet and would impress not only in their size but in their potential to reign supreme in the Pacific. He called for a fleet of eighteen large submarines capable of making three round trips to the west coast of the United States without refuelling, or one round trip to any point on the globe. They also had to be able to store and launch at least three attack aircraft armed with one torpedo or one 1,800lb (800kg) bomb. By March general design plans for the submarines had been finalised. Construction of the I-400 commenced at Kure Dockyard on 18 January 1943 followed by four more, the I-401 (April 1943), I-402 (October 1943), I-403 (September 1943) and the I-404 (February 1944), but only the first three were ever completed.

The I-400 class submarines were fitted with four 2,250hp engines and carried enough fuel to go round the world one-and-a-half times, more than enough to reach the United States travelling east or west. Measuring more than 400ft (122m) in length overall, the I-400 class displaced 5,900 tons (6,500 short tons), more than double that of the American submarines. The cross section of the hull had a unique figure-of-eight shape that afforded the necessary strength and stability to handle the weight of the large aircraft hangar built amidships on the top deck. The hangar was a cylindrical watertight compartment 55ft (16m) long and 11ft (3.5m) in diameter. The outer access door could be opened hydraulically from within or manually from the outside by turning a large hand-wheel connected to a rack and spur mechanism. The door was made waterproof with a 2in (51mm) rubber gasket. The conning tower was offset to port to allow three aircraft to be stored along the boat's centreline.

On top of the hangar were mounted three waterproof Type 96 triple mount 1in (25mm) cannon for anti-aircraft defence, two aft and one forward of the conning

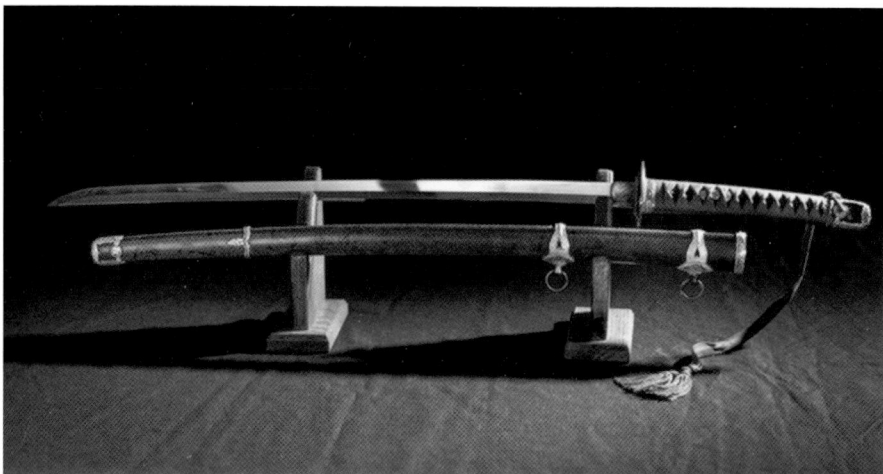

Nobuo Fujita's sword on display. (*Author*)

tower. One Type 11 5.5in (140mm) deck gun was also positioned aft of the hangar and had a range of 16,333 yards (15,000m). Eight torpedo tubes were mounted in the bow, four above and four below, but no aft tubes were fitted. Originally the hangars of the I-400 class were designed to hold two specially designed Aichi M6A Sieran aircraft. However, in 1943, Commander Yasuo Fuijimori, Submarine Staff Officer of the Naval General Staff, put forward a suggestion that the hangar could be enlarged and lengthened to take three aircraft. This was deemed to be feasible and work was started on extending the hangars to take three Sierans.

The Sieran had been specifically modified for use aboard the submarines and could carry a 1,800lb (800kg) bomb over a distance of 620 miles (1,000km) at a speed of 295mph (475km/h). To fit the aircraft inside the narrow confines of the hangar, the wings rotated 90 degrees downwards and folded backward hydraulically against the fuselage. The horizontal stabilisers folded down and the top of the vertical stabiliser folded over so that the overall forward profile of the aircraft was within the diameter of its propeller. When deployed for flight the Sieran had a wingspan of 39ft (12m) and a length of 38ft (11.6m). A crew of four could prepare and launch all three aircraft in 45 minutes (15 minutes if the aircraft's floats were not attached). Because the aircraft would normally be launched at night, small key areas of the aircraft were coated with waterproof luminescent paint to assist the crew when assembling in the dark.

Located just below the main deck on either side of the catapult track were two special watertight containers containing the floats for the Seiran aircraft. These could be easily and quickly slid out on ramps and attached beneath the aircraft's wings. A third set of floats and additional spares were also kept inside the hangars. With the increased hangar size to accommodate a third aircraft, this of course meant that additional spares had to be stored, making space within the hangars very limited.

The I-402 with a US Navy prize crew aboard, coming alongside the USS *Proteus*. Note the small HA-20 submarine alongside. (*USN*)

The Sieran floatplanes were launched by means of an 85ft (26m) Type 4 No. 2 Model 10 compressed air catapult mounted on the forward deck of the submarine. Underneath the catapult track were four high-pressure air cylinders connected in parallel to a piston. The aircraft was mounted on top of a collapsible carriage via attachment points along the fuselage and when the launch pressure was reached and released, the aircraft would be hurled along the track and into the air, although the piston itself would only travel between 8 and 10ft during the operation.

One major problem that faced the designers of the aircraft was that the engines had to be run for at least 20 minutes before take-off. This was because the viscosity of the oil in the cold engine was so thick that it had to be heated and thinned before it would travel round the narrow channels inside the engine. Running up the engine inside the hangar would subject the submarine's crew to deadly carbon monoxide fumes. To overcome this, engineers devised a heating system that could be attached to each engine so that the oil could be pre-heated prior to engine start and launch. The system was a complete success. Once the aircraft had been launched the submarine submerged, but because of the vastness of the open sea, it required pinpoint navigation accuracy on the part of the aircraft's observer to enable the crew to find the submarine again.

The I-400 class submarines were equipped with the very latest technology and the electronics on board included a Mark 3, Model 1 air-search radar equipped with two antennas. This unit was capable of detecting aircraft out to a range of 43 miles (80km). The submarines were also equipped with Mark 2, Model 2 air/ surface radar seta with distinctive horn-shaped antennas. Each boat carried an E27 radar-warning receiver connected to both a trainable dipole antenna and a fixed non-directional antenna made up of a wire basket and two metal rods. The submarines were all equipped with two periscopes of German manufacture, about 40ft (12.2m) long, one for use during daylight hours, the other for night-time use.

Strung along the submarine's gunwales were two parallel sets of demagnetisation cables running from the stern to the bow planes. These were intended to dissipate the static charge that built up when the hull sliced through the water, which caused the steel in the hull to deteriorate over time. A special anechoic coating, made from a mixture of gum, asbestos and adhesives, was applied to the hull from the waterline to the bilge keel. This coating was apparently based on German research, though completely different in composition from the German anechoic coatings such as Alberich or Tarnmatte. The use of this mixture was intended to absorb or diffuse the enemy's sonar pulses and dampen down the reverberations from the boat's internal machinery. Theoretically this made detection whilst submerged more difficult, though its effectiveness was never conclusively established because none of the I-400 class submarines ever saw action.

In May 1944, the I-401 was fitted with a German-supplied snorkel, a hydraulically-raised air intake device allowing the boat to run its diesel engines and recharge its batteries while remaining at periscope depth. This retrofit occurred while the boat was laid up at Kure for repairs after being damaged by an American mine in April during sea trials. The I-402 was completed shortly before the war ended, but had been converted to a tanker and was never equipped with an aircraft.

The I-400 class submarines were unwieldy and relatively difficult to manoeuvre whilst on the surface because of their small rudders. The large conning tower

The launching rail on the I-400 submarine. (*USN*)

The launching rail of the I-401 submarine. (*USN*)

superstructure, which was offset to accommodate the aircraft hangars, also caused the sub to veer off course during any strong winds. The maximum safe diving depth of the I-400 class was only 82 per cent of its overall length, which presented a problem if the submarine dived at too steep an angle in an emergency. Because of the large aircraft hangars and conning towers, all I-400 class submarines had a significant radar signature whilst on the surface, and could be detected by aircraft relatively easily. Dive time was 56 seconds; nearly double that of the US fleet submarines, which made the Japanese boats susceptible to attack if caught on the surface.

When submerged and travelling at a slow speed of 2 knots, the offset superstructure forced the helmsman to steer seven degrees to starboard in order to steer a straight course. When conducting a torpedo attack the captain had to take into account his larger turning circle into starboard than to port, again because of the offset design. Like in other Japanese submarines, crewmembers had no air-conditioning to control the temperatures in tropical waters and no flush toilets. Lack of cold storage and inadequate sleeping quarters greatly limited the crew's diet and forced some of the crew to sleep on deck or in the passageways.

Looking back towards the conning tower aboard the I-400. (*USN*)

As the war turned against the Japanese and their fleet no longer had free rein in the Pacific, the late Admiral Yamamoto's daring plan to attack the cities of New York, Washington D.C. and a number of other large American cities was reintroduced. It was decided that, although the plan had merit, it was too risky and fraught with logistical problems. Captain Tatsunoke Ariizumi who, through his persistence, had persuaded the Japanese High Command to abandon their plans for an attack on the US mainland and attack the Gatun Locks instead. He argued that a successful attack on the Panama Canal lock gates would cause more damage to key equipment and to morale that any attack on the US mainland. Then, in August 1943, Captain Chikao Yamamoto and Commander Yasuo Fujimori conceived the idea of using the I-400 submarines in a *Sen Toke* (secret submarine attack) to destroy the locks of the Panama Canal in an attempt to cut American supply lines to the Pacific Ocean and disrupt the passage of US ships. The whole force was put under the command of Captain Tatsunoke Ariizumi. Intelligence-gathering on the proposed target began later that year. The Japanese were well aware that American fortifications existed on both sides of the canal. On the Atlantic side the large coastal batteries of Fort Sherman had a range of 30,000 yards (17km), preventing enemy ships from getting

The conning tower of the I-401 showing her radar scanner. (*USN*)

near enough to shell the locks. In the months following Pearl Harbor, air and sea patrols had been strengthened around both entrances and barrage balloons and anti-submarine nets had been erected in August 1942. The 88th Coast Artillery Unit (Anti-Aircraft) had been added to help defend against any aerial attacks.

As the war continued and Japan's military strength declined, security around the Canal became increasingly lax. The Japanese knew this when in January 1944, Commander Fujimori personally interrogated an American POW who had carried out guard duty on the locks. He told Fujimori that defensive air patrols had virtually ceased, since it was considered increasingly unlikely that the Axis powers would ever attack the locks. This information further convinced Fujimori that his plan to attack the Panama Canal was feasible.

A Japanese engineer who had worked on the Panama Canal during its construction handed over hundreds of documents, including blueprints of the Canal's structure and construction methods, to the Naval General Staff. A team of three shipping engineers studied the documents and concluded that the locks at Miaflores on the Pacific side were the most vulnerable to aerial bombing, but the Gatun Locks of the Atlantic side offered a greater chance of causing substantive damage, since it would be harder to halt any outflow of water. They estimated that the Canal would be unusable for at least six months following a successful attack on the locks.

To increase the size of the airborne attack forces, Commander Fujimori requested that two additional fleet submarines still under construction at Kobe, the I-13 and

Image showing the large 140mm gun mounted on the aft deck of the I-401 and also the many anti-aircraft guns mounted around the conning tower. (*USN*)

I-14, be modified to carry two Sieran bombers each, bringing the total numbers of aircraft available to ten. It was originally planned that two of the Seiran bombers would carry torpedoes and the other eight would carry 1,800lb (800kg) bombs. They were to make a combined torpedo and glide bombing attack against the Gatun Locks. Eventually the torpedo bombing method was dispensed with, because only one of the Sieran pilots managed to master the technique.

The Panama Canal strike plan called for four aircraft-carrying submarines (I-400, I-401, I-13 and I-14) to sail eastward across the Pacific to the Gulf of Panama, a journey expected to take two months. At a point 100 miles (185km) off the coast of Ecuador, the submarines would launch their Seiran aircraft at 0300 hours on a moonlit night. The Seirans, without their floats, would fly at an altitude of 13,000ft (4,000m) across the northern coast of Columbia to the vicinity of Colón on the Caribbean side of the isthmus close to the entrance of the Panama Canal. They would then turn westward on a heading of 270 degrees, then turn south-west and make their final approach to the canal locks at dawn. After completing their bombing runs, the Seirans would return to a designated rendezvous point and ditch alongside the waiting submarines where the aircrews would be picked up.

At the beginning of April 1945, Captain Tatsunasuka Arizumi decided that the Seiran pilots would make kamikaze attacks by ramming the gates, rather than the conventional bombing runs, a tactic becoming increasingly common as the war continued to go against the Japanese. The Seiran squadron leader had already suggested as much to Arizumi earlier that month, though for a time this was kept secret from the other aircrew members. At the end of May however, one pilot happen to observe a Seiran having its bomb-release mechanism being removed and replaced with a fixed mount. Realising the implications of this change, he angrily confronted the executive officer of the squadron, who explained that the decision to withhold this intention from the other crewmembers was made to 'avoid mental pressures on the aircrews'.

By 5 June 1945 all four aircraft-carrying submarines had arrived at Nanao Wan, where the Maizuru Naval Arsenal had built a full-scale wooden model of the Gatun Lock gates. It was placed on a raft and towed out into the bay. The following night formal training commenced with the Seiran deck and flight crews practising rapid assembly, catapult launch and recovery of their aircraft together with rudimentary formation flying. From 15 June the Seiran pilots made practice daylight bombing runs against the wooden mock-up gates and by 20 June all training ended and preparations made for the operation. The beginning of July 1945 brought the first submarine flotilla together, which consisted of the I-400, I-401, I-13 and the I-14. The task force was equipped with ten aircraft. The two smaller submarines, the I-13 and the I-14, did not have the fuel capacity for the round trip to the Panama Canal, and were to be refuelled from the bigger boats. Using the same route that was used by the Pearl Harbor attack force, the four submarines, provisioned for a four-month cruise, set sail for Oahu. It was intended that they would head southwards down towards the Colombian coast, then the submarine force would alter course and move in a northerly direction hugging the coastline. When they were in range of the locks, the submarines would surface and launch their Sieran aircraft. Each aircraft would carry either a torpedo or a 1,800lb (800kg) bomb. After take-off the pilots would jettison their floats so as to increase their diving speed when they attacked.

The attack was to take place in two phases. The first, codenamed *Hikari* (Light),

The I-400 at sea during the war. (*Author*)

involved disassembling, crating and loading four Nakajima C6N Saiun ('Myrtle') single-engined, high speed reconnaissance aircraft into the watertight hangars of the I-13 and I-14 and taking them to Truk where they would be reassembled. They would then carry out a number of reconnaissance flights over Ulithi Atoll to confirm the presence of the American aircraft carriers anchored there. The two submarines would then make their way to Hong Kong where they would take on board four Seiran bombers and then head to Singapore to join up with the I-400 and the I-401.

The second phase of the attack, codenamed *Arashi* (Storm), was planned for daybreak on the 17 August 1945 where the I-400 and I-40,1 after a rendezvous with the remainder of the submarine attack force, would launch their six Seiran bombers on a kamikaze mission against the carriers. The six aircraft had been painted all over silver with American star and bar insignias, so as to confuse the enemy in the event they were spotted as they made their approach. The pilots, on discovering this subterfuge, complained bitterly saying that it was a personal insult to them to fly their aircraft under American markings, as well as being dishonourable under the rules of war. Each aircraft had a 1,800lb (800kg) bomb bolted to the fuselage and were to fly at less that 150ft (50m) above the water in an effort to avoid detection by radar. It was assumed that the American fighters on CAP would be patrolling at around 13,000ft (4,000m).

On 26 March 1944 an American task force had started a ferocious bombardment of the south-east coast of Okinawa. All Japanese submarines were ordered into the area to engage the enemy but sailed right into an overwhelming anti-submarine operation. The submarine radio traffic had been intercepted and relayed to the task force who were waiting for them. The I-44 and I-56, both of whom were carrying *Kaiten* human torpedoes, had been sunk by destroyers before they got near the task force, while the I-47, also carrying *Kaiten*s, was attacked by aircraft from one of the aircraft carriers and forced to return to Kure to repair extensive damage without launching any of her *Kaiten*s. The I-8, I-46, RO-41 and RO-46 were also lost. One submarine, the I-58, under the command of Commander Mochitsura Hashimoto, reported being attacked over fifty times by aircraft making it almost impossible to get close to the task force, such was the control that the Americans had gained over

Submarine I-14 in Tokyo Harbour. (*JMSDF*)

the sea and air. The I-58 and the I-36 had been tasked to attack ships at anchor off Iwo Jima with their *Kaitens*, but the intense ASW activity in the area made it extremely difficult to get close to their objective. When the two submarines were finally in a position to launch their *Kaitens*, their operation was cancelled and they were ordered to proceed to Okinoshima and assigned to act as a wireless link for the Combined Fleet during an operation that had been planned for 11 March. The two submarines turned reluctantly and headed for Okinoshima, jettisoning their *Kaitens* as they did so. After completing their assignment, the I-58 returned to Kure, and a disappointed Commander Hashimoto complained that he had just been in a position to launch his *Kaitens* when recalled. He was told that the High Command never realised that he had got that close, which once again highlighted the failure of communication that had plagued the Japanese Navy throughout the war.

Then Japanese scout submarines came back with greatly exaggerated information that the Americans had assembled a fleet of fifteen aircraft carriers and supporting ships at Ulithi Atoll in preparation for an attack on the Japanese homeland. But before the attack on the Panama Canal could be realised, reports came through that Okinawa had fallen to the Americans. In Japan the word had reached the Japanese people that the Americans were preparing a massive assault on the home islands. The Japanese Naval High Command decided that an attack on the Panama Canal would have little or no impact on the outcome of the war and a more direct and immediate action was necessary to stem the Allied advance. The Panama Canal mission was aborted and the submarines reassigned to attack the Americans fleet at Ulithi Atoll. The two giant I-400 class submarines were not sent and neither were used again operationally.

For all their technical sophistication and potential, the I-400 class had major basic problems that had never been addressed. Although the I-400s may have been considered to be a major threat had they become operational, there is no doubt they would have been relatively easy targets for the ASW) aircraft that were becoming increasingly more successful.

American aircraft carriers at Ulithi Atoll. (*USN*)

The I-58 and I-53 at Kure in 1945. (*USN*)

The I-400 aircraft-carrying submarine in dry dock at Pearl Harbor. This gives a good indication of its immense size. (*USN*)

Bow shot of the I-400 submarine on speed trials.

Close-up of the I-400 conning tower with a US Navy prize crew aboard and the submarine's crew on deck. (*USN*)

Captured I-class submarines alongside the USS *Euryale*. (*USN*)

I-401 alongside a dock in Tokyo Bay. (*USN*)

Commander Toshiwo Kusaka of the I-400 being questioned by US Naval Intelligence officers. (*USN*)

The launching ramp on the I-400 submarine with the recovery crane stowed alongside to the right. (*USN*)

The I-400 and I-401 alongside the USS *Proteus*. (*USN*)

Some of the officers and men from the
I-401 after surrendering. (*USN*)

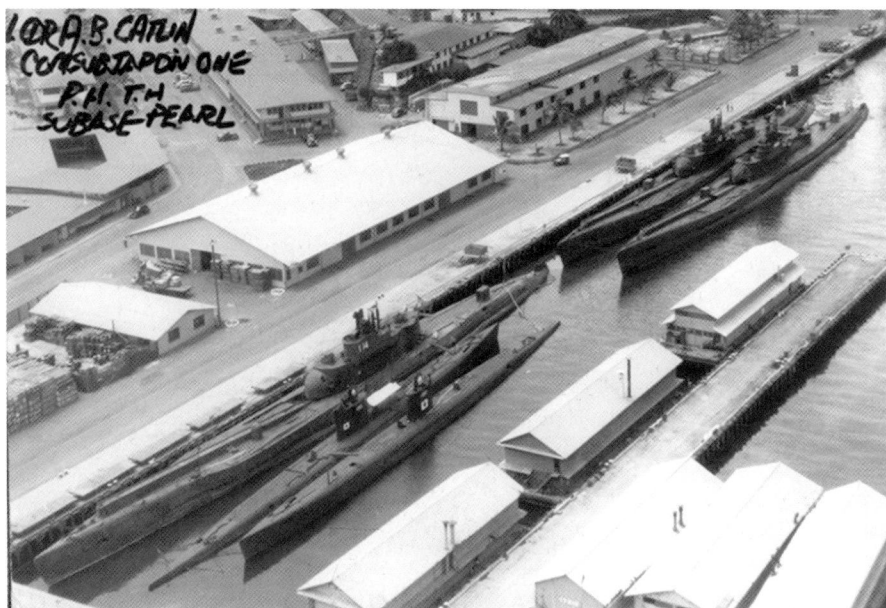

Aerial shot of the I-14, two I-400 class and two transport submarines at Pearl Harbor after the war. (*USN*)

Japanese crews of the I-400 and I-401 assembled on the deck of the I-400. (*USN*)

The Japanese crew of the I-400 assembled on deck on reaching Pearl Harbor. (*USN*)

I-400 submarines moored alongside the USS *Euryale* giving a good example of the tremendous size of these submarines. (*USN*)

Chapter 9

The Final Days

The submarine war against the Americans had never really achieved expectations and, as the war progressed, the Japanese submarine force became less and less of a problem to the Allies. One of the main reasons for this was the ever-increasing use of radar by American ships and aircraft. The veteran Japanese submarine commanders were constantly complaining about the lack of technical equipment including radar. Most submarines were equipped with surface radar but once submerged the submarines were, for all intent and purposes, running blind. Numerous attempts were made to persuade the Naval Technical Department to expedite the tests they were carrying out, but this was rejected on the grounds that the tests could not be hurried. One submarine commander, Lieutenant Commander Hashimoto, said that after numerous attempts at meetings with the Naval Technical Department regarding the fitting of radar, the only thing he managed to get from them was a pair of binoculars for lookout purposes. Such was the intransigence of the Headquarters Staff that even at this late stage of the war, their pride and dignity was an overriding factor and they would not be harassed into making decisions.

The Japanese High Command was considering even more desperate measures and that was the use of explosive paper balloons. As ridiculous as it may have at first appeared, it was not without its supporters. The project called *Fu-Go* had been activated at the end of 1944 and had been sending explosive paper balloons on the prevailing western wind across the Pacific to America. On 6 December 1944 a violent explosion was heard on the southern slopes of Gearhart Mountain just east of Bly, Oregon. The local sheriff investigated and discovered the bodies of the wife of the Reverend Archie Mitchell and their five children. It was later discovered that this was the 240th recorded discovery of a balloon bomb. Balloon bombs had been reported along the west coast of America from Alaska to Montana and remnants had been sent to the US Naval Research Laboratory for examination. It was quickly established that they were of Japanese origin but the question was how were they being sent. An immediate news blackout was imposed.

US Naval Intelligence had known for some time that the Japanese had used balloons to carry explosives and that they had been used in the Russo-Japanese War using the upper air current. It was the attack on Tokyo by Doolittle's raiders that had prompted the High Command to find a retaliatory way of attacking the

American mainland. The only attack so far on the mainland was in September 1942 by Warrant Flying Officer Nobuo Fujita in his Yokosuka E14Y1 aircraft after being launched from the I-25. He had dropped four incendiary bombs on the Siskiyou National Forest, Oregon, but with little effect. By August 1943 the Japanese Navy had an arsenal of some 200 balloons, ready to be launched from submarines. Each balloon had a diameter of about 100ft and an inflated capacity of 19,000ft^3 giving the balloon a lifting power of around 1,000lbs at sea level and 200lbs at 36,000ft. The explosive payload consisted of two 11lb thermalite incendiary bombs and one 33lb anti-personnel fragmentation bomb, all suspended from a metal circular ring that was suspended by nineteen shroud lines and triggered by three androids which were attached to a battery-powered circuit.

The whole affair was extremely hit and miss, because the balloons had no other form of propulsion other than the winds, and depended entirely on the strength and the direction of them. Records later showed that of the 9,300 balloons that were released only 285 arrived in America although a couple did manage to reach Canada. The project was abandoned as being totally ineffective and producing no significant results. It is interesting to note that the American public in the main were completely unaware of the balloon threat.

In Tokyo in an effort to boost the people's morale, the Navy claimed that in the previous couple of months they had sunk two cruisers, five destroyers, one seaplane

Koryu submarine at the Yokosuka Naval Base. (*USN*)

A number of *Koryu* midget submarines at the Yokosuka Naval Base. (*JMSDF*)

tender, fifteen oil tankers and a number of transports plus a few minor vessels. The Allies denied all but one of the claims, as there were no recorded incidents of any of their ships being attacked during this period. There was one recorded unsuccessful attack by a *Kaiten* on the fleet tug USS *Sioux*, which sank the *Kaiten* with 40mm gunfire.

The lack of success of the Type C *Kaiten* prompted the development of a larger version, the Type D or, as it became known, the *Koryu* (The Nation). This 55ft (16.7m) version had a displacement of 19 tons, a range of 450 miles on the surface at 5 knots and 36 miles submerged at 3 knots, and capable of diving to 330ft. It carried two 18in torpedoes, one each side of the lower section of the hull. The midget submarine was powered by an 85hp Izusu automatic petrol engine whilst on the surface and a 80hp electric engine when submerged. With a crew of five the *Koryu* could either be lowered into the water by crane or launched from a ship by launching rails. They were initially designed for the defence of Okinawa, but as the war rapidly deteriorated for Japan it was decided to pack the bows with explosives and use the *Koryu* as a Kamikaze weapon. The Japanese High Command, now desperate, ordered 542 to be built, but shortage of materials reduced that number to 115 and none ever saw service.

But the war was deteriorating rapidly for the Japanese as the Allies made sweeping advances across the Pacific. Japanese garrisons, starved of food, medical supplies and ammunition, were surrendering faster than the Allies could cope. What was becoming even more critical was the flow of oil that was being drastically reduced by American submarine attacks on Japanese oil tankers. The Japanese Navy required 1.6 million barrels of oil per month to function, so the effect the losses of their tankers had on them was almost catastrophic. So much so in fact that in 1943 the import of oil had fallen from 1.75 million barrels per month to just 360,000 barrels per month. As the war around the Philippines started to favour the Allies and Japanese forces were being forced to retreat and suffer substantial losses, the flow of oil became even smaller. In fact it was reduced to just 9 per cent during the last 15 months of the war and the government were reduced to carrying out experiments of trying to extract a form of petrol from potatoes – unsuccessfully.

The attack on Okinawa by the Americans had sent shock waves through the Japanese High Command as they realised that the Allies were getting closer and closer to Japan. The submarines I-8, RO-46 and RO-41 were immediately despatched to search for enemy transports. It was decided to increase the number of *Kaitens* to each submarine to six, with the result that modifications were made to the I-36 and the I-47. They were joined by the *Kaiten*-carrying submarines I-56, I-58 and I-44, each with six redesigned human torpedoes. Word came through that the first three submarines that had been sent to Okinawa had been sunk with all hands. As the *Kaiten*-carrying submarines approached Okinawa they came under attack, first from fighter aircraft and then destroyers. The I-58 suffered some damage from the depth-charge attacks and was leaking oil. On returning to Kure for repairs, not having launched one of her *Kaiten*s, the crew found that of all the submarines sent to Okinawa she and the I-47 were the only ones to return. This was a bitter blow to the Japanese, they were losing submarines and crews faster than they could replace them, and of those that were replaced, the crews were so inexperienced that they were turning out to be more of a danger to themselves than to the enemy. In addition the I-363, I-367 and I-165 were also modified to take five *Kaiten*s and ordered to sea to look for targets. The I-165 was sent to the Marianas and on 23 June the minelayer USS *Champion* (AM-314) with her destroyer escort USS *Gilligan* (DE-508), detected an underwater contact and carried out a series of depth-charge and Hedgehog attacks. A small amount of diesel oil and debris appeared some minutes later but nothing else. Then three days later a Lockheed PV-2 of VPB-142 spotted a submarine with a midget submarine on its deck on the surface and dropped three depth charges followed by a 'Fido' acoustic torpedo. On a second pass, the crew of the PV-2 saw a large amount of oil and debris on the surface and two *Kaiten*s. The I-165 was sunk with the loss of 106 crew and five *Kaiten*s and their pilots.

The I-363 returned to Kure for repairs and then left for Sasebo. Just 10 miles off the Miyazaki coast, it hit a mine and sank. Ten sailors were rescued, but the remainder of the crew were lost. The I-367 carried out a few more missions but to no effect and surrendered to the Americans at the end of the war.

News about the desperate situation now facing the Japanese Army, together with the Navy's continuing loss of submarines and surface vessels, sent waves of serious concern to the other member of the Axis Alliance who too was experiencing serious difficulties. Germany's reply to Japan's urgent request for U-boats to be sent to assist the Japanese Navy in the Pacific and Indian Oceans was disappointing to say the least when the offer of just two U-boats, the U-234 and the U-876, in the next

The I-367 with two *Kaiten* human torpedoes on the deck.

four months was made. The U-234 (Type XB), commanded by Kapitänleutnant Johann-Heinrich Fehler, was the first to be assigned and left Kristiansand, Norway on 16 April 1945. On board was General der Flieger Ulrich Kessler of the Luftwaffe, who was to take up liaison duties in Tokyo, two Japanese naval officers, Lieutenant Commander Hideo Tomonaga, a naval architect and submarine designer, and Colonel Shōji Genzō, an aviation expert. together with a dismantled Messerschmitt Me 262 jet fighter and a cargo of 530kg of uranium oxide. Both the Japanese engineering officers had been in Germany learning about new submarine technology and jet and rocket aviation developments.

Then on 8 May 1945 news came through that Germany had capitulated and all German naval vessels were to surrender to the Allies – the war in Europe was over. The two Japanese officers aboard the U-234 committed suicide by taking an overdose of luminal, a barbiturate sedative and antiepileptic drug, and were buried at sea. The U-234 then surrendered to the USS *Sutton* (DE-771) and was escorted to the Navy Yard at Kittery, Maine. The U-876 (Type IX D-2), commanded by Kapitänleutnent Rolf Bahn, was attacked and seriously damaged by Typhoon fighter aircraft and subsequently scuttled by her crew on 4 May 1945 at Eckernförde in northern Germany.

At the end of the war in Europe, the Japanese interned all German U-boat officers and men and their submarines were taken over to become part of the Imperial Japanese Navy. The U-862 became the I-502, U-181 the I-501, U-219 the I-505, and U-195 the I-506. The U-181 (I-501) also carried a Focke-Achgelis Fa 330 *Bachstelze* (Wagtail) rotor kite, but it is extremely unlikely that the Japanese ever used it as they would have to had a trained pilot/observer to fly it and an experienced crew to assemble and dissemble it. The Italian submarines UIT-24

(*Commandante Capellini*) and UIT-25 (*Luigi Torelli*) became the I-503 and I-504 respectively. They were also the only submarines ever to sail under three flags – Italian, German and Japanese.

On 30 July 1945 one of the major successes by a Japanese submarine was made when the I-58 came across the heavy cruiser USS *Indianapolis* (CA-35), without escort, on its way from Tinian to Leyte after undergoing damage repairs due to being hit by a Kamikaze aircraft. Shortly after midnight on 29 July the I-58 closed to attack and fired six Type 95 torpedoes, two or three of them hitting the cruiser on the starboard bow causing massive damage. Within minutes the *Indianapolis* took on a heavy list to starboard and started to settle by the bow. Ten minutes later she suddenly rolled over completely and plunged to the bottom with her stern high in the air. Of the 1,196 members of her crew, 300 went down with the ship, leaving the remaining members of the crew struggling in the water, most of who were without life-jackets. It was later thought that all six *Kaiten*s had been launched against the USS *Indianapolis* and not torpedoes as were stated in the captain's report.

The *Indianapolis* managed to send distress calls before sinking and a message was intercepted from the Japanese claiming to have sunk a heavy cruiser. Of the three listening stations that received the signals, one commander was said to have been drunk, another had ordered his men not to disturb him and a third thought it was a Japanese trap. For a long time the US Navy denied that distress calls had been sent but the information came to light after the release of declassified records. Only 312 members of the crew actually survived and then only after a massive search and rescue mission. The first of the rescue missions was by Lieutenant Adrian Marks, who had spotted the survivors in the water during a routine patrol flight and radioed for help. On seeing sharks attacking the survivors, he ignored an order not to land his Catalina flying boat on the water, but landed and taxied towards them. Hauling as many of them as he could from the water, he managed to save a large number of lives by placing them all over his aircraft. He stayed on the surface until the first of the rescue ships arrived, the destroyer USS *Doyle* (DE-368).

It was widely believed that the USS *Indianapolis* had just delivered the atomic bomb that was destined to be dropped on Hiroshima, an important area containing many factories producing military equipment. The then Secretary of State, Henry Stimson, denied it, but in President Harry S. Truman's memoirs he stated that it was true. At the end of the war the captain of the *Indianapolis*, Captain Charles McVay III, was court-martialled for 'hazarding his ship's safety'. One of the main witnesses called was Captain Mochitsura Hashimoto, the captain of the I-58 that had sunk the heavy cruiser. His testimony was instrumental in McVay's partial acquittal. Captain McVay was, however, found guilty of hazarding his ship through negligence by failing to order the running of a zigzag course. This was despite the testimony of Captain Hashimoto, who, when asked if zigzagging would have made any difference, replied that it would have not, because as there was no escort he was able to get very close when he fired his torpedoes. The incident begs the question as to whether or not this would have happened had the *Indianapolis* had been given the escort she should normally would have expected? The court martial's verdict was widely criticise by other ship commanders, stating that Captain McVay was made a scapegoat to cover up the failure of the Navy to protect the *Indianapolis*.

The I-58 continued to search for enemy warships and although it claimed to have sunk a destroyer (not confirmed) it found a single merchant ship and launched one of the *Kaiten*s. Some minutes later a loud explosion was heard and black smoke was seen rising. When it had dissipated nothing could be seen of the merchant ship.

On 6 August 1945 the United States B-29 bomber 'Enola Gay' dropped 'Little Boy', an atomic bomb, on the Japanese city of Hiroshima, devastating the area for miles and causing thousands of casualties (approximately 160,000 by the end of the year and 69 per cent of the city was destroyed). Three days later another B-29 bomber, 'Bocks Car', dropped 'Fat Man', a plutonium bomb, on the secondary target the city of Nagasaki (Kokura had been the primary target), again causing widespread casualties and devastation (approximately 80,000 people and 80 per cent of the city was destroyed). At the same time as the first bomb was dropped, the Soviet Union declared war on Japan and immediately invaded Manchuria, breaching the Soviet-Japanese Neutrality Act. The Russians had already agreed with Britain and America to attack Japan during the Potsdam Conference and that they would invade Manchuria.

The 'Enola Gay' returning from Hiroshima. (*USAF*)

Side view of 'Little Boy' atomic bomb. (*USAF*)

The loss of their merchant ships had been devastating to Japan causing the import of key materials to fall from 20 million tons in 1941 to 10 million tons in 1944 and 2.7 million tons the following year. The effect on the people of Japan was also becoming a serious cause for concern for the government. In 1944 the average caloric intake of the Japanese people had fallen 12 per cent below what

'Fat Man' plutonium bomb that was dropped on Nagasaki by Boeing B-29 Superfortress 'Bock's Car'. (*USAF*)

was deemed to be necessary for the daily requirement. The effect on the Japanese people was devastating to say the least and, such was the desperation, that Emperor Hirohito ordered the Supreme Council for the Direction of War to accept the terms of surrender that the allies had put forward. On 15 August 1945 Emperor Hirohito made a radio broadcast to his people informing them of Japan's surrender to the allies. This was the first time the vast majority of the Japanese people had ever heard the voice of their emperor who was regarded by then as almost a god.

In the Pacific, just before the attack on Ulithi Atoll was about to take place, the Japanese military were told to lay down their arms and surrender. All submarines were ordered to return to Kure. There were some who wanted to continue fighting to the death, but the majority realised that there was no point in continuing as the Navy as a fighting force no longer existed and the air force had been decimated. The war was over and Japan had been defeated. The crews on the submarines were ordered to destroy all their weapons. Torpedoes were fired without aiming and on the aircraft-carrying submarines the aircraft were catapulted off still in their folded configuration. The I-400 surrendered at sea to the destroyer USS *Blue* (DD-744) and was boarded. With a prize crew aboard, the submarine was taken under escort to Sasebo Bay. The three other I-400-class submarines were together at Sasebo Bay with a number of other aircraft-carrying submarines. When the Americans received word that the Russians were demanding to see these giant aircraft-carrying submarines and wanted to examine them, all but four of the submarines were taken to a point 32 miles (60km) west of Nagasaki, packed with C-2 explosives and sunk in 660ft (200m) of water. The remaining four submarines, the I-400, I-401, I-201 and I-203, were sailed to Hawaii by American crews for further detailed inspection. When completed they were all sunk in the waters off Kalaeloa near the island of Oahu in Hawaii, by torpedoes from the submarine USS *Trumpetfish* (SS-425) to prevent the Russians gaining access to them. The I-402 was sunk off Nagasaki after being used as target practice for the destroyer USS *Everett F. Larson* (DD-830).

The US Pacific submarine campaign achieved three major successes. First, the Japanese merchant marine losses were so heavy that Japanese shipbuilding industry was unable to keep up with the demand for new ships. Secondly the destruction of the merchant marine and naval forces dramatically reduced Japan's ability to control the vast Pacific Ocean. Thirdly the submarine enabled the US Navy to take the offensive into Japanese-controlled waters with the result that they accounted for 60 per cent (4.9 million tons) of merchant shipping in addition to 30 per cent (700,000 tons) of naval ships, which included eight aircraft carriers, one battleship and eleven cruisers. But the cost was still relatively high: of the total of 288 US submarines deployed throughout the war zones, 52 were lost, 48 in the Pacific theatre of the war.

The Japanese reliance on the submarine force to help neutralise the American fleet never materialised. The attack on Pearl Harbor was in essence the point in which the submarine should have taken control, but didn't. Despite encircling the island of Oahu, not one of the ships entering or leaving Pearl Harbor or Honolulu was attacked. Fifteen of the twenty I-class submarines that were patrolling the waters south of Oahu returned to Japan after a few days. The remaining five were assigned to patrol the west coast of America and one of these, the I-170, was lost when an SBD Dauntless from the aircraft carrier USS *Enterprise* caught her on the surface and sank her with a direct hit. The commanders of the returning submarines claimed that the main reason they were unsuccessful was because of the extremely aggressive patrolling and depth-charging by US Navy ships and aircraft. The returning submarines' only successes were a couple of unarmed merchant ships that they happened to come across during their trip back to Japan. American submarines started to dominate the Pacific and Indian Oceans and caused major problems by going after Japanese merchant ships who were supplying the Japanese-held islands with food, medicine and ammunition. The rapid Japanese advance at the beginning of the war had stretched her supply lines to almost breaking point and the sinking of her supply ships had a detrimental effect.

In an interview at the end of the war, Vice Admiral Shigeyoshi Miwa, Commander-in-Chief of the Sixth Submarine Fleet, said at the beginning of the war the Japanese submarine force was at its strongest, but the numbers decreased as the war dragged on and production could not keep up with demand. The Allied campaign of attacking and sinking Japanese merchant ships, thus depriving the now-starving Japanese garrisons on the various islands, was highly effective. This

Japanese submarine I-10 arriving in Penang. (*IJN*)

resulted in Japanese submarines being used to transport food, medical supplies, transport the sick and wounded, senior officers and rescuing downed aircrew, but not for seeking out enemy warships. Despite vociferous complaints from almost all the submarine commanders their voices went unheard. One of the other reasons given was that Japanese submarines had been built with inferior materials and fitted with sub-standard weapons. Although their torpedoes were far superior to those of the Allies, this was countered by the sonar and radar that was fitted in the American submarines. This technology meant that the Japanese submarines were often only aware of the enemy's presence after they were attacked. Poor leadership, the bitter in-fighting between the Army and the Navy and the intransigence of the senior commanders to listen to commanders on the front line, was also a major contributing factor. As one Japanese senior officer said at the end of the war:

The Japanese failed because their men and officers were inferior, not in courage, but in the intelligent use of courage. Japanese education, Japanese ancestor worship, and the Japanese caste system, were reflected time after time in uninspired leadership and transfixed initiative. In a predicted situation, which could be handled in an orthodox manner, the Japanese were always competent and often resourceful. Under the shadow of frustration however, the obsession of personal honour extinguished ingenuity.

As the defeated population of Japan started to come to terms with the occupying forces, the Kamikaze sacrifices made by so many young men was bitterly resented by many families. This was echoed by many former members of the 'Cherry Blossom Squadron', who openly criticised their superiors over the strategy of kamikaze. Parents of those who died carrying out kamikaze attacks publicly berated the members of the fanatical High Command who had instigated the programme, saying that they had 'violated the basic tenets of humanity' and had given the Japanese people the name of being barbaric savages who had no regard for human life.

Appendix 1

Japanese Submarine Losses in the Second World War

I-1

On 29 January 1943 the I-1 was sighted and attacked by the much smaller 607-ton New Zealand minesweepers HMNZS *Kiwi* and *Moa*. Unable to penetrate the I-1's hull with their deck guns, the minesweepers rammed and sank her in shallow water at Kamimbo Bay, Guadalcanal, with the bow of the wreck partially protruding from the water.

I-2

On 7 April 1944 the I-2 was cruising submerged in the Bismarck Sea, 50 miles west-north-west of New Hanover, when at 0630 the USS *Saufley* (DD-465), on patrol in the Emirau-Massau area, picked up a sonar contact on a submerged submarine. At 0645 the destroyer dropped a pattern of nine depth charges, followed by nine more 30 minutes later. Seconds later her sonar operator reported two underwater explosions. Minutes later oil was spotted covering the area where the sonar contact had been made. The I-2 was reported sunk with the loss of all hands.

I-3

On 16 November 1942 Vice Admiral Komatsu convened a meeting of his submarine captains and announced that the submarine force has been ordered by Admiral Yamamoto, CinC Combined Fleet, to organise a supply system for the Seventeenth Army garrison on Guadalcanal. The I-2, under the command of Lieutenant Commander Togami, carried out four supply runs of medical and food supplies to the beleaguered garrison. On the fifth run, the submarine contacted the local

I-1 on sea trials. (*Author*)

garrison and then launched a Daihatsu barge from her deck and prepared to deliver her cargo. At 0652 the lookouts on *PT-59*, which was patrolling the area with the *PT-44*, spotted the barge next to the surfaced submarine. Within minutes the *PT-59* had launched two 21in Mark 15 torpedoes from 400 yards distance, the first of which hit the stern of the I-3. This was followed seconds later by a tremendous explosion. The second torpedo missed but fortunately passed under *PT-44*, which was on the other side of the Japanese submarine raking it with gunfire. The I-3 sank immediately together with 90 officers and men. Her gunnery officer Ensign Takeichi and three seamen were blown overboard by the explosion. They managed to swim ashore and join the Japanese forces on Guadalcanal. They were the only known survivors.

I-4

On 18 December 1942 at 2215 the I-4 arrived at the mouth of the Mambare River, on her fourth supply run to the garrison at Buna, but was detected by torpedo boats *PT-121* and *PT-122*. The PT boats immediately opened fire and two torpedoes were fired at the surfaced submarine with no success. The I-4 quickly submerged and left the area. A few hours later the I-4 returned, but failed to contact the Japanese garrison. On 21 December 1942, off St. George's Channel, New Guinea, the USS *Seadragon* (SS-194) was alerted by an 'Ultra' message of the sighting of an I-class submarine on a northerly course at the southern entrance of St. George's Channel. The submarine was making 14 knots, was painted black and carried a white '4' on her conning tower. The *Seadragon* commenced an approach and fired three Mark 10-3 torpedoes from a range of 850 yards. The lookouts on the I-4 spotted the incoming torpedoes and the submarine attempted to take avoiding action. The first torpedo missed because of a gyroscope failure, the second exploded prematurely after 18 seconds, but the third hit the submarine in the stern causing a massive explosion followed by a large ball of flame. The I-4 sank very quickly by the stern with her bows in a vertical position as she slid beneath the waves. There were no survivors.

I-5

I-class submarines' duties changed into acting as supply boats and the I-5 was no different. At the beginning of 1944 the I-5's role became one of general duties and over the next six months she carried out over six food, ammunition and supply runs to desperate units. Then on 8 July 1944, 300 miles east of Saipan, the escort carrier USS *Hoggatt Bay's* (CVE-75) task group, a hunter-killer group, was conducting ASW operations off the Marianas. The carrier's radar picked up a contact on the surface at 21,000 yards. Two of the four screening escorts, USS *Wyman* (DE-38) and USS *Reynolds* (DE-42), were sent to investigate the carrier's radar contact 360 miles east of Guam. The *Wyman* closed the range on the contact until but lost radar contact at 4,000 yards as the submarine dived. The *Wyman* switched to her sonar and picked up a strong echo at 1,600 yards. The destroyer then fired a barrage of twenty-four Mark 10 Hedgehog projector charges followed by a second barrage of twenty-four. Five small underwater explosions were followed by a much heavier detonation that rocked the *Wyman*. Attempts to regain sonar contact were made, but the sonar's returns indicated the contact has been destroyed. The I-5 was presumed lost with all 130 hands east of Saipan.

I-6

The I-6 was a further experimental development of the J1M lass (J2 class) long-range cruising submarine (*Junyo sensuikan*). She was completed at the Kawasaki yard in Kobe in 1935 and seems to have retained her seaplane facilities (a deck tube for the seaplane and an aft catapult) throughout her career. She was deployed east of Oahu when war broke out, and put a torpedo into the USS *Saratoga* (CV-3) on 11 January 1942, putting the aircraft carrier out of action and ensuring she would not be available for the Coral Sea and Midway operations. At 2233 on 16 June 1944, the converted Japanese sub-chaser *Toyokawa Maru* sighted a submarine surfacing near the convoy. A submarine alert was given so the *Toyokawa Maru* made a sharp turn and rammed the submarine's starboard side slightly abaft the conning tower. The submarine took on a heavy list, turned turtle and sank within a few minutes. The crew of the *Toyokawa Maru* opened fire with machine guns and dropped some depth charges not realising that they were attacking one of their own submarines. There were no survivors of I-6's crew of 104.

I-7

On 22 June 1943, the USS *Monaghan* (DD-354) was patrolling south of Kiska, when it picked up a surface target 14,000 yards away. Making out the shape of a submarine in the heavy fog the destroyer closed and opened fire. It was the Japanese submarine I-7 and coming under fire again and again she received several hits to her conning tower on her port side, her deck gun bulwark and aft ballast tanks. The commanding officer, Lieutenant Sekiguchi, was severely wounded and Engineering Officer Lieutenant Handa Masao was killed. Such was the confusion that lookouts on the submarine reported that the I-7 was being attacked by no less than three separate ships from different directions. Gunnery officer Lieutenant (jg) Shindo Yoshio assumed command and ordered return fire from deck guns and machine guns. Lookouts spotted what they took to be a small fire on one of the attackers. Ten minutes later, the *Monaghan* ceased firing. Within minutes the destroyer resumed firing at the same target, this time illuminating it with star shells. One shell disabled the I-7's steering engine, which caused the submarine to commence a wide turn during the engagement, in which the deck gun crew fired over 70 main calibre shells and about 2,000 machine-gun rounds. Another hit from the *Monaghan*'s guns detonated the ready-to-use ammunition for the submarine's deck gun, starting a small fire. The flames were sucked into the diesel engine ventilation intakes, endangering the galley and the forward head. Two more shells from the destroyer holed the aft deck casing on the port side, so that I-7 developed a 30-degree list as the water poured in. Realising the position was hopeless Lieutenant Yoshio ordered the I-7 to return to Kiska. The *Monaghan* realised that she was close to rocks off Kiska and broke off the chase. The I-7 reported its damage and estimated time of arrival but because of the damage to its steering engine and the continuing taking on water, it ran aground on the Twin Rocks off Vega Bay, sinking rapidly by the stern. Several sailors were trapped inside the submarine and a bag containing codebooks and other secret documents was left suspended on a ladder at her No. 3 after access hatch. Only 50ft of the bow protruded out of the water. A Daihatsu barge was launched and evacuated all forty-three survivors (including ten wounded), but a total of eighty-seven officers and crewmen had been killed in the engagement. The following day soldiers in a Daihatsu from Kiska blew up the bow of I-7 in the midst of the fog, using demolition charges. Divers attempted to locate the codebooks prior to the scuttling, but failed to retrieve them. US divers later retrieved them.

I-8

On 31 March 1945 off Kerama Retto, Okinawa, the USS *Stockton* (DD-646) was screening a task group assisted by ASW Martin PBM Mariner seaplanes from the seaplane tender USS *Chandeleur* (AV-10). Then the *Stockton* picked up a surface radar contact. She immediately engaged the contact – a surfaced submarine – which crash-dived. The destroyer soon made a sound contact and then attacked again with a salvo of depth charges. In seven attacks over the next four hours, the *Stockton* expended all of her depth charges. Her place was taken by the USS *Morrison* (DD-560) just as the I-8 surfaced, but then submerged immediately on seeing the destroyer. The *Morrison* dropped a pattern of eleven charges that forced Lieutenant Commander Shinohara to the surface only 900 yards from the destroyer. He engaged the *Morrison* with his deck guns but after a 30-minute fight, *Morrison*'s main armament of five 5in quick-firing guns blasted holes in the conning tower and stern of the submarine causing it to start to sink. The boat capsized and went down by the stern. A small boat from the *Morrison* rescued an unconscious survivor, PO2C Mukai Takamasa, one of I-8's gun crew. He was the only survivor.

The I-8 had been involved in one of the worst atrocities by a submarine crew in the Second World War. On 26 March 1944, the Dutch-registered merchant ship SS *Tjisalak* was torpedoed by the I-8 whilst sailing from Melbourne to Ceylon with 103 passengers and crew. The full description of what happened is in the main text. Two months later, I-8 was involved in another atrocity when she torpedoed the 7,176-ton American Liberty ship SS *Jean Nicolet*. The 100 crewmen abandoned their burning ship and took to the life rafts. The full details of this incident are also in the main text.

I-9

Like other I-class submarines the I-9 was redesignated from being part of the battle fleet to becoming a supply boat. On 2 June 1943 the I-9 arrived at Kiska, unloaded its cargo and then departed on that same day carrying seventy-nine passengers (fifty-five sailors, ten soldiers and ten construction workers). After delivering its supplies and passengers the I-9 returned to Paramushiro. Two days later the I-9 departed Paramushiro for Kiska on its second supply run and to evacuate the personnel of the local midget submarine base. No contact was made with the I-9 after this. On 13 June 1943, 15 miles east of Sirius Point. At 1758 the USS *Frazier* (DD-607) detected a target 6,900 yards away with her radar. The destroyer closed the range in dense fog at 20 knots and soon established sonar contact with a submarine. At 2009 a lookout sighted two periscopes at just 100 yards. The *Frazier* opened fire on the submarine, scoring a hit on one periscope. The destroyer attacked the I-9 with depth charges and within minutes air bubbles, oil and debris were seen to rise to the surface. The *Frazier* made two more attacks to ensure that the submarine was sunk. The I-9 was lost with all hands.

I-10

On 4 July 1944, 65 miles east-north-east of Saipan, the Task Group 50.17 with six tankers and the escort carrier USS *Breton* (CVE-23) was refuelling at sea, when the soundman on the escort destroyer USS *Riddle* (DE-185) detected an underwater contact bearing 250 degrees, range 1,900 yards. The Task Group Commander ordered his formation to execute an emergency turn to port. After firing a five depth-charge urgent barrage the *Riddle* commenced a new approach, but the submarine foiled her attack by turning into the wakes of the retiring formation. Then 18 minutes later the contact was regained at 1,250 yards. Three patterns of Hedgehog projectiles were fired, but the submarine avoided being hit by diving deeper and by frantic manoeuvring. At 1812, the *Riddle* made another depth-charge attack with a full pattern set deep, without any obvious results. With almost all her depth charges gone, the estimated range, bearing and target course were passed to another destroyer, the USS *David W. Taylor* (DD-551), who made a contact at 1822 and dropped eleven depth charges set to medium depth. At 1828, the *Riddle* was about to commence another attack, when a heavy underwater explosion occurred directly ahead. No further contacts were obtained despite intensive searching. Oil and debris were seen to break the surface just before sundown and the following day an oil slick was seen stretching 9 miles downwind from the point of attack.

I-11

The I-11 was reported missing on 11 January 1944. Her last report placed her off Funafuti, close to the Gilbert Islands. No Allied reports of contact were ever made so her disappearance remains a mystery.

I-12

The I-12 was one of the rare I-class submarines that was used for its intended purpose which was to intercept Allied merchant ships and sink them. On 30 October 1944 the I-12 torpedoed and sank the Liberty ship SS *John A Johnson*. After ramming and sinking the lifeboats and rafts they machine-gunned the seventy survivors in the water, killing ten. A Pan American Airways aircraft spotted the remaining men soon thereafter, and the USS *Argus* (PY-14) a brig, rescued them. The hunt was on for the submarine and on 13 November, just 10 days after the sinking of the *John A Johnson*, the I-12 was located near Kauai in the Hawaiian Islands by the minesweeper USS *Ardent* (AM-340) and the USCG cutter *Rockford*. The *Ardent* and the *Rockford* were escorting a six-ship convoy midway between Honolulu and the United States when the *Ardent* picked up a sonar contact. The minesweeper immediately fired a 24-charge Hedgehog pattern into the area, followed by a second pattern some 10 minutes later as they tracked the contact. The *Rockford* also joined in the attack and fired another Hedgehog barrage. Within minutes two violent underwater explosions rocked both vessels. *Ardent* made another run, this time dropping thirteen depth charges, seconds later a series of underwater explosions followed. Minutes later wreckage appeared on the surface – deck planks covered with diesel oil, pieces of varnished mahogany inscribed in Japanese, and a piece of deck planking containing Japanese builders' inscriptions. All the evidence of a 'kill' and retribution for the atrocities carried out by the crew of the I-12 were claimed by the *Ardent* and *Rockford*.

I-13

On 16 July 1945 TBF Avenger aircraft from the escort carrier USS *Anzio* (CVE-57), accompanied by the destroyer escort USS *Lawrence C. Taylor* (DE-415), carried out an ASW operation close to the island of Truk. During the operation they picked up the sonar signal of a submarine and carried out a bombing and depth-charge attack. The I-13 was known to be operating in the area at the time and as no contact was made with her after that date it is assumed that she had been the target and was sunk with all hands. The I-13 was also one of the submarines that had been converted to carry two Aichi M6A1 Sieran bombers.

I-14

The I-14 was one of the aircraft-carrying submarines that was converted to carry two Aichi M6A Sieran bombers in a watertight hangar on the deck. The submarine saw very little service until the very end of the war and then surrendered at sea when hostilities ceased. The submarine was taken under escort and with an American crew aboard to Hawaii for a detailed examination by submarine experts. When all the examinations were completed the submarine was taken to a deep-water section of the Pacific off Oahu and sunk. Such was the secrecy surrounding its location

The I-14 with a prize crew aboard after surrendering. (*USN*)

that it wasn't until 2009 that a team of divers from the Hawaii Undersea Research Laboratory and National Oceanic and Atmospheric Administration discovered the remains of the submarine.

I-15

The I-15 was a B1 type submarine and was built at Kure Navy Yard on 30 September 1940. Her first and only commanding officer was Commander Nobuo Ishikawa. I-15 operated off the north coast of Oahu during the raid on Pearl Harbor. Her second wartime patrol, in May and June 1942, took her to the Aleutians, where she conducted reconnaissance of several islands. I-15's third and final patrol took place from August to November 1942, when she operated in the vicinity of the Solomon Islands in the South Pacific, supporting the Japanese efforts to hold Guadalcanal. One source suggested that I-15 hit the battleship USS *North Carolina* (BB-55) with a torpedo on 15 September 1942, but it is more likely that the torpedo came from another submarine operating in the area, the I-19. On 10 November 1942 the I-15 surfaced to recharge her batteries when it was spotted by the USS *Southard* (DMS-10), which was taking supplies to Guadalcanal. Closing on the submarine quickly the *Southard* opened fire with its 4.5in main guns. The submarine immediately crash-dived and went into the attack, firing two torpedoes in reply which both missed. The *Southard* picked up a sonar contact and attacked again, this time with depth charges, forcing the badly-damaged I-15 to the surface. The *Southard* opened fire with her battery of guns, hitting the I-15 in the conning tower with a salvo. The submarine immediately sank by the bows – there were no survivors.

I-16

The I-16 left Truk on a supply mission to Buin, Bougainville, carrying rice in 75lb rubber bags. The submarine signalled that her ETA at Buin was 2000, 22 May. The signal was intercepted by FRUPAC (Fleet Radio Unit, Pacific) at Honolulu and passed through channels to Commander Escort Division 39, at Tulagi Harbor, Florida Island near Guadalcanal, Solomons. Orders were issued to the destroyers USS *George* (DE-697), USS *Raby* (DE-698) and USS *England* (DE-635) to operate as a hunter-killer group and intercept the I-16. That same day, the Americans intercepted radio traffic that indicated the Japanese had established a new submarine picket 'NA line' between Truk and the Admiralty Islands to intercept American carriers. 140 miles NE of Cape Alexander, Solomons, an American patrol plane sighted the I-16 running on the surface and signalled its position. The *England*, *Raby* and *George* conducted a line-abreast sonar sweep until the *England* picked the I-16 on her sonar. She began the first of five attacks – each with a barrage of twenty-four throw-ahead Mark 10 Hedgehog charges. After the fifth attack, a huge underwater explosion lifted the *England's* stern out of the water by 6in as the I-16 exploded and sank. The explosion must have been at a depth of over 500ft because over 20 minutes passed before the first pieces of debris appeared. Deck planking, pieces of cabinets and various other objects appeared, then finally a sealed rubber container with a bag of rice inside surfaced. More an hour later, a small oil slick started to appear and by the following day, the slick was three miles wide and six miles long. The I-16 was declared sunk with all 107 hands.

I-17

On 9 August 1943, the I-17, under the command of Captain Kōzō Nishino, spotted a small convoy en route from Noumea to Espiritu Santo. Concentrating on the convoy, the I-17 failed to spot the minesweeper HMNZS *Tui* of the Royal New Zealand Navy 25th Minesweeping Flotilla, providing ASW escort to the cargo ship USS *Taganak* (AG-45) and Liberty ship SS *Wiley Post*. The *Tui* made an ASDIC contact bearing, 3,400 yards away from the convoy causing the convoy to take evasive action by zigzagging. *Tui* made three runs over the position of the contact, dropping four depth charges. The contact was lost so the *Tui* carried out another ASDIC sweep but failed to regain the contact and rejoined the convoy. Whilst the *Tui* was making her sweep of the area, a Chance-Vought OS2N-1 Kingfisher of Scouting Squadron VS-57, which was on a routine ASW sector search, had joined her,. The pilot, Lieutenant (jg) Robert Clinton, flew over the *Tui* and received a visual signal indicating that they had made a submarine contact. Landing his floatplane alongside the minesweeper, Clinton verified the contact and took off again. Within minutes he had sighted a periscope cutting the water. Diving into the attack, he dropped two depth charges ahead of the periscope. By this time another Kingfisher had joined the hunt and dropped two more depth charges. Two of them exploded close to the periscope trail and then air bubbles and an oil slick suddenly appeared in the water. The I-17 was forced to the surface, breaking the water bow first at a steep angle. Lieutenant Clinton strafed the deck of the submarine with his single .30-cal machine gun to keep the crew from manning their guns, but it jammed. The I-17's crew reached their 25mm twin AA mount and opened fire while the submarine was running at 18 knots. Clinton climbed out of range and radioed for assistance and within minutes four more Kingfishers arrived. The submarine tried to take evasive action, firing her AA guns. One of the Kingfishers attacked from astern and dropped two depth charges, one missed but the other exploded 30ft aft of the conning tower. One of the other aircraft made a pass and dropped a depth charge that hit within 10ft of the submarine's starboard side. The blast sent a plume of water up over 50ft. In less than a minute the I-17 had sunk with the loss of ninety-seven crewmen. Later the *Tui* rescued six survivors.

I-18

When an American carrier task force was spotted by a Japanese reconnaissance aircraft 200 miles south of San Cristobal Island, the I-18 was ordered to intercept and attack the carriers. Nine miles from the task force an OSU Kingfisher from the light cruiser USS *Helena* (CL-50) spotted the submarine on the surface, contacted the destroyer USS *Fletcher* (DD-445) then dropped a smoke marker. The I-18 immediately dived as the destroyer closed at full speed. At 2,900 yards the *Fletcher* picked up her sonar contact and dropped a large pattern of depth charges. A violent explosion followed and minutes later a patch of oil appeared on the surface, at which point the destroyer dropped another three depth charges in the middle of the oil slick. The resulting explosions brought wreckage to the surface, which was identified as coming from the submarine. There were no survivors.

Submarine I-18 on patrol. (*JMSDF*)

I-19

The invasion of the Gilbert Islands commenced on 20 November 1943 with an invasion fleet consisting of 200 ships, which included 13 battleships and 11 aircraft carriers. On hearing of the invasion, the I-19, together with the I-21, I-35, I-39,

I-40, I-169, I-174 and I-175 and RO-38 were ordered to proceed to Tarawa in the Gilbert Islands at full speed to attack the American fleet. On 25 November the USS *Radford* (DD-446) made a night radar contact with a submarine just 8 miles from the fleet, but minutes later lost it as the submarine submerged. Then a sonar contact was made with the submarine and the *Radford* made seven depth-charge attacks over the sonar contact area. Contact was lost but no wreckage was found. Japanese post-war records however confirmed that the I-19 was the submarine that was sunk at the location on that day.

I-20

When a torpedo attack on the American tanker SS *W. S. Rheem* 10 miles north of Bougainville was reported on 3 September 1943, the destroyer USS *Ellet* (DD-398) left her base in Espiritu Santo and started to search for the Japanese submarine responsible. Within hours the destroyer picked up a contact on her radar at 13,000 yards, but in the darkness they were unable to identify the boat so they attempted to make contact with a blinker gun. Getting no response they fired star shells over the area to illuminate the sea, but the radar reported the target had disappeared. Minutes later the destroyer's sonar picked up a contact at 3,000 yards and the *Ellet* started a depth charge pattern until the contact disappeared. As dawn broke, the *Ellet*, still on station, saw a large slick of oil slowly spreading across the depth-charged area together with a considerable amount of debris. After the war Japanese records stated that the I-20 had been operating in the area and contact with her was lost around the time of the *Ellet*'s attack on an unknown submarine. The I-20 was presumed lost with all 101 crew off Espiritu Santo.

I-21

The I-21 was one of the few submarines that were equipped to carry a reconnaissance aircraft and in May 1942 launched her E14Y 'Glen' to reconnoitre Sydney harbour. At 0420, it circled twice over the harbour near where the heavy cruiser USS *Chicago* (CA-29) was anchored. The 'Glen' was first thought to be an American plane, but then Royal Australian Air Force (RAAF) fighters were eventually sent to intercept, but were unsuccessful. The 'Glen' returned to the I-21 and reported the sighting of a 'battleship'. Like many of the other I-class submarines it was only occasionally used for the purpose for which it had been assigned, a general duties boat. But when the invasion of the Gilbert Islands commenced on 20 November 1943 with an invasion fleet consisting of 200 ships, which included 13 battleships and 11 aircraft carriers, the I-21 together with other submarines were ordered to proceed to Tarawa in the Gilbert Islands at full speed to attack the American fleet. On 27 November, the I-21 reported that they had sighted the American fleet: this was the last transmission sent by the boat. That same day TBF Grumman Avengers of Air Group 35 from the escort carrier USS *Chenango* (CVE-28) were supporting

The I-21 on patrol. (*JMSDF*)

The I-21 submarine showing the cable cutter mounted on the bows. (*Author*)

the invasion when they spotted the partially-submerged I-21 moving towards the fleet. They immediately went into the attack and dropped their torpedoes into the submarine – sinking it. There were no reports of any survivors.

I-22

After sighting a convoy 40 miles south-east of Malaita, Solomons, the I-22 reported her position and prepared to engage the enemy. It was the last signal received from her. On 6 October 1942 a PBY-5A Catalina flying boat, had been delivering oxygen bottles and personnel to Henderson Field, Guadalcanal, when it spotted a Japanese submarine starting to dive. Going into the attack the Catalina dropped four depth charges in the area. Two explosions followed and then two very large explosions. After circling area for about 15 minutes there appeared a large oil slick, some debris and a mass of air bubbles. Nothing else was seen so it was assumed the submarine was sunk with all hands. As the I-22 was known to be in the area it is assumed that it was the I-22 that was sunk.

The I-22 in Tokyo Harbour. (*USN*)

I-23

The I-23 disappeared off the coast of Hawaii on 28 February 1942 and was lost with all hands. Her last position was radioed on 24 February and nothing was heard from her again. There were no reports of contacts or sightings of a Japanese submarine around this time, so her disappearance was put down to a diving accident or engineering mishap.

I-24

On 7 June 1943 the I-24, on patrol in the Kiska area of the Aleutian Islands, came across a large number of American ships. This was her last message. As the I-24 made her way towards Paramushiro in the Kuril Islands in dense fog, the sub-chaser USS *Larchmount* (PC-487) made a sonar contact, followed by a radar contact and then visual contact of the submarines periscopes as they cut through the water. Immediately the *Larchmount* fired depth charges, which forced the I-24 to the surface. Realising that he only had minutes before the submarine's gun crew opened fire, the captain of the sub-chaser put on full power and raced towards the submarine at 20 knots, ramming it then riding over the I-24's hull. Before the gun crew could react he rammed the submarine again, this time crashing into the conning tower. The I-24 rolled over and sank together with her entire crew.

I-25

The submarine I-25 will go down in history as the boat that was responsible for the only aerial attack ever carried out in wartime on the United States of America. It was equipped to carry a reconnaissance aircraft, a Yokosuka E14Y1 'Glen' that was carried in a watertight hangar mounted in front of the conning tower. Prior to the attack on America, the I-25 and her aircraft carried out a number of reconnaissance flights over Australia. The first was a reconnoitre of Sydney Harbour on 17 February 1942, when the 'Glen', flown by Warrant Flying Officer Nobuo Fujita, crossed the coast at La Perouse, southern Sydney, flew across Botany Bay and then headed north, counting twenty-three ships in the harbour. A three-funnelled warship, two destroyers, and five submarines were sighted. The 'Glen' finally crossed the coast at North Head. The second mission, on 26 February, took the 'Glen' over Melbourne's Port Phillip

Bay. Fujita broke out of the cloud cover directly over the RAAF's Laverton airfield. Two aircraft were scrambled to intercept but never found him. The next flight over Melbourne took place on 26 February 1942. On 9 September 1942 with the sea conditions calm just west of the Oregon coast, the I-25 surfaced and launched her aircraft. Nobuo Fujita dropped three incendiary bombs near Mount Emily, but overnight heavy rain had saturated the woods and the bombs failed to ignite the timber. Then on 29 September another attempt to start a forest fire in the Oregon woods was made. Fujita's plane was launched by catapult and although the entire western coast of Oregon was blacked out, the Cape Blanco lighthouse was still operating. Using the light as a reference point the aircraft flew over the coast and dropped another three incendiary bombs. The rain had saturated the forest once again reducing the small fire created by the bombs. The raid, although showing that the United States was vulnerable to attack from the air, came to nothing and no more attempts were made. Nobuo Fujita was returned to Japan and was replaced by another pilot. On 25 August 1943 the destroyer USS *Patterson* (DD-392) was escorting a convoy from the New Hebrides Islands to the lower Solomons, when it made radar contact with a surfaced submarine. The destroyer closed to 4,000 yards, but the submarine dived and contact was lost. Minutes later sonar contact was made with the submarine and the destroyer dropped several depth charge patterns that sank the submarine. The I-25's last contact put it in the area and so it is presumed lost with all 100 officers and men.

I-26

On 25 October 1944 the I-26 reported sighting four enemy carriers together with escort destroyers off Leyte. This was the last message received from the submarine. Late in the evening a lookout aboard the destroyer escort USS *Richard M. Powell* (DE-403) reported seeing a periscope wake off the starboard side. Immediately all the ships in the task force were notified of the presence of a submarine and other escort ships started to search the area, whilst the aircraft carriers in the task force started to take evasive action. Then, as the escort carrier USS *Petrof Bay* (CVE-80) made a turn, two torpedoes were seen to pass either side of the ship. The *Richard M. Powell* immediately picked up a sonar contact and initiated a depth-charge pattern followed by launch of Mark 10 Hedgehog projectiles. Minutes later a large patch of oil was spotted on the surface. The destroyer stayed on station in case it was a ruse by the submarine and then, in the early hours of the morning, picked up another sonar contact. She dropped sixteen depth charges and fired several Hedgehog projectiles. Almost immediately all sonar contact was lost followed by the discovery of a large patch of oil the following morning.

I-27

After sinking the cargo ship the SS *Khedive Ismail* on 12 February 1944, the I-27, commanded by Commander Toshiaki Fukumura, started to search amongst the rest of the convoy. Numerous periscope sightings were reported by different vessels causing confusion. Then one of the escort destroyers, HMS *Paladin*, made a sonar contact just north of the position of the now-sunken *Khedive Ismail*. After dropping a pattern of depth charges in the area, the *Paladin* chased after another reported contact and dropped a single depth charge in the area where a periscope had been detected by the steamer SS *City of Paris*. In the meantime, another

The sinking of a merchant ship as seen through a periscope. (*Author*)

destroyer, HMS *Petard*, made another sonar contact and dropped a pattern of seven depth charges, followed by eight depth charges five minutes later. Suddenly the I-27 surfaced about a mile and a half off *Petard*'s and *Paladin*'s starboard quarter and was down by the stern, her deck awash. Both destroyers opened fire with all guns, claiming numerous hits. *Petard* then passed close to the I-27's stern and fired a pattern of three depth charges set to 50ft. These caused no visible damage and the submarine started to move, correcting its trim constantly. The captain of *Paladin* decided to ram the submarine to prevent it from diving again but at the last minute he turned away to port, colliding with the submarine's port foreplane on her starboard side. The impact tore an 80ft long gash below the destroyer's waterline, flooding her engine and gearing rooms, two fuel tanks, and the after magazine. The destroyer became dead in the water, but managed to fire two depth charges, one of which exploded right under the I-27's bows. Two minutes later five gunners scrambled from I-27's conning tower in an attempt to man the deck gun, but *Paladin*'s No. 2 Oerlikon AA gun opened fire from 400 yards, blowing one of them overboard and killing the others. I-27 increased her speed to 8–10 knots, going round in circles and still down by the stern. HMS *Petard* fired a number of 4in rounds that riddled the I-27's conning tower, disabling one of the periscopes and the deck gun. *Petard* then launched six torpedoes one by one, all of which missed the target. Then a seventh torpedo finally struck the crippled submarine, blowing her in half. There were no survivors.

I-28

On 11 May 1942 the I-28 was ordered to return to Truk with I-22 and I-24. The I-28 reported trouble with its diesel engines, which was the last message received from her. The message was picked up by American code-breakers and relayed to US Naval Headquarters. The submarine USS *Tautog* (SS-199) was ordered to intercept the Japanese ships returning from the Battle of the Coral Sea, including the damaged aircraft carrier *Shokaku*. Soon after receiving the message the *Tautog* sighted two I-class submarines (probably I-22 and I-24) separately heading towards Truk. Then the *Tautog* sighted a third Japanese submarine making 12 knots, on the same northerly track with I-28 clearly marked on its conning tower. The *Tautog* fired two Mark XIV torpedoes, one hit and halted the I-28. With both her engines stopped the Japanese submarine took on a heavy list to starboard. At least fifteen officers and sailors appeared on the bridge. The *Tautog* closed to 800 yards and fired another torpedo, hitting the submarine right under the conning tower. Within minutes the I-28 had sunk with all hands. The *Tautog* circled the area for 15 minutes, then heard a succession of sharp cracking noises, followed by a single tremendous explosion, which almost lifted the *Tautog* out of the water. Then a large slick of oil and debris appeared. There were no survivors.

I-29

The I-29 was unique inasmuch as it was one of only three Japanese submarines to visit the Germans in France and her captain, Commander Takakazu Kinashi, was presented with the Iron Cross 2nd Class by Adolf Hitler for sinking the aircraft carrier USS *Wasp*. The visit to Lorient was not just social, the submarine carried urgent special supplies for the Germans and in return came away with blueprints for jet and rocket aircraft that the Germans had developed. They also had on board a rocket motor that was used on the Komet fighter and a Juno 004B jet engine that was used on the Messerschmitt Me 262. On the way back to Japan, signals concerning the I-29 were picked up by Allied code-breakers who informed the US Navy COMSUBPAC (Commander Submarine Force US Pacific), who in turn contacted a wolfpack consisting of the USS *Sawfish* (SS-276), USS *Tilefish* (SS-307) and USS *Rock* (SS-274) to intercept the I-29. On 25 July the I-29 reported sighting a surfaced enemy submarine. Almost at the same time the I-29 was seen by the *Sawfish*, who immediately launched four torpedoes. Japanese crewmembers spotted the incoming torpedoes and Commander Kinashi attempted to take evasive action, but it was too late. The three torpedoes had hit and the I-29 sank almost immediately. Three of I-29's crewmen were blown overboard by the explosion, but only one managed to swim ashore to a 'small Philippine island' and report the loss. Commander Kinashi was promoted posthumously to Rear Admiral.

I-30

The I-30 was one of only three Japanese submarines to visit the German submarine base at Lorient. When she departed she carried one passenger, a Japanese engineer who had been looking at new electronic equipment that was being made available under the tripartite agreement. The I-30's cargo included blueprints of the Würzburg air defence ground radar plus a complete set, five German G7a aerial torpedoes and three G7e electric torpedoes, five *Torpedovorhalterechner* (torpedo data computers),

The I-30 meeting with a German supply ship in the Indian Ocean. (*JMSDF*)

240 Bolde sonar countermeasure rounds, rocket and glider bombs, anti-tank guns, a Zeiss anti-aircraft artillery director, 200 20mm AA guns, industrial diamonds valued at one million yen and fifty top-secret 'T-Enigma' coding machines. The I-30's navigator received maps of the mineswept area around Singapore but they were not accurate and three miles east of Keppel Harbour she hit a British mine and quickly sank. Commander S. Endo and ninety-six crewmen were rescued, but thirteen men were lost. Divers recovered some of the I-30's cargo including most of the 20mm guns, torpedo data computers and radar blueprints, but the model of the Würzburg radar was destroyed and the drawings for it were rendered unusable by the salt water. Berlin was informed of the loss of the forty Enigma machines (ten having been taken off in Singapore) aboard the I-30.

I-31
On 11 May 1943, after discharging her cargo of supplies, the I-31 was ordered to attack the American Task Forces 16 and 51 as they carried out the invasion of Attu in the Aleutian Islands. As the submarine approached Attu the battleship USS *Pennsylvania* (BB-38) was spotted shelling the islands, so the I-31 fired a torpedo at her. Overhead a PBY Catalina on anti-submarine patrol spotted the wake of the torpedo and radioed the *Pennsylvania* which took immediate evasive action and watched the torpedo pass under her stern. The PBY Catalina dropped a smoke marker at the point of the torpedo being fired. The destroyer USS *Phelps* (DD-360) immediately raced to the spot and after making a sonar contact, dropped two depth charges. With contact lost, two more destroyers, USS *Farragut* (DD-348) and USS *Edwards* (DD-619), joined in the hunt. After suffering a pattern of depth charges

the I-31 was forced to the surface where the *Edwards* opened fire. The submarine sank almost immediately after receiving numerous hits to the conning tower and hull. Within minutes a large spread of diesel oil rose to the surface covering an area of about five square miles. There were no survivors.

I-32

After finishing a supply run to Wotje, Marshall Islands, the I-32 was ordered on 17 March 1944 to proceed to an area east of the Marshall Islands to attack enemy communications in that area. As the I-32 approached the islands they reported sighting the enemy task force, but the US Naval Fleet Radio Unit's code-breakers intercepted the signal and immediately a signal was flashed to the hunter-killer destroyer group with the task force. The destroyers USS *Halsey Powell* (DD-686), USS *Manlove* (DE-36) and the submarine-chaser *PC-1135* were dispatched to intercept and destroy the submarine. Just 50 miles off Wotje the *Manlove's* radar picked up a submarine running on the surface just five miles away. She closed quickly but the submarine suddenly crash-dived. However, contact was quickly established again by the sonar on the *Halsey Powell* which immediately dropped an extensive depth charge pattern. She was joined by the *Manlove* who dropped depth charges and Mark 10 Hedgehog charges and the *PC-1135* who attacked with mortar-fired Mousetrap bombs. After cruising the area for a couple of hours a large patch of diesel oil was spotted rising to the surface. Nothing more was heard of the I-32 and no survivors were found.

I-33

The submarine I-33 seemed fated from day one. A series of accidents and mishaps marred the life of the boat. After colliding with a coral reef on 26 September 1942, which damaged a forward torpedo tube, a valve was inexplicably opened in the stern during repairs, which flooded the aft section of the boat causing in to sink to a depth of 108ft and the loss of thirty-three members of the crew who were trapped in the forward compartment. At the end of December 1943 the submarine was raised and refitted. The I-33 was then taken out on acceptance trials and on the second crash dive the main induction valve on the starboard side failed to close, causing all the section aft of the control room to be flooded. In an effort to clear the water the crew managed to partially blow the main ballast tanks allowing the submarine's bows to break the surface. However, the flooding continued and within minutes the submarine had slid back and settled on the bottom in 180ft of water. Officers and crew were trapped in various section of the submarine, but only ten were in the control room and had the means to escape. Of the ten only eight reached the surface and of these only two managed to reach shore and be rescued. A suicide note was later recovered from one of the compartments. Later divers located the wreck and found the bodies of two sailors entangled in the bridge enclosure. They also found

Suicide notes found in the engine room of the I-33. (*Author*)

a piece of 2in-diameter wooden scaffolding that had slipped into the air-induction line during the refitting and had jammed the main induction valve open during the final dive. One hundred and two crewmembers lost their life in the accident.

I-34

On 3 October 1943 the I-34 departed Kure on the first leg of a mission to the Lorient submarine base in France, the third such mission to be undertaken by a Japanese submarine. Radio traffic between Tokyo and Berlin was constantly being monitored and the details about the mission were intercepted and deciphered by Allied code-breakers. On arriving in Singapore, the I-34 was loaded with a cargo of tin, tungsten, raw rubber and opium. The opium was stored in wooden boxes in the floatplane hangar after the E14Y1 'Glen' aircraft had been removed. The initial diving tests reveal that the additional cargo had upset I-34's trim, preventing crash-dives. After the problem had been resolved the I-34 departed Penang early in the morning. The Germans planned to refuel I-34 in the Indian Ocean from the supply ship SMS *Bogota*. Allied intelligence, who had been monitoring radio traffic in the area, picked up an 'Ultra' special intelligence signal. The British submarine HMS *Taurus* had been alerted and just 30 miles outside Penang sighted I-34 running on the surface at 14 knots. Six torpedoes from *Taurus* were fired, one hit I-34's starboard side just below her conning tower and seconds later she sank. Twenty of the crew of the I-34 in the forward crew space survived the attack and were trapped inside the submarine. One of the crew managed to open a deck hatch, allowing them to escape. Of these, fourteen were picked up by a native junk and arrived at Penang that same evening, but eighty-four crewmembers were lost. The I-34 was the first IJN submarine to be sunk by a Royal Navy submarine.

I-35

On 20 November 1943 Operation Galvanic (the invasion of the Gilbert Islands) started when the Americans invaded Tarawa and Makin Islands. The invasion fleet of 200 ships included 13 battleships and 11 carriers. The I-35 was ordered to the area to engage the enemy and sighted the enemy Task Force 53, consisting of the escort carriers USS *Suwanee* (CVE-27), USS *Chenango* (CVE-28) and USS *Sangamon* (CVE-26) together with its destroyer screen. As the I-35 approached the task force its sonar signal was picked up the destroyer USS *Meade* (DD-602) on anti-submarine patrol. Two aircraft were launched from cruisers whilst the USS *Frazier* (DD-607) joined the *Meade* and both launched intensive depth-charge attacks, which forced the I-35 to the surface. The submarine found itself between the two destroyers who immediately opened fire with their 5in and 40mm guns. The two aircraft carried out bombing runs and one bomb hit an ammunition box on the deck of the submarine. Then the *Frazier* rammed the submarine just aft of the conning tower, rupturing the hull. As the *Frazier* backed off, with her bow badly damaged, the I-35 sank quickly stern first. The destroyers launched rescue boats to pick up survivors. The survivors identified the submarine as the I-35. A total of ninety-two crewmembers were lost.

Crewmembers about to be rescued from their makeshift lifeboat after their ship was torpedoed. (*USN*)

E14Y1 'Glens' from submarines on patrol. (*Author*)

I-36

The I-36 was one of the Japanese submarines equipped with an E14Y1 'Glen' reconnaissance floatplane. After one incident, on 22 April 1943, the floatplane after spotting a number of American aircraft carriers and battleships, failed to return to the I-36. It was later discovered that the aircraft had been forced to land on the sea after being hit by gunfire and scuttled to prevent it being captured. What happened to the crew of the aircraft is not known. The I-36 was then assigned to carry *Kaiten* human torpedoes, but after a series of unsuccessful attempts to sink enemy ships and suffering damage from carrier aircraft, the I-36 returned to Kure. Its reconnaissance aircraft was launched again in March 1944 when it carried out a reconnaissance flight over the Majuro Atoll. The aircraft failed to locate the submarine after the flight and alighted on the water, but was recovered the following morning. It was while moored at Kure that the crew witnessed the atomic bomb over Hiroshima. Shortly afterwards the Emperor announced an end to hostilities and the I-36 and her crew surrendered to the Americans.

I-37

On 8 November 1944 Operation Kikusui (Floating Chrysanthemum) – Tokko (special attack) on Palau-Ulithi anchorage was launched with the I-36, I-37 and I-47 against enemy shipping. The I-37 carried four *Kaiten* suicide torpedoes, piloted by Lieutenant Kamibeppu Yoshinori, Lieutenant jg. Murakami Katsutomo, Ensign Kondo Kazuhiko and Ensign Utsunomiya Hideichi. Ten days later, just hours before the attack, the I-37 was spotted and two American destroyers USS *Conklin* (DE

439) and USS *McCoy Reynolds* (DE-440) immediately started a search and within hours had picked up a sonar signal. The two destroyers attacked with a pattern of Mark 10 Hedgehog projector charges. A series of violent underwater explosions followed and minutes later debris and oil came to the surface. There were no further contacts and no survivors were found.

I-38

On 11 November 1944 the I-38, under the command of Captain Eitarō Aku, was ordered to the Ngulu Islands to find out if the American fleet was using them. The IJN staff needed the information to plan future *Kaiten* missions. Whilst east of Luzon, the I-38 reported sighting an enemy task force. This was her last known transmission. Some time later the destroyers USS *Nicholas* (DD-449) and USS *Taylor* (DD-468) were escorting the cruiser USS *St. Louis* (CL-49) from Ulithi to Kossol Roads, Palau when the *Nicholas's* SG radar picked up a surface contact at 22,000 yards. The destroyer closed quickly and opened fire with its 5in main armament, but the contact disappeared. Some hours later, the *Nicholas* picked up the target again by a sonar contact and dropped a pattern of eighteen depth charges. Contact was lost but regained some time later. As the destroyer prepared to attack again, the contact turned hard right. The destroyer also went hard right and found itself practically on top of the contact. A salvo of depth charges quickly followed. A few minutes after the last charge went off, a huge underwater explosion that sank the submarine rocked the *Nicholas*. Some hours later debris and human remains were sighted in the attack area. The I-38 was lost with all of her 110 crewmen.

The aircraft-carrying submarine I-38 on patrol. (*Author*)

I-39

On 20 November 1943 the American Operation Galvanic (the invasion of the Gilbert Islands) started when they invaded Tarawa and Makin Islands. The invasion fleet of 200 ships included 13 battleships and 11 aircraft carriers. The following day the I-39, together with the I-19, I-35, I-169 and the I-175, was ordered to proceed to Tarawa in the Gilbert Islands to engage the enemy fleet. The I-39, carrying an E14Y1 'Glen' floatplane, approached the area and reported its arrival. This was the last message received from the I-39. Then 60 miles south-west of Tarawa, the destroyer USS *Boyd* (DD-544) detected a submarine and dropped a pattern of depth charges and sunk the I-39 with her entire crew of ninety-six men.

I-40

The I-40 departed Truk for the Makin area on her first war patrol on 26 November 1943 and was ordered, together with the I-19, I-40, I-169 and the RO-38, to form a picket line north of Makin. A signal to the I-40, I-19 and the I-20 inquiring as to their respective locations was sent on 21 February 1944 but no reply was received from the I-40. It was presumed lost in the Gilberts with all ninety-seven crewmen. There are conflicting accounts as to the I-40's demise; some accounts state that the I-40 was sunk on 25 November 1943 off Makin Island by the USS *Radford* (DD-446), but some sources indicate that the submarine sunk there was the I-19.

I-41

The last message received from the I-41 reported attacking an American task force and sinking the *Casablanca* class escort carrier USS *Anzio* (CVE-57) on 12 November 1944. However, it was the cruiser USS *Reno* (CL-96) that had been hit and only damaged. The attack alerted the task force to the presence of a Japanese submarine. The USS *Anzio*'s aircraft conducted an ASW sweep of the area and one of the aircraft reported a radar contact with a submarine on the surface. The aircraft and destroyers mounted a hunt for the submarine that lasted 14 hours, and then a sonar contact by the destroyer USS *Lawrence C. Taylor* (DE-415), resulted in a coordinated depth-charge attack with her sister-ship the USS *Melvin R. Nawman* (DE-416) and two planes from the *Anzio*. They sank the I-41 with the loss of all hands.

I-42

On 5 March 1944 the I-42 departed Truk on a supply run to Palau. On arrival the submarine embarked cargo and personnel and then departed on a supply run to Rabaul, carrying a total of 102 personnel. In an attempt to avoid detection the captain, Commander Ogawa, zigzagged on the surface at 18 knots. Also in the area was the USS *Tunny* (SS-282), which had been alerted by an 'Ultra' signals-intelligence message from COMSUBPAC at Pearl Harbor. The USS *Tunny* then picked up a surface contact at 13,000 yards on her SJ radar and closed on the target. It was visually identified as an I-class submarine, but the I-42's lookouts also sighted the *Tunny*. For almost an hour and a half, the two submarines manoeuvred for position, attempting to obtain a shot. Then, 6 miles south-west of Angaur, Palau the *Tunny* found itself in position and fired four torpedoes from a distance of 1,900 yards. The American submarine then came hard to starboard to prevent a collision and then crash-dived to avoid a possible return attack. Even before the *Tunny*'s hatch was closed, two hits were heard and a brilliant flash was seen. The *Tunny* dived to 150ft and began to circle the area. The soundman reported that the screws of the Japanese submarine had stopped, followed by breaking-up noises, which continued for an hour. The I-42 was reported sunk with all 102 hands.

I-43

On 4 February 1944, Vice Admiral Takagi Takeo's Sixth Fleet Headquarters signalled the I-43 to proceed to Truk carrying fifty-nine sailors from the 2nd Platoon of the 101st Sasebo Special Naval Landing Force aboard. The USS *Aspro* (SS-309) was submerged on station as part of the forthcoming Operation Hailstone when the soundman picked up the I-43's propeller noises. Minutes later a surfaced 'I-9' class submarine was sighted zigzagging at 17 knots. She carried a numeral marking identified her as the I-43 and a *Hinomaru* (Japanese flag) painted on the conning tower. Also observed was a midget submarine mounted just aft of the conning tower. The *Aspro* was unable to close for an attack while submerged so it waited until the I-43 had passed, then surfaced in the daylight and tracked her at flank speed. After a long radar-assisted chase, the *Aspro* gained a position ahead of the target and fired four Mark XIV-3A torpedoes at a range of 2,100 yards. One minute later two hit the I-4 and the submarine exploded and sank by the stern. The I-43 was presumed lost in the Truk area with all 166 hands.

I-44

With the tide of war in the Pacific now turning in favour of the Allies, the Japanese had now resorted to desperate measures and on 3 April 1945 a fifth *Kaiten* mission was devised. The plan called for the I-44, I-47, I-56 and I-58, each carrying six *Kaiten*s, to attack anchored American shipping off Okinawa. On 4 April 1945 the I-44 departed Otsujima for Okinawa on her fifth war patrol with the same *Kaiten* crew as previous missions. On 21 April 1945 the Sixth Fleet HQ ordered the I-44 to return to her base. There was no reply. On the same day 220 miles south-east of Okinawa Lieutenant (jg.) Donald L. Davis of Composite Squadron VC-92 took off from the USS *Tulagi* (CVE-72) on an ASW patrol in his Grumman TBM Avenger torpedo-bomber. Later in the mission, Davis sighted a submarine on the surface. He dived on it from 4,000ft and released a depth bomb that exploded next to the diving submarine's conning tower. On

The I-44 on patrol. (*Author*)

The I-44 leaving to go on a mission with her *Kaiten* pilots lined up on deck. (*Author*)

his second pass, Davis released a Mark 24 'Fido' acoustic homing torpedo that exploded against the submarine's hull and sank it. The I-44 was lost off Okinawa with all 130 crewmen plus four *Kaiten* pilots.

I-45

On 28 October 1944, 60 miles off Dinagat Island, Philippines, the destroyers USS *Eversole* (DE-404), USS *Richard S. Bull* (DE-402) and USS *Whitehurst* (DE-634) were returning from San Pedro Bay to rejoin their unit. At 0210, the *Eversole* made a sonar contact with a submarine, but it was lost soon after. At 0228 another contact was made, then half a minute later *Eversole* received two successive torpedo hits causing immediate loss of power and a 15-degree list. The captain, Lieutenant Commander Marix, ordered Abandon Ship. The *Eversole* remained afloat for about 15 minutes before sinking stern first. Minutes later the I-45 surfaced to circle the area, firing her 25 mm AA gun at the survivors in the water, then dived 20 minutes later. Shortly afterwards a massive underwater explosion followed, killing or wounding many of the men in the water. (It was later assumed that it was the *Eversole* blowing up.) The *Richard S. Bull*, alerted by the explosion, arrived at the scene of sinking and rescued 139 officers and men out of the crew of 213 (three of the survivors died later). While the rescue was being carried out the *Whitehurst* arrived and provided anti-submarine cover, and during this picked up a sonar contact east of Siargao Island. Immediately the destroyer carried out a series of attacks with barrages of 7.2in Mark 10 Hedgehog projector charges. The first three were unsuccessful but the fourth attack resulted in several underwater explosions that were so violent that they damaged the destroyer escort's sound gear. Later the lookouts on both ships observed wooden damage control plugs, various bits of deck planking, rags, bags of rice and other debris in a widening oil slick. The submarine sunk in these attacks was probably the I-45 with the loss of all 104 crewmembers.

I-46

On 8 October 1944 the USS *Helm* (DD-388) was part of the screen of the carrier Task Group 38.4 consisting of the USS *Enterprise* (CV-6), USS *Franklin* (CV-13), USS *Belleau Wood* (CVL-24) and USS *San Jacinto* (CVL-30) that was engaged in direct support of ground operations on the invasion of Leyte. During the engagement the USS *Helm* and USS *Gridley* (DD-380) detected a submarine trying to penetrate TG 38.4's screen. As the task group's carriers cleared the area, the two destroyers carried out depth-charge attacks. On 30 October all IJN submarines stationed east of Leyte were ordered to report their respective locations to Sixth Fleet HQ. The I-46, I-26 and I-54 failed to answer. On 1 November 1944 the I-46, I-26 and the I-54 failed to report for a second time. The I-46 was known to be in the area of the attack so was presumed lost with all 112 hands off the Philippines.

I-47

The I-47's role was as a *Kaiten* mother boat and as such was rarely involved in attacks on enemy shipping. On 30 July 1945 the I-47 was caught by a typhoon whilst on the surface recharging its batteries. Unable to complete the recharge, it was forced to stay surfaced and became swamped on a number of occasions. On 1 August 1945, after recharging its batteries, it was discovered that the heavy seas had washed *Kaiten* No. 1 away, causing damage to its mother submarine. The remaining human torpedoes, it was discovered later, had developed leaks. The I-47 returned to Hikari where the five remaining *Kaiten*s and their pilots were disembarked, then proceeded to Kure. On 15 August 1945 the Emperor Hirohito broadcasted an Imperial Rescript that called for an end to hostilities. The crew of I-47 refused to surrender and boarded a Kaibokan (an escort ship) in Kure harbour and confiscated her food supply, several rifles and machine guns. They intended to proceed to Rabaul to continue fighting, but the plan failed because of the lack of fuel. The submarine was abandoned by her crew and later surrendered at Kure

I-48

On 9 January 1945 the I-48 departed on its second *Kaiten* mission with four *Kaiten*s as part of the Kongo group with I-36, I-47, I-53, I-56 and I-58 for a planned attack on the USN Third Fleet anchorage at Ulithi. On 21 January, north-east of

The I-48 with *Kaiten*s on board being prepared for launching. (*Author*)

Yap Island, a Martin PBM-3D Mariner of VPB-20 based at Tinian made a radar contact with a surfaced submarine heading for Ulithi. It attempted to establish the nationality of the sub, which immediately crash-dived. The Mariner attacked the sub with two depth charges and then released a Mark 24 'Fido' acoustic torpedo. The I-48 (evidently with some *Kaiten*s already manned) received serious damage and was forced to abort the mission. The crew of the PBM Mariner reported their sighting to Ulithi and a three-strong hunter-killer group of destroyer escorts, the USS *Conklin* (DE-439), USS *Corbesier* (DE-438) and USS *Raby* (DE-698), was dispatched. It was assumed that the damaged submarine would head directly for Japanese-held Yap Island at an estimated submerged speed of three knots during the first night and day. After no contacts were made it was decided to expand the search. On 23 January the *Corbesier* made a surface radar contact at about 9,800 yards. The target was heading 210 degrees making 18 knots and then crash-dived. The *Corbesier* then obtained a sound contact and fired a salvo of Mark 10 Hedgehog projector charges but missed. The *Conklin* and *Raby* joined in the chase and five more Hedgehog attacks were made, all with negative results and contact was lost. The *Conklin* regained contact and carried out another Hedgehog attack from a distance of 550 yards. Seventeen seconds later, four or five explosions were heard from an estimated depth of 175ft. Then a violent explosion occurred, temporarily disabling *Conklin*'s engines and steering gear. Then huge air bubbles come up alongside; soon thereafter oil and debris surface. Large quantities of human remains were sighted. A whaleboat from *Conklin* picked up pieces of planking, splintered wood, cork, interior woodwork with varnished surfaces, chopsticks and a seaman's manual. The I-48 was sunk with her 122-strong crew along with four *Kaiten* pilots.

I-49 and I-50
Both cancelled.

I-51
Used extensively for trials with an aircraft aboard.

Yokosuka E6Y1 on the deck of the I-51 during trials. (*Author*)

I-52
Sunk on 25 July 1944 by TBM Avengers from the escort carrier USS *Bogue*.

The I-52 alongside the dock at Kure. (*USN*)

I-53
Surrendered in 1946.

The I-53 and I-36 tied up alongside the dock in Kure. (*USN*)

I-54

Within just a few months of coming off the blocks at the Kure Naval Yard after being launched on 4 May 1943, the I-54 was assigned to Group A and ordered to attack the aircraft carriers of Task Force 38 and the crippled USS *Houston* (CL-81), but was later reassigned to patrol 120 miles east of the Philippines between the areas assigned to the I-38 and the I-46. With the American Operation King Two (the invasion of Leyte, Philippines) under way, the I-54 and twelve other submarines were ordered to take up patrol station east of Leyte, Philippines. Admiral (later Fleet Admiral) William F. Halsey's Third Fleet of 738 ships including 18 aircraft carriers, 6 battleships, 17 cruisers, 64 destroyers and over 600 support ships landed the Army's X Corps (24th Infantry and 1st Cavalry Divisions) and the XXIV Corps (7th, 77th and 96th Infantry Divisions) to begin the campaign to retake Leyte. Just east of Leyte, the USS *Helm* (DD-388) was part of the screen of Rear Admiral Ralph E. Davison's carrier Task Group 38.4 comprising the USS *Enterprise* (CV-6), USS *Franklin* (CV-13), USS *Belleau Wood* (CVL-24) and USS *San Jacinto* (CVL-30) that was engaged in direct support of ground operations on Leyte. The *Helm* and USS *Gridley* (DD-380) detected a submarine that was trying to penetrate TG 38.4's screen. As Davison's carriers cleared the area, the two destroyers carried out depth charge attacks. Within minutes debris appeared with a large oil slick. The I-54 was presumed lost with all 107 hands as no signal was received from her and she was known to have been operating in the area

I-55

Some sources credit the USS *Gilmer* (APD-11) and the USS *William C. Miller* (DE-259) with the sinking of the I-55 on 28 July 1944, but some sources considered it to be the RO-48. The fate of the I-55 is not known.

The I-55 on sea trials. (*JMSDF*)

I-56

On 31 March 1945 the I-56 was assigned to the Tatara Unit with the I-44, I-47 and I-58 each carrying six *Kaiten*s. The unit then departed for Okinawa where the American Operation Iceberg (the invasion of Okinawa) was under way with Admiral Raymond A. Spruance's Fifth Fleet, included more than 40 aircraft carriers, 18 battleships, 200 destroyers and over 1,000 support ships that had surrounded the island. The fleet were there to support Lieutenant General Simon B. Buckner Jr's Tenth Army (7th, 77th and 96th Infantry and 1st and 6th Marine Divisions) when they made their amphibious landings to take the island from the Japanese. Just east of Okinawa, radar aboard Task Force 58's battleship USS *Missouri* (BB-63) detected a submarine 12 miles from the task force. The report set off a hunter-killer operation by USS *Bataan* (CVE-29) and destroyers USS *Heerman* (DD-532) who made a radar contact and the USS *Uhlmann* (DD-687) attacked with depth charges. Two aircraft from the *Bataan*, the USS *Collet* (DD-730), USS *McCord* (DD-534) and USS *Mertz* (DD-691) repeatedly depth-charged the submarine. After several hours, debris and a large oil slick appeared and the I-56 was presumed lost with 116 crewmen and six *Kaiten* pilots.

I-57

Cancelled.

I-58

Surrendered in 1946.

I-59
Cancelled.

I-60
Sunk by depth charges by HMS *Jupiter* on 17 January 1942.

I-61
Sunk in a collision with a gunboat off Iki Island on 2 October 1941,

I-62
Changed to I-162.

I-64
Changed to I-164.

I-65
Changed to I-165.

I-66
Changed to I-166.

I-67
Lost on 29 August 1941 during an exercise off the Bonin Islands, reason unknown.

I-68 and I-69
Changed to I-168 and I-169 respectively.

The I-68 on sea trials.(*Author*)

The I-69 on sea trials. (*Author*)

I-70

One of the first Japanese submarine casualties of the war was the sinking of the I-70 (sometimes incorrectly referred to as the I-170). On 10 December 1941 the I-70 had been shadowing the aircraft carrier USS *Enterprise* (CV-6) when it was spotted on the surface by a Douglas SBD Dauntless dive-bomber from VT-6 on an ASW patrol. The SBD bombed the submarine, causing enough damage to prevent the submarine from diving. Some time later another SBD from the *Enterprise* found the submarine still on the surface and sank it with a direct hit. There were no survivors.

I-71 and I-72

Changed to I-171 and I-172 respectively.

I-73

On 27 January 1942 the USS *Gudgeon* (SS-211) was returning to Pearl Harbor from her first war patrol to the Bungo Straits off Japan when they received an Ultra message advising them of the approach of three Japanese submarines, the I-18, I-22 and I-24. The *Gudgeon* was submerged when her sound operator reported fast propeller sounds on the port bow. Going to periscope depth a visual contact was made at a distance of about 5,000 yards, and the target was identified as the I-73 submarine with a deck gun mounted forward, making 15 knots. The *Gudgeon* fired three Mark 14 steam torpedoes from 1,800 yards. Due to heavy seas visual contact was temporarily lost, but minutes later two explosions were heard. The propeller noises stopped immediately and when *Gudgeon* came to periscope depth again, the target was gone. The I-73 was sunk with all hands. She was the first warship ever sunk by an American submarine.

I-74 and I-75

Changed to I-174 and I-175 respectively.

I-76, I-77, I-78, I-79, I-80. I-81, I-82, I-83, I-84 and I-85

Changed to I-176, I-177, I-178, I-179, I-180, I-181, I-182, I-183, I-184 and I-185 respectively.

I-121

Surrendered in 1945.

I-122

The I-122 was directly involved in the 'First China Incident' on 7 July 1937 (known also as the Marco Polo Bridge Incident). The submarine was on exercise with Japanese troops on the Hun River, Lugouqiao, China. The Japanese troops on night manoeuvres are said to have fired blank cartridges at the shoreline. Nearby Chinese troops fired back, but did not cause casualties. The following morning at roll call, the Japanese discovered that one of their soldiers was missing and assumed that the Chinese had captured him. They demanded entry to a Peking suburb to look for the soldier. When the Chinese refused, the I-122 opened fire with its deck gun and shelled the city and an undeclared war on China began. On 9 June 1945 the I-122 departed Maizuru for a training cruise in Nanao Bay, Sea of Japan. The following day a group of nine American submarines, including the USS *Skate* (SS-305), penetrated the minefields guarding the entrance to the Tsushima Strait, using a new FM sonar. The I-122 was returning to the Nanao base, zigzagging at about 15 knots, when she was sighted by the *Skate*. The submarine was soon positively identified as I-121 class and the *Skate* fired four torpedoes at 800 yards. Two hit amidships and the I-122 sank instantly with all hands. Five minutes later breaking-up noises were heard and a large air bubble appeared on the surface, followed by a large slick of oil. An IJN observation post at Rokugo Lighthouse witnessed the sinking, but attributed it to an onboard explosion of torpedoes.

I-123

Like most of the I-class submarines the I-123 was being used more as a supply boat than anything else. On 29 January 1942, the I-123, which was on patrol with the I-124, attacked the 5,375-ton tanker USS *Trinity* (AO-13) which was being escorted by the destroyers USS *Alden* (DD-211) and USS *Edsall* (DD-219). Three corvettes of the Royal Australian Navy (RAN) 24th Minesweeping Flotilla were ordered to proceed to sea at full speed. HMAS *Deloraine* was approaching the scene of the attack when she was targeted by the I-124, who fired a single torpedo. The *Deloraine* turned to starboard and evaded the torpedo which missed her stern by 10ft. Minutes later the *Deloraine* established an Asdic contact and commenced her first counter-attack with six depth charges. Oil and air bubbles appear to the surface but nothing else and the I-123 made he escape. On 24 August 1942 a message was received ordering the I-123 to deliver food to an Army coastwatcher post on

Florida Island. The submarine failed to locate the unit and was redirected to the east of Savo Island. On 29 August a message was sent stating that the submarine had been forced to dive after spotting a reconnaissance seaplane. This was the last message received from I-123. Just 60 miles east of Savo Island that same morning, the lookouts on the destroyer-minelayer USS *Gamble* (DM-15), spotted the conning tower of a diving submarine. The *Gamble* tracked the I-123, using her magnetic anomaly detection system. Then closing in, the destroyer-minelayer conducted several depth-charge attacks. After the last attack, the *Gamble* ran through a large oil slick. Her crew spotted a large air bubble break the surface and later recovered broken deck planking. No survivors were found and it is assumed that the I-123 was sunk. The Japanese submarine RO-34, patrolling to the west of that area, registered a number of explosions coming from I-123's location.

I-124

On 10 January 1942, the I-124 departed Davao for Darwin on her third war patrol. That same day, one of the mines laid by I-124 the previous month in Manila Bay sank the 1,976-ton Panamanian-flagged converted steamer SS *Daylite*. On 16 January 1942 the I-124 laid twenty-seven mines near Darwin where twenty Allied ships were in the harbour. The following day the USS *Houston* (CA-30) reported sighting two Japanese submarines that were probably I-124 and I-123. Allied code-breakers intercepted a signal from the I-124 reporting that three Allied transports escorted by a single destroyer had arrived at Darwin. This was the last message received from the I-124.

Following HMAS *Deloraine*'s second attack on the I-123, the I-124 briefly exposed her periscope and bow. The submarine had a five-degree trim by the stern and a list of 20 degrees to port. One depth charge launched from *Deloraine*'s port thrower exploded within 10ft of the submarine's periscope. Before I-124 disappeared, a Vought-Sikorsky OS2U Kingfisher floatplane from USS *Langley* (AV-3) dropped a small bomb in the same location. More oil and air bubbles were sighted rising from the now-stationary submarine lying on the bottom at 25 fathoms depth. The *Deloraine* carried out another depth-charge attack and then more bubbles were sighted. The corvette slowed down to observe the area and collected samples of oil and a number of TNT particles were observed floating in the water. The *Deloraine* made another contact off to the south-east and used her last depth charges in two attacks against that target. More oil and air bubbles were sighted.

Later HMAS *Lithgow* replaced the *Deloraine* and the second corvette conducted seven attacks, using all her forty depth charges. Diesel oil and air bubbles were once again sighted. The *Lithgow* was then joined by HMAS *Katoomba* who attempted to drag for the submarine, using a grapnel. A contact was made with the submarine, but the grapnel broke free when recovered. Later that evening USS *Alden* and USS *Edsall* arrived on the scene. *Edsall* detected a contact on the edge of the oil slick originating from the I-124 and immediately launched a pattern of five depth charges; three explosions were recorded. The *Alden* also attacked the contact. The following morning the *Deloraine* returned to the location of the I-124, now marked with a DAN buoy, and detected another submarine echo and conducted three successive attacks. She was joined by the *Katoomba* but at midday the attacks were finally called off as a result of deteriorating weather.

The RAN boom vessel HMAS *Kookaburra* arrived on the scene and commenced a series of attempts to locate the submarine on the seabed. The sinking of the I-124 was claimed to have been made by both *Deloraine* and *Katoomba* and it was the first IJN warship sunk by the RAN. One week later the *Kookaburra*, carrying a team of sixteen divers from the submarine tender USS *Holland* (AS-3), returned to the location of the proposed site of the sinking of the I-124 and after a number of dives located the wreck of a large submarine with the forward hatch blown open.

I-167
Lost during exercises off the Bonin Islands, reason unknown.

I-168
In April 1943 the American retaliation for Pearl Harbor and their advance in the Pacific was beginning to have a marked effect on the Japanese. So much so that the Japanese submarine force was increasingly being used for supply runs instead of the hunting down of enemy ships. Rear Admiral Kouda Takero's SubRon 1 with the I-2, I-7, I-31, I-34, I-35, I-168, I-169 and I-171 in the Northern District Force, Fifth Fleet were given the mission to reinforce and re-supply the isolated Japanese garrisons in the Aleutian Islands. The I-168 departed Attu with a cargo of ammunition and mail for Kiska and after arriving there unloaded its cargo and returned to Yokosuka. Loaded with another cargo, the I-168 departed for Rabaul and upon entering the Isabel Strait sent a situation report. This was the last message from the I-168. At dusk on 27 July the I-168 sighted a surfaced enemy submarine in the Steffen Strait between New Ireland and New Hanover. Lieutenant Commander Nakajima, captain of the I-168, fired a torpedo at the submarine, but missed. The submarine the USS *Scamp* (SS-277) spotted the incoming torpedo and crash-dived to 220ft. The torpedo passed overhead and the *Scamp* immediately returned to periscope depth. Catching the I-168 on the surface, the *Scamp* fired four torpedoes, all of which struck home, sinking her instantly with all ninety-seven crewmembers.

I-169
After carrying out a number of supply runs, the I-169 arrived at Dublon Island, Truk to replenish her own supplies and carry out repairs. Whilst at her anchorage in the lagoon the CO and twenty sailors went ashore in Dublon. In addition to the remaining crew were some workmen who were also aboard. On the morning

of 4 April 1943 an air raid warning was issued. On the I-169 the watch officer ordered the I-169 to dive immediately, although most deck hatches were still open. As the first wave of PB4Y Liberator bombers arrived overhead, I-169 submerged. The main induction valve was not secured and the aft compartments flooded immediately. Despite a desperate attempt to re-surface the submarine settled at the bottom of the lagoon in 125ft of water. The remainder of the crew sealed off the flooded area. Once the raid had passed, an unsuccessful attempt was made to contact the trapped crew of the I-169. A diver was sent down who contacted the survivors by tapping on the hull. The following day the headquarters of the Japanese Sixth Fleet issued an order to rescue the survivors. A repair ship with a 30-ton crane and the tug Futagami were dispatched to lift the bow to the surface. The initial search failed to locate the submarine but once they found her they attempted a lift, but the flooded submarine was too heavy and the crane's cable broke. Divers made further attempts to contact the crew but tapping only came from the aft compartment. Air hoses were lowered and holes were drilled in the ballast tanks, but it was impossible to signal the crew to open the air valves to the ballast tanks. By the end of the day there were no further responses from the entombed crew. All had suffocated. In the next weeks, thirty-two bodies were recovered from the forward compartments. Two days after the incident USN code-breakers intercepted and decrypted a message that read:

> Interim report about the I-169 incident. 1. The bodies of the Army officers have been recovered and the causes of the accident have been investigated. It is regrettably the case that, as far as can been seen, the hatchway and outboard ---- were closed, but the cover of the engine room was left open. Compressed air was driven thence through the storm ventilator -----. Through some mistake or other the flood – controller there was left open, for that reason ---- (blanks) --- the engine room and after torpedo compartment hatchway was open.

The threat of invasion by the Americans was deemed to be imminent so the wreck was bombarded with depth charges to prevent the submarine's technology from falling into enemy hands. The bow and conning tower were heavily damaged by the depth charges but nothing else.

I-170 (I-70)
See I-70.

I-171 (I-71)
On 30 January 1944 the I-171 (formerly I-71) departed Rabaul on a supply run to Buka, carrying rubber containers on her deck. The I-171 was the second submarine (after the I-181) to supply the garrison. The

use of submarines as supply boats was now becoming the norm. Then 15 miles west of Buka Island two destroyers, USS *Guest* (DD-472) and USS *Hudson* (DD-475) were covering the transports that were landing Marines on Green Island. The two destroyers picked up a surface contact on their SG radars at 3,500 yards. The I-171 realised that she had been spotted and dived, but the destroyers maintained a contact on their sonar and made depth-charge runs that sank the I-171. Confirmation of the sinking was obtained when USN code-breakers intercepted and decrypted a message that read:

> I-171 departed Rabaul January 30th to engage in transportation operations to Buka but she had not arrived at Buka by February 5th at 1800 as scheduled. After 3rd, she was called a number of times but there is no response. We have no further information on her ----- personnel items------ I-171 is presumed lost with all ninety-one hands off Buka.

Another message was intercepted by USN code-breakers and decrypted that read:

> I-171 departed Rabaul January 30, arrived Buka Feb. 2 (blurred number might be 1 or might be 2). Completed unloading men and cargo and (continued on special transportation duties). Has not been heard from since February 1. According to report of naval force at Buka, an enemy destroyer was (sighted) to west of Buka that date. It is assumed that Captain and all hands died in battle. -----.

I-172 (I-72)

On 10 November 1942, during a period of heavy submarine losses being suffered by the Japanese, the I-172 (formerly the I-72) was sunk by the destroyer-minesweeper USS *Southard* (DMS-10). The last signal received from the submarine was when she was off Guadalcanal and involved in the Battle of Santa Cruz. 'It was increasingly being thought that these heavy losses were caused by the lack of submarine reconnaissance of the American fleet as the submarines were otherwise engaged as supply boats.'

I-173

See I-73.

I-174 (I-74)

After surviving two near-misses from depth-charging destroyers, the I-174 left Kure for the Marshall Islands on 3 April 1944 on her ninth war patrol. On 11 April Patrol Bombing Squadron VB-108, equipped with twelve Consolidated PB4Y-1 Liberators, relocated to Eniwetok. Whilst on early morning patrol, a Liberator from VB-108 spotted a submarine on the surface and depth charged it with depth bombs. The submarine disappeared and some minutes later a large oil slick and debris appeared, increasing over the next two days. The I-174 was sunk with all 107 hands. Japanese records later confirmed that this submarine was sunk.

I-175 (I-75)

On 1 January 1944 the American Operation Flintlock (the invasion of the Marshall Islands) took place under the command of Vice Admiral (later Admiral) Marc A. Mitscher's Task Force 58 who landed the 4th Marine Division and the Army's 7th Infantry Division and captured Kwajalein, Roi-Namur and Majuro Atolls. The same day the, I-175 and RO-39 were ordered to proceed to Wotje in the Marshall Islands to attack the Task Force. The I-175 was reconnoitring the Wotje Atoll when she was picked up on the USS *New Jersey's* (BB-61) radar at a range of 21 miles. The destroyer USS *Charrette* (DD-581) was ordered to detach from the screen and investigated the contact. When she was just 300 yards from the contact it disappeared from the radar. The *Charrette* then switched to her sonar and quickly acquired a target. A pattern of eight depth charges was dropped in the area, but contact was lost. The destroyer USS *Fair* (DE-35) was ordered to assist the *Charrette* and attacked with 7.2in ahead-thrown Mark 10 Hedgehog' projector charges. Four explosions were heard and an hour later a large spreading slick of oil appeared on the surface with other debris. Japanese records later showed that it was the I-175 that had sunk with the loss of 100 crewmembers.

I-176 (I-76)

The I-176 was the only Japanese submarine to sink an American submarine when it torpedoed the USS *Corvina* (SS-226) off Truk in 1943. With the invasion of the Marshall Islands the I-176 was ordered to try and intercept Vice Admiral Marc A. Mitscher's Task Force 58 and attack. Then north of Buka Island an American patrol plane spotted the I-176 and her position and signalled her position to DesDiv 94 in the Treasury Islands. The destroyers USS *Franks* (DD-554), USS *Haggard* (DD-555), USS *Hailey* (DD-556) and USS *Johnston* (DD-557) were ordered to search and destroy the submarine. The *Haggard* made a sonar contact on her starboard bow at a range of 2,800 yards and together with the *Franks* they made five separate attacks. Such was the ferocity of the attacks that the *Haggard* suffered slight damage from exploding depth charges, when her gyrocompass was knocked out. Then between the last two attacks, a heavy underwater ripple explosion was heard. The USS *Franks* dropped a further pattern of thirteen depth charges. An oil slick covering seven miles of ocean together with various debris, including splintered wood, cork and a geta sandal were sighted. The attack was initially assessed as a 'probable kill' but Japanese records later showed that it was the I-176 that was lost, with all 103 hands, north-west of Buka.

The I-176 underway. (*JMSDF*)

I-177 (I-77)

The I-177 will be remembered for the sinking of the Australian hospital ship HMAHS *Centaur* on 14 May 1943. The torpedo ignited a fuel tank setting the ship ablaze. She rolled to port and sank within three minutes. Of the 332 crew, patients, medical staff and passengers on board, 268 died – only 64 were rescued. On 19 September 1944 the I-177 departed Kure on her fourth war patrol off Palau, Halmahera and Mindanao, Philippines. When she arrived at her assigned patrol area off Palau, she was redirected to reconnoitre Ulithi. On returning from Ulithi a PBM-3D Martin 'Mariner' of VPB-16 on ASW patrol made radar contact on a submarine. As it approached, the submarine crash-dived, but a positive identification was made. The PBM dropped a Mark 24 'Fido' acoustic homing torpedo that damaged I-177 badly. The PBM relayed the target's location to a nearby hunter-killer group that immediately started to search for the submarine. The USS *Hoggatt Bay's* (CVE-75) radar picked up a contact at 20,000 yards, and the escort destroyer USS *Samuel S. Miles* (DE-183) was dispatched from the carrier screen to investigate. Lookouts on the *Samuel S. Miles* sighted a surfaced submarine, and as the submarine crash-dived, the *Samuel S. Miles* locked on to the I-177 with her sonar and attacked with a salvo of twenty-four ahead-thrown Mark 10 Hedgehog projector charges. A second salvo was followed by a violent explosion and some minutes later a large oil slick appeared on the surface together with a vast amount of debris. Records later showed that the I-177 failed to reply to a radio signal call to return after completing the reconnaissance of Ulithi. It was presumed lost with all 101 hands in the Palaus area.

I-178

On 4 June 1943 the I-178 left Truk to carry out her second patrol off the eastern coast of Australia. Two weeks later the captain Commander Utsugi sent a routine signal to the Sixth Fleet giving his position. That same evening, a Bristol Beaufort of the RAAF's No. 32 Squadron was on patrol when it came across a surfaced submarine and, after identifying it as a Japanese submarine, attacked it causing considerable damage. Another Bristol Beaufort from No. 32 Squadron came across the same submarine that was still proceeding on the surface and inflicted further damage. Then a couple of hours later an oil slick was sighted off Nambucca Heads. The attacked submarine must have been the I-178 because she was known to have been in the area and failed to answer signals from Headquarters, Sixth Fleet. No signal was ever heard from the submarine again and it was presumed lost off the eastern coast of Australia with all eighty-nine hands.

I-179

In June 1943 the I-179 started its shakedown trials in the western Inland Sea and then departed for Kure for the next stage of its shakedown trials in Iyo Nada, in the western part of Inland Sea. The I-179 began transmitting a report about conducting a cargo debarking test in the area of the Inland Sea, when contact was suddenly lost. A number of IJN vessels in that area attempted to contact I-179 both visually and by radio but without success. A rescue vessel from Kure was sent to the area and located the wreck of the I-179 in 265ft of water. Divers were sent down and they discovered that several hatches in the bow area, as well as the bow buoyancy tank vent valve, had been left open. The subsequent inquiry concluded that the submarine was lost as a result of a handling error when the bow buoyancy tank was accidentally flooded. The I-179 was refloated in 1957 and scrapped. The remains of all eighty-five sailors were recovered.

I-180

On 20 March 1944 the I-180 departed Ominato to patrol east of Unalaska and south of Kodiak in the Aleutians. Just south of Alaska the I-180 torpedoed and sank the 7,176-ton American Liberty ship SS *John Straub*. The same day the USS *Gilmore* (DE-18) and the USS *Edward C. Daley* (DE-17) were escorting a convoy from Dutch Harbour to Kodiak, Alaska when the *Gilmore*'s SG radar picked up a surfaced submarine at 8,000 yards. At 4,000 yards, the 'pip' disappeared and contact was broken. The *Gilmore* quickly picked up a sound contact at 2,600 yards. Over the next hour, the *Gilmore* laid down three separate barrages of Mark 10 'Hedgehogs', each of twenty-four projector charges, but without result. Some hours later the *Gilmore* dropped a pattern of thirteen depth charges, but again without result. One hour later another pattern of thirteen depth charges was dropped followed minutes later by a heavy underwater explosion that rocked the destroyer escort. No more signals were received from the I-180. As it was known to be in the area it was presumed lost with all hands.

I-181

On 3 January 1944 Major Gregory 'Pappy' Boyington, the 26-victory 'ace' CO of the famed Marine 'Blacksheep' squadron (VMF-214), was shot down while on a fighter sweep over Rabaul. Boyington ditched his Chance-Vought F4U-1A 'Corsair' about five miles from shore and was injured in the crash. After spending eight hours in the water, the I-181 surfaced near Boyington and he was taken aboard as a POW. Two hours later, I-181 arrived at Rabaul. Boyington was flown on a Nakajima L2D 'Tabby' via Saipan to Japan where he spent the next 18 months at Ofuna prison camp near Yokohama. Years later, he said the treatment he received aboard the I-181 was the best he received in captivity. The I-181 departed Rabaul on a supply run to Gali, New Guinea with the RO-104, carrying ComSubDiv (Commander Submarine Division) 22 and his staff. That evening, the I-181 was damaged in a running battle with an unidentified American destroyer and a PT boat. After numerous attempts to try and contact her she was presumed lost south-west of New Guinea with all eighty-nine hands.

I-182

On 22 August 1943 the I-182 departed Truk to patrol off the New Hebrides. At the end of August the USS *Wadsworth* (DD-516) arrived from Espiritu Santo as part of a hunter-killer group and commenced searching on a north-south axis. On 1 September the *Wadsworth* made a strong sonar contact and dropped a full pattern of ten depth charges with 150ft depth settings, but with negative results. Not to be daunted, the *Wadsworth* carried out a second attack that developed into a stern chase. The submarine turned left just before the depth charges, set at 250ft, were fired. The submarine continued on a zigzag course, creating a wake that adversely affected the sonar's reception. The destroyer made several runs without dropping depth charges, trying to get into the right position, and then fired a deep pattern, set at 425ft. As the destroyer turned to clear the area, a huge bubble surfaced, but no oil slick or debris. Determined to get the submarine, the *Wadsworth* carried out a fourth attack, which like the previous attacks developed into a stern chase, with the submarine manoeuvring to create underwater disturbances. After dropping ten charges with a mean setting of 250ft, the destroyer turned away to try and pick up another sonar contact. Then a Consolidated PBY Catalina patrol plane reported an oil slick and debris just south of the last depth-charge pattern. Closing in on the area the destroyer checked on the slick, which smelt like diesel fuel and was about 400 by 600 yards and spreading. Wooden debris was also seen, but the identity of the submarine that the *Wadsworth* sank remained unknown. It was later confirmed that no further communication was made with the I-182 despite messages being sent ordering it to return to Truk and it was presumed lost with all eighty-seven crew off Espiritu Santo.

I-183

On 6 October 1943 the I-183 was carrying out a series of diving exercises in the area west of Ozu Island during its shakedown trials. During a crash-dive test one of sailors failed to close the main induction valve. The engine room flooded and despite an emergency main tank blow, the I-183's stern hit bottom with the bow sticking out of the water. The I-183's engineering officer managed to close the watertight hatch leading to the aft crew compartment, so that the flooding was limited to main engine and electric motor rooms. Sixteen sailors were trapped in the aft section of the submarine. Most of the crew escaped through the forward torpedo tubes and were picked up by the local fishermen. The following day a floating crane and a team of divers arrived from Kure Navy Yard. The submarine was refloated, but the sixteen sailors in the aft compartment were found dead. After being refitted the I-183 was assigned to SubRon 11 with the I-42, I-43, I-45, I-52, I-184, RO-40, RO-41, RO-43, RO-113 and RO-114. Following an air raid on Palau, I-183 departed for Kure with the I-44, but was forced to return because of a mechanical failure. After repairs the I-183 arrived at Kure and was reassigned to SubDiv 22, Sixth Fleet. The I-183 departed Kure for Truk via Saipan and was zigzagging at 17 knots after exiting the Bungo Straits when she was picked up by the USS *Pogy*'s (SS-266) SJ radar. The American submarine immediately commenced a surfaced chase at flank speed. Then 30 miles south of Cape Ashizuri, the *Pogy* closed to 1,300 yards and fired four Mark 23 torpedoes set to 6ft. Two minutes later the second torpedo hit the target and the I-183 sank in less than 40 seconds. Minutes later four or five loud explosions were heard. The *Pogy* doubled back and ran through a large oil slick, which they described as 'smelling like the new 100-octane aromatic aviation gasoline'. The I-183 was presumed lost with all of her ninety-two crew in the mid-Pacific.

I-184

In 1944, with the Japanese situation now desperate, all the I-class attack submarines were now assigned to the role of supply boats. On 20 May the I-184 departed Yokosuka with food and supplies for the starving garrison on Mili Atoll, Marshall Islands. After unloading the supplies Admiral Toyoda Soemu, CINC, Combined Fleet, ordered Vice Admiral Takagi to re-deploy his boats to the Marianas. From his headquarters on Saipan, Takagi ordered all available submarines to deploy east of the Marianas. The I-184 was ordered to proceed immediately to the east of Guam and patrol between the areas allotted to I-5 and the I-185. On 15 June 1944 the invasion of Saipan started when Task Force 52 landed. The I-184 was ordered to proceed to Saipan and acknowledged the message, signalling his ETA as 18 June (JST). This was the last message received from the I-184. The Battle of the Philippine Sea was well under way with the escort carrier USS *Suwanee* (CVE-27) supporting the invasion of the Marianas. A Grumman TBF Avenger torpedo-bomber of VT-60 from the aircraft carrier was flying an ASW patrol when, as it dropped below the cloud cover, it spotted a surfaced Japanese submarine. Lookouts on the submarine saw the Avenger and the I-184 crash-dived, but too late. The Avenger dropped depth bombs just ahead of the submarine's track and seconds later the I-184 exploded and sank with all ninety-six hands.

I-185

The I-185 departed Kure on 11 June 1944 on her supply mission, her decks piled high with drums of rice, but en route heavy seas washed most of them overboard. She was then diverted to the Saipan area to take part in the Defence of the Marianas when Admiral Toyoda Soemu CinC, Combined Fleet, ordered Vice Admiral Takagi Takeo CINC, Advance Expeditionary Force (Sixth Fleet) to redeploy his submarines to the Marianas. From his headquarters on Saipan, he ordered all available submarines to deploy east of the Marianas to attack Task Force 52 as they carried out the invasion of Saipan. Communications between Takagi's Sixth Fleet were disrupted by the invasion mainly because of the vast amount of radio traffic and during this the I-185 transmitted her last situation report. The I-185 received orders to abort her supply mission to Wewak and join up with the I-5, I-6, I-41 and I-184 to take up station in a north-south picket line 300 miles east of the Marianas. Heading for the same area were American troop transports guarded by the destroyer USS *Newcomb* (DD-586) and the minesweeper USS *Chandler* (DMS-9). As they approached Saipan the *Newcomb* made a sonar contact with a submarine and together with the *Chandler*, commenced an attack with depth charges. The contact was then lost momentarily until the *Chandler's* depth-charge attack brought up some oil. The *Newcomb* carried out another attack, followed by one from the *Chandler*. After a few minutes after the last attack made by *Chandler*, a deep-sea explosion was heard followed minutes later by debris consisting of cork slabs, wood, diesel oil and human remains. Records later showed that the I-185 was operating in the area but was never heard from again.

I-201, I-202 and I-203
Surrendered in 1945.

Sen Taka (ST) class I-202 submarine. (*Author*)

I-204
Destroyed by B-29 bombers during a raid on Kure shipyard in 1945.

I-205
Destroyed during air raid in 1945.

I-206
Sunk in storm during sea trials in 1945

I-207
Not completed, 1945.

I-208
Not completed, 1945.

I-351
The I-351 was the first of the planned class of the 'Sen-ho' avgas tankers, capable of carrying 132,000 gallons of gasoline. It was also used to ferry personnel and supplies and on the morning of 11 July 1945 it left Singapore with forty-two pilots amongst its cargo. As it entered the South China Sea on a zigzag course it was picked up on the radar of the American submarine USS *Blower* (SS-325). The *Blower* dived and launched four torpedoes in two spreads. The first two are thought to have hit the target, but did not explode. The I-351 dived and made its escape. The *Blower* alerted the nearby submarine the USS *Bluefish* (SS-222) who was patrolling east-north-east of Natuna Besar. Within hours of its first encounter with the *Blower*, the I-351 was running on the surface and was picked up on the radar of the *Bluefish*. For over an hour the *Bluefish* tracked the I-351, closing all the time. When it was in range four torpedoes were fired from 1,850 yards. Two missed but the other two struck home and the I-351 exploded and broke in two, sinking by the stern. The following morning whilst looking for debris the *Bluefish* picked up three survivors. All three were lookouts and were blown into the water when the torpedoes struck, one of the torpedoes striking the aviation fuel tank. A total of 110 sailors and aircrew were lost.

I-352
Sunk by B-29 bombers during raid on Kure shipyard, 1945.

I-353
Not built.

I-368
Sunk on 26 February 1945 by a TBM Avenger torpedo bomber from the escort carrier USS *Anzio* (CVE-57), using a 'Fido' acoustic homing torpedo. All eighty-six crewmembers were lost.

I-361

The I-361 was one of the large transport submarines that were converted to carry *Kaiten* submarines on her deck. On 24 May 1945 the I-361, together with the I-36, I-165 and I-363 left on her ninth *Kaiten* mission, with five *Kaitens* aboard, to a position just off Okinawa. As they approached the area, an American minesweeper detected the I-361. The minesweeper alerted the nearby Task Force's escort carrier the USS *Anzio* (CVE-57) and her four screening destroyer escorts warning them of a possible Japanese submarine in the area. The *Anzio* headed for the contact's last reported position and launched a series of searches by Composite Wing VC-13's TBM Avenger aircraft. 400 miles south-east of Okinawa the radar operator on one of the Avengers picked up a contact. Dropping out of the cloud cover the submarine was spotted on the surface at about 6,000 yards. The pilot fired four 5in rockets at the submarine, striking it twice. The target was identified as an I-161 class submarine without a deck gun, but no *Kaitens* were sighted during the attack. The I-361 crash-dived, but the Avenger dropped sonobuoys and a Mark 24 'Fido' acoustic tracking torpedo, which homed in on the propeller sounds and exploded. Two destroyers, the USS *Oliver Mitchell* (DE-417 and the USS *Tabberer* (DE-418), were closing in on the area when at a distance of 15 miles, the crew of the *Oliver Mitchell* felt a massive underwater shock. When both the destroyers arrived on the scene they found a large, heavy oil slick, bits of deck planking and other debris. The I-361 sank with all seventy-six crewmen and five *Kaiten* pilots.

The I-361 submarine with two *Kaiten* human torpedoes on her deck with their pilots waving their swords. (*Author*)

I-362

On 1 January 1945 the I-362 departed Yokosuka on a supply run via Truk to Meleyon Island, located in the Woleai Atoll in the Caroline Islands between Truk and southern Palau with the supplies for the beleaguered garrison. Just off the Eastern Carolines the escort destroyer the USS *Flemming* (DE-32) was on convoy duty as one of two escorts for a pair of oil tankers bound from Ulithi to Eniwetok when a radar contact was made with a surface target at a range of 14,000 yards. Closing to 4,000 yards, the *Flemming* challenged the target but got no response. The target faded from the radar, but switching to sonar the *Flemming* picked up a clear sonar echo at the same range and bearing. The destroyer closed to 1,000 yards and illuminated the area with her port searchlight, but found the area clear. The *Flemming* then made a depth-charge attack, followed by four Mark 10 Hedgehog barrages, each of twenty-four charges. Some minutes after the fourth Hedgehog attack, three violent underwater explosions were felt and heard. The deep rumbling blast shook the *Flemming* and damaged her sound gear. Debris was sighted and a large diesel oil slick started to spread on the surface. The submarine – probably I-362 which was known to have been operating in the area was sunk with all hands.

I-363

On 30 March 1945 after being used as a transport boat running supplies to troops the I-363 returned to Yokosuka. Her deck guns and Daihatsu landing craft fittings were removed and she was converted to carry five *Kaiten* human-torpedoes. By the end of May the I-363 had carried out eight *Kaiten* missions, then at the beginning of June, together with the I-36, I-165 and I-361 she went on patrol in an area between Okinawa and Ulithi Atoll. Just south-east of Okinawa, the I-363 sighted a convoy, but the sea was too rough to launch the *Kaitens*, so it was decided to attack with conventional torpedoes but with no results. The I-363 was diverted to the Sea of Japan to defend against a possible Soviet invasion and whilst patrolling off Kyushu the submarine was strafed by aircraft from Task Force 38 and received minor damage, but two crewmembers were killed. The I-363 returned to Kure for repairs and then left for Sasebo. Just 10 miles off the Miyazaki coast, the I-363 hit a mine and sank. Ten sailors were rescued, but the remainder of the crew were lost.

I-364

On 4 September 1944 the I-364 departed Yokosuka for Wake Island on her maiden supply voyage with a crew of seventy-seven aboard. Her estimated time of arrival at Wake was 'late September'. Then 250 miles east of the Boso Peninsula, the I-364 was running on the surface making 9.5 knots when she was picked up on the radar of the USS *Sea Devil* (SS-400), also on her first patrol. The *Sea Devil* began tracking and identified the target as an I-58 class submarine with a large Rising Sun insignia painted on the side of her conning tower. The I-364 commenced zigzagging, unaware of the *Sea Devil* making an approach. As the I-364 passed in front at 1,800 yards, the *Sea Devil* fired four Mark 18-2 torpedoes. Two hit their target and were followed by a large explosion. The I-364 sank almost instantly, leaving just a large pall of brown smoke where the target had been and a rapidly spreading oil slick. There were no survivors.

I-365

The I-365 was commissioned in August 1944 as a transport submarine and attached to Yokosuka Naval District. Its first mission was on a transport mission carrying medicine and mail to Truk. On 16 November it departed Truk for Yokosuka via the Ogasawara (Bonin) Islands carrying sixty-five crew and thirty-one passengers. The I-365 sent a routing signal when just east of the Ogasawara (Bonin) Islands, this was the last message received from the submarine. Just 75 miles south-east of Yokosuka the USS *Scabbardfish* (SS-397) was on lifeguard duty off Japan, when it sighted through the high periscope the I-365 running on the surface. The American submarine tracked the Japanese submarine for over three hours and attempted to outrun the target and reach a favourable firing position. A Japanese reconnaissance aircraft then spotted the *Scabbardfish* but it failed to warn the I-365 that it was being tracked. Realising that it had been spotted, the *Scabbardfish* was forced to dive, and finished its approach submerged. It then launched two torpedoes from a distance of 1,625 yards. Seconds later one of the torpedoes exploded on the Japanese submarine's starboard side in the forward battery compartment. The I-365 sank within 30 seconds. After surfacing to look for debris the *Scabbardfish* discovered five survivors amongst the oil-strewn debris. Four of the survivors refused to be rescued and subsequently drowned; the fifth, Petty Officer Sasaki, did not and was the sole survivor. He identified the submarine as the I-365.

I-366

Surrendered 1946.

I-367

Surrendered 1946.

I-368

On 19 February 1945 the American Operation Detachment – the invasion of Iwo-Jima – began and the Fifth Fleet of over 450 ships landed the 54th Amphibious Corps (3rd, 4th and 5th Marine Divisions). The following day the order came from the Headquarters of the Japanese Sixth Fleet to form the next *Kaiten* group. The American landing on Iwo Jima had been earlier than expected, so the *Kaiten* training was cut short. The I-368, I-44 and I-370 were ordered to launch their *Kaiten*s at anchored American shipping off Iwo Jima. The I-368 was on her first sortie (the very first *Kaiten* carrier to do so), and 35 miles west of Iwo Jima was running on the surface when it was picked up on radar by a Grumman TBM-1C Avenger torpedo bomber from the USS *Anzio*'s (CVE-57) Composite Wing VC-82. The I-368 was not moving and the Avenger overshot her on the first pass. The submarine quickly dived and on the second pass the pilot of the Avenger dropped a float light marker and sonobuoys followed by a Mark 24 'Fido' acoustic homing torpedo. The I-368's conning tower broke the surface near the marker, but quickly dived again. A second Avenger arrived and dropped more sonobuoys and another 'Fido'. Minutes later a violent explosion erupted followed by a large spreading oil slick and debris. The I-368 sank with her crew of eighty-six: there were no survivors.

I-369
Surrendered 1946.

I-370
The I-370 was the first cargo-carrying submarine to be converted to carry *Kaiten* submarines. Trials were underway when on 19 February 1945 the invasion of Iwo Jima started. The American Fifth Fleet of over 450 ships, landed the 54th Amphibious Corps (3rd, 4th and 5th Marine Divisions). The I-370 was in the 'Chihaya' group with I-44 and I-368 and their mission was for the group to launch their *Kaiten* at the anchored American shipping off Iwo Jima. The I-370 departed Hikari for Iwo Jima with five *Kaiten* aboard and was expected to attack the American fleet five days after departure. Running on the surface the I-370 saw nine empty American transports that had departed Iwo Jima for Saipan. As they prepared to launch all the *Kaitens* the I-370 was picked up on radar by the destroyer USS *Finnegan* (DE-307). The destroyer immediately detached from the escort screen and closed in on the submarine. Within minutes of being spotted, the I-370 crash-dived and broke the contact. The *Finnegan* picked up the submarine by sonar

The I-370 with *Kaiten* human torpedoes on her deck. The pilots are waving goodbye to those on shore which was rather prophetic as the submarine and the entire crew were lost when depth-charged by a destroyer. (*Author*)

and launched an ahead-thrown Mark 10 Hedgehog attack that failed. This was followed by thirteen deep-set depth-charge attacks and a new series of Hedgehog charges. Minutes later thirteen depth charges set to medium depth were released. Five minutes later a deep underwater rumbling sound was heard and a mass of air bubbles rose to the surface. Then fuel oil started to come to the surface and a slick covering an area four miles long and two miles wide slowly spread. The I-370 with her crew of seventy-nine and five *Kaiten* pilots were destroyed. The I-370 was the first cargo submarine converted to carry the *Kaiten* to be lost.

I-371

The I-371 was the second Japanese supply submarine to reach the badly starved Japanese army garrison of Mereyon. Such was the situation that, that month, 467 men had died of starvation. After unloading 50 tons of food and mail the I-371 left for Truk. The USS *Lagarto* (SS-371) was on an anti-picket boat sweep to aid Task Force 38's carrier planes in remaining undetected as they approach to strike Japan, when the submarine's radar picked up a surfaced submarine at 5,000 yards. The *Lagarto* closed and fired torpedoes and sunk a submarine – most probably the I-371. It was known that the I-371 was operating in the area and as there was no further contact from her it is assumed that it was she that was sunk in this attack.

I-372

On 15 June 1945 the I-372 left Yokosuka on her second supply run to Wake. The same day the USN Fleet Radio Unit, Melbourne, Australia provided the following information: 'A Japanese submarine left Tokyo Bay at 0900 on 5th to pass 5 miles south of Nojima Saki at 2000 on passage to Wake Island.' The I-372 was on its return to Yokosuka when it suffered a near miss during an attack on Yokosuka by Grumman TBF Avenger torpedo-bombers and F6F Hellcat fighter-bombers from Task Force 38's USS *Essex* (CV-9), USS *Randolph* (CV-15), USS *Shangri-La* (CV-38) and USS *Belleau Wood* (CVL-24). The near miss ruptured the I-372's starboard cargo hold amidships. Despite the desperate efforts of her crew to keep her afloat the I-372 started to sink slowly and finally sank in shallow water. Later the hulk of I-372 was raised, towed to deep water and scuttled. There was one casualty but the rest of the crew escaped.

I-373

On 17 June 1945 the I-373 arrived at Sasebo to be converted to carry aviation fuel. The I-373 departed Sasebo on 13 August on her first tanker run to Formosa. Entering the East China Sea on a zigzagging course at 10 knots the I-373 was picked up on the SJ radar of the submarine USS *Spikefish* (SS-404). Within minutes the *Spikefish* had made visual contact but lost sight when the I-373 submerged. Two hours later the *Spikefish* regained radar contact at 8,600 yards and tracked the target until it was sighted on the surface. The silhouette identified the target to be a large I-class submarine. The *Spikefish* manoeuvred itself into firing position and launched a full salvo of six bow torpedoes, obtaining two hits that sank the I-373 by the stern. The *Spikefish* surfaced and picked up one survivor of I-373's crew of eighty-five. The I-373 was the last Japanese submarine to be sunk in the Second World War.

I-374
Construction ceased in 1945.

I-400
Surrendered 1946.

Excellent shot of the I-400 in dry dock in Pearl Harbor. (*USN*)

USS *Blower* alongside the I-400 showing the difference in size. (*USN*)

I-401
Surrendered 1946.

I-402
Surrendered 1946.

The I-401 tied up alongside the I-400 at Pearl Harbor. (*USN*)

The large watertight door of the I-400's aircraft hangar showing its construction. (*USN*)

I-403
Not built.

I-404
Destroyed during raid on Kure shipyard, 1945.

I-405
Scrapped before completion, 1945.

RO series

RO-1–24
All scrapped.

RO-25
Sunk in collision with the cruiser *Tatsuta* in 1924, refloated and used as a test boat until 1938 then scrapped.

RO-26
Scrapped in 1940.

RO-27
Scrapped in 1940.

RO-28
Scrapped in 1940.

RO-29
Scrapped in 1938.

RO-30
Surrendered in 1945.

RO-31
Surrendered in 1945.

RO-32
Surrendered in 1945.

RO-33

The RO series of submarines were involved in the first actions in the Pacific. The RO-33 was one of the submarines that supported the invasion of Java. At the beginning of August 1942 the RO-33 left Rabaul on her fourth war patrol to operate in the Coral Sea in the Port Moresby area and south-east coast of New Guinea. Just off Murray Island the submarine spotted the Australian 300-ton motor vessel MV *Mamutu*, which was sailing without an escort from Port Moresby to Daru, Papua, carrying 103 passengers, a crew of 40 and general cargo. The submarine surfaced and commenced shelling the fleeing vessel from her 3in deck gun. The first shell destroyed the radio room; the second shot hit the bridge, killing the captain. Within minutes the ship was ablaze and starting to sink. The RO-33 passed the sinking *Mamutu*, machine-gunning and killing the survivors in the water. All were lost. Ten days later the RO-33 came across the 3,310-ton merchant ship SS *Malaita* being escorted by a destroyer, HMAS *Arunta*, that had left Port Moresby for Cairns. The RO-33 moved into attack the *Malaita*, and fired a torpedo that struck the ship below the bridge on her starboard side. The ship took on a heavy list to starboard causing the crew to abandon ship fearing that she was about to capsize. Later the crew re-boarded her and the *Malaita* was taken in tow back to Port Moresby. In the meantime HMAS *Arunta* raced to the area, made a sonar contact on the submarine and immediately made four attacks with Mark VII depth charges. Minutes later a large slick of heavy oil started to spread, together with debris from the submarine. The RO-33 was sunk with all seventy officers and men.

RO-34

On 2 April 1943 the RO-34 departed Rabaul on her eleventh war patrol to provide weather reports and perform lifeguard duty east of the Russel Islands during the Operation I-GO. Just 40 miles off Russell Island, Solomons, the destroyers USS *O'Bannon* (DD-450) and USS *Strong* (DD-467) of DesRon 21 returning from shelling the shore installations in the New Georgia area, made radar contact with a surfaced submarine at 9,350 yards. The *O'Bannon* was detached to investigate the contact and as she approached the submarine rapidly and prepared to ram her, it occurred to the captain that it could be a minelayer, so at the last minute the USS *O'Bannon* went hard over to avoid a collision. Turning to fire, the destroyer was too close to depress her guns. The RO-34 started crash-diving immediately. Drawing away to approximately 1,000 yards, the *O'Bannon* brought her 5in main armament to bear and started firing, as did the *Strong*, which had arrived to assist. At least one hit was observed before the submarine managed to crash-dive. As the *O'Bannon* closed to fire her K-guns, she passed less than 100 yards ahead of the submarine, and fired depth charges at it. Contact was broken, but sonar contact with the submarine was soon re-established. A second pattern of eight depth charges was then dropped and minutes later the RO-34 was seen sinking by the stern. Early next morning a large, widening oil slick was sighted. Later that morning the *Strong* made a radar contact with a surfaced submarine at range of 9,320 yards. After illuminating the submarine with flares the destroyer opened fire with its 5in guns, scoring at least three direct hits. After the submarine dived, the destroyer dropped two patterns of depth charges. Minutes later debris was observed on the surface. The *Strong* was credited with the sinking of an enemy submarine. It was later thought that there must have been two submarines in the area at the time but it was never confirmed.

RO-35

The RO-35 departed Truk on 6 August 1943 to reconnoitre the Espiritu Santo area, New Caledonia. Later that day reports from the RO-35 speak of sighting a convoy of six transports off Espiritu Santo. This was the last signal received from the RO-35. Just east of the Solomons, 170 miles from Santa Cruz Island, the USS *Patterson* (DD-392) was screening a convoy of Task Unit 32 from the New Hebrides toward the lower Solomon Islands. The *Patterson's* radar picked up a surface contact and she was ordered to close and investigate. At 4,000 yards, the contact – a diving submarine – disappeared. The *Patterson's* sonar remade contact with the target at 3,800 yards and the destroyer commenced dropping depth-charge patterns. Some minutes later the crew of the *Patterson* heard a deep underwater explosion followed by debris coming to the surface and a large, ever-increasing slick of diesel oil.

RO-36

At the beginning of May 1944, with the tide of the war in the Pacific turning against the Japanese the defence of the Marianas became a priority. The CINC, Combined Fleet, Admiral Toyoda Soemu, ordered Vice Admiral Takagi Takeo, CINC Sixth Fleet (Submarines) to re-deploy his boats to the Marianas. The Japanese detected the presence of an American task force off the Marianas, so the RO-36 was redirected to the Saipan area with RO-43 and reassigned to SubRon 7 at Truk. The RO-36 sent a regular situation and weather report that day to ComSubRon 7. It was the last report received from RO-36. Just 75 miles east of Saipan the destroyer USS *Melvin* (DD-680) was part of the screen of Task Group 52.17's battleships that were approaching to bombard Saipan. The *Melvin's* radar detected a surfaced submarine and closing within firing range, opened fire with her 5in main armament. Scoring a number of hits on the outer casing the *Melvin* then depth-charged the submarine as it started to submerge. Minutes later there was a tremendous explosion as the submarine sank. A large oil slick and debris appeared later. The RO-36 was presumed lost with all seventy-seven crew.

RO-37

On 3 January 1944 the RO-37 departed Truk to patrol off the New Hebrides. Near to San Cristobal Island, Solomons, the RO-37 sighted and torpedoed the fleet oiler USS *Cache* (AO-67) en route to Espiritu Santo. The torpedo struck the *Cache* on its port side and immediately the tanker sent out a distress call. The destroyer USS *Buchanan* (DD-484) that was enroute to Espiritu Santo from Purvis Bay, Florida Island picked up the call. The *Buchanan* immediately went to flank speed and made a radar contact at 12,750 yards. As the destroyer closed to 2,000 yards her searchlight illuminated a diving submarine. Momentarily the *Buchanan* lost radar contact, but her sonar picked up the target at 1,250 yards. For the next two hours the destroyer laid down a succession of depth-charge attacks, then the following morning at first light a large oil slick and debris was sighted in the attack area. No signal was ever received from the RO-37 and it was presumed lost with all sixty-one hands in the New Hebrides area.

RO-38

The RO-38 left Truk on 19 November 1943 on its first and last war patrol. There were no further contacts with RO-38 after its departure. The following day saw the start of Operation Galvanic (the invasion of the Gilbert Islands) when American forces invaded Tarawa and the Makin Islands with an invasion fleet of 200 ships including 13 battleships and 11 aircraft carriers. Vice Admiral Takagi Takeo, Commander, Sixth Fleet (Submarines) ordered the I-19, I-21, I-35, I-39, I-40, I-169, I-174 and I-175 and RO-38 to proceed to Tarawa and attack the invasion ships. The RO-38, I-19, I-40 and I-169 were to form a picket line north of Makin. The RO-38 failed to answer a general order from Sixth Fleet to report. It is thought that the American destroyer USS *Cotton* (DD-669), which was known to be in the area, depth-charged a submarine around this time and it was presumed to be the RO-38, missing with all seventy-seven hands off the Gilberts.

RO-39

On 26 January 1944, after carrying out a number of supply runs the RO-39 was ordered to rescue downed aircraft crews of 531st NAG (Woleai) and 755th NAG (Maloelap) who had been attacking the American invasion fleet off the Marshall Islands. Then it was ordered to proceed to an area 200 miles north-east of Wotje, Marshall Islands and attack the American invasion fleet. Vice Admiral Marc A. Mitscher's Task Force 58 landed the 4th Marine Division and the Army's 7th Infantry Division and captured Kwajalein, Roi-Namur and Majuro Atolls. Just off Wotje the destroyer USS *Walker* (DD-517) picked up a surface contact on radar. As the destroyer closed it fired star shells that illuminated a submarine. As the submarine crash-dived, it sent off an emergency signal to Sixth Fleet at Truk. The *Walker* tracked the submarine for some hours on sonar and then destroyed her with a single depth-charge attack. This was confirmed when debris and an ever-widening oil slick appeared on the surface. There were no survivors.

RO-40

At the beginning of 1944, with the invasion of the Marshall Islands well under way, the RO-40 departed from Truk on 12 February for an area east of the Gilbert Islands via the Marshall Islands on her first war patrol. She was to join up with the RO-39 and after sending an acknowledgement of the order no messages were received from her thereafter. When 45 miles north-west of Kwajalein, Marshall Islands as it approached an American convoy, the destroyer USS *Phelps* (DD-360) made a sonar contact at 1,700 yards. The destroyer immediately dropped a pattern of thirteen depth charges on the contact. The *Phelps* was quickly joined by the destroyer USS *MacDonough* (DD-351) and the minesweeper USS *Sage* (AM-111) who joined in the hunt and laid down patterns of depth charges. Some minutes later a series of violent explosions rocked the sea and a large oil slick mixed with debris came to the surface. It was known that the RO-40 was operating in the area and after receiving no reply to the signals sent to it, it was assumed that it had been sunk with all sixty-nine hands in the Gilberts area.

RO-41

On 18 March 1945 the RO-41 left Saeki followed by the I-8, RO-49 and RO-56 to intercept the damaged aircraft carrier USS *Franklin* (CV-13) in the Okinawa area. Then, 320 miles east of Okinawa, the RO-41 reported sighting an enemy destroyer. This was the last message received from RO-41. The destroyer USS *Haggard* (DD-555) was acting as a picket 12 miles ahead of Task Force 58. The destroyer made a contact detected by radar on the surface at 25,000 yards. The *Haggard* and the USS *Uhlmann* (DD-687) were detached to investigate. The contact dived and disappeared, but the *Haggard* made contact again this time by sonar and dropped a pattern of depth charges. A couple of minutes later a submarine surfaced off the destroyer's port beam. The destroyer's 40mm anti-aircraft gun raked the submarine's conning tower and then went hard left rudder ramming the sub's starboard side abaft the conning tower. Minutes later the RO-41 sank by the stern – there were no survivors.

RO-42

The RO-42 departed Yokosuka on 15 May 1944, its mission to reconnoitre Majuro and then proceeded to north-north-east of Kwajalein, Marshall Islands. Just 40 miles east of Roi at 2330, the escort destroyer USS *Bangust* (DE-739) made a surface contact with her SL radar and minutes later her Officer of the Deck visually sighted a submarine and blinked a challenge. The submarine immediately crash-dived. For the next eight hours the *Bangust* searched the area and then regained contact. The submarine used all the evasive tactics it knew, making full rudder throws and sudden changes of speed. The *Bangust* made three unsuccessful attack runs with barrages of twenty-four Mark 10 Hedgehog projector charges, but then on her fourth run, there came a tremendous underwater explosion that cracked a seam in the destroyer's hull. The submarine tried desperately to surface but failed and sank with all seventy-three of the crew. Hours later a large oil slick was seen spreading in the area.

RO-43

On 13 February 1945 the RO-43 prepared to deliver a shipment of 450mm Type 97 torpedoes for the midget submarine unit stationed on Cebu, but the mission was cancelled because of enemy activity in the Okinawa area. The American invasion of Iwo Jima started three days later when the fifth Fleet of over 450 ships, landed the 54th Amphibious Corps (3rd, 4th and 5th Marine Divisions). The RO-43 was ordered to patrol within an area 75 miles off Iwo Jima and attack the fleet. The destroyer USS *Bennion* (DD-662) reported a sonar contact with a submarine. The escort carrier USS *Anzio* (CVE-57) launched one of VC-82's radar-equipped Grumman TBF Avenger torpedo-bombers to conduct a search of the area. This was followed by a second Avenger of VC-82 to continue the ASW search. The second Avenger's radar operator picked up a contact and as the aircraft passed over the contact, he recognised the shape of a diving submarine. A pair of sonobuoys was dropped followed by a Mark 24 'Fido' acoustic homing torpedo. A violent explosion followed sending a plume of water high in the air. Some hours later a large oil slick covered the area where the submarine sank – probably the RO-43 as no further contact was made with the submarine. Presumed sunk with all seventy-nine hands off Iwo Jima, the RO-43 was the first IJN submarine lost during the Iwo Jima campaign.

RO-44

The RO-44 was one of the Japanese submarines that experienced the war in the Pacific for longer than most. On 17 April 1944 when B-24 Liberators raided Truk, both the RO-44 and RO-42 had to crash dive, but only received minor damage by near misses underwater. When Truk was bombed again, the RO-44 and other submarines submerged to the bottom of the shallow 75ft deep anchorage, but when the submarine surfaced the periscope had been damaged so badly in the raid that it could only be repaired in Japan. Whilst en route to Kure she was bombed and strafed by an American aircraft, but only damaged slightly by the machine-gun bullets. After repairs the RO-44 was sent to reconnoitre the invasion of Saipan and sent a report, which was the last contact made by the submarine. Also covering the invasion was the escort destroyer USS *Burden R. Hastings* (DE-19) who made radar contact with a surfaced submarine. The destroyer closed and challenged with her Aldis lamp, but there was no reply and the submarine crash-dived. The destroyer fired two barrages of twenty-four Mark 10 Hedgehog ahead-thrown projector charges and dropped four depth charges. A series of violent explosions followed and the following day an aluminium plaque with 'RO-44' on it was recovered from the debris. The RO-44 was presumed lost with all seventy-two hands.

RO-45

Early in the morning of 29 April 1944, a Mitsubishi G4M 'Betty' patrol plane from Truk sighted an American task force (TF 58) heading north at 18 knots for Truk. Rear Admiral Ōwada Noboru ordered the RO-45, RO-44, I-16, I-176, RO-106, RO-108 and RO-115 to intercept it, but the RO-45 was the only submarine that managed to make contact with the Americans. Task Force 58, including five fleet carriers and seven light carriers, began a two-day attack on shipping, fuel and ammunition dumps, aircraft facilities and other installations at Truk. The destroyers USS *MacDonough* (DD-351) and USS *Stephen Potter* (DD-538) were on radar picket duty screening the carriers. The *MacDonough* made a radar contact on a surfaced submarine but lost the contact when the submarine dived. Minutes later sonar contact was made and the two destroyers made a series of depth charge attacks. A Grumman F6F Hellcat from the aircraft carrier USS *Monterey* (CVL-26) provided spotting support. Minutes later several loud explosions were heard, then oil and debris came to the surface close to where the depth charges had been dropped. The RO-45 was sunk with all hands.

RO-46

The RO-46 was one of those Japanese submarines that just disappeared without trace. It was involved in the invasion of Okinawa as a reconnaissance submarine but was never heard from again.

RO-47

On 17 September 1944 the RO-47 departed Kure with orders to attack the American amphibious forces that were invading Peleliu, Palau. That was the last communication with the RO-47. On 26 September the destroyer USS *McCoy Reynolds* (DE-440) was making a solitary run from Peleliu to Guam to join Task Force 57 when the SL radar detected a target on the surface at 9,200 yards. Realising that it had been spotted the submarine dived and the contact disappeared from the radar. Minutes later sonar reported, an underwater contact at 2,500 yards. The *McCoy Reynolds* fired a barrage of twenty-four Mark 10 ahead-thrown Hedgehog projector charges. When the first salvo missed, six more attacks were made, followed by an extremely heavy underwater explosion. Some time later diesel oil and splintered wood planking spread across the surface. There were no survivors the RO-47 had sunk with all hands.

RO-48

The RO-48 was assigned on 5 July 1944 to stand by to rescue IJN pilots from Tinian during the attack on Saipan by the Americans. After being attacked whilst on the surface and forced to dive, the captain informed HQ that he was going to change his position. The Sixth Fleet ordered the RO-48 to return. Just 300 miles east of

Saipan, the USS *Hoggatt Bay*'s (CVE-75) task group 12.2, a hunter-killer group, were conducting ASW operations off the Marianas. The carrier's radar picked up a contact on the surface at 21,000 yards. Two of the four screening destroyer escorts, the USS *Wyman* (DE-38) and USS *Reynolds* (DE-42), were sent to investigate the radar contact. The *Wyman* closed the range but lost radar contact at 4,000 yards when the contact dived. The destroyer immediately switched to her sonar and picked up a strong echo at 1,600 yards. The destroyer fired a barrage of twenty-four Mark 10 Hedgehog projector charges, but without results. On 19 July 1944, the *Wyman* closed for a second attack and fired a second barrage of twenty-four Hedgehogs. Seconds later the destroyer was rocked by five violent underwater explosions as the Hedgehogs blew the submarine apart. Attempts were made to regain sonar contact but the sonar's returns indicated that the contact had been destroyed. However, it was later discovered that the submarine had signalled that the RO-48 had undergone a severe depth-charging and had been forced to leave her station north of Saipan. This was the last message received from RO-48.

RO-49

On 1 April 1945 Vice Admiral Raymond A. Spruance's Fifth Fleet, including more than 40 aircraft carriers, 18 battleships, 200 destroyers and over 1,000 support ships, began the invasion of Okinawa. Lieutenant General Simon B. Buckner Jnr's Tenth Army (7th, 77th and 96th Infantry and 1st and 6th Marine Divisions) made amphibious landings and took the island from Lieutenant General Ushijima Mitsuru's 32nd Army. The RO-49 was on patrol in the area when the destroyer USS *Hudson* (DD-475), which was on radar picket duty, received a signal of a submarine sighting from LCS-115. The destroyer immediately switched on her SG radar and approached the area to investigate. Getting a contact, the *Hudson* fired a star shell that forced the submarine to dive. The contact was lost. The *Hudson* continued to search until she regained contact on sonar and began the first series of attacks that ranged over the next six hours. In all, she dropped six barrages of depth charges that sank a submarine – possibly the RO-49. Japanese sources later suggested that the RO-49 was already missing in action (MIA) on 5 April 1945 and that the submarine *Hudson* sank was the I-56.

RO-50
Surrendered 1945.

RO-51, 52, 53, 54
Cancelled.

RO-55

The life of the RO-55 was a very short one. On 27 January 1945 the submarine left Kure on its first war patrol for an area west of Mindoro. On 2 February 1945 whilst patrolling off Luzon the RO-55 was attacked by enemy aircraft, but managed to dive and escape. The submarine signalled that its arrival at the patrol area would be delayed. This was the last signal received from the RO-55. Three days later whilst off Iba, Luzon, Philippines, the RO-55 attempted to attack a convoy of ships headed for Leyte Gulf. One of the convoy's destroyer escorts, the USS *Thomason* (DE 203), picked up a surfaced submarine on her SL radar. The destroyer attacked with barrages of twenty-four ahead-thrown Mark 10 Hedgehog projector charges and sank the submarine on the first pass. This was probably the RO-55, which was declared lost with all eighty hands.

RO-56

At the beginning of April 1945, like the RO-49 the RO-56 was sent to attack the American Fifth Fleet in their invasion of Okinawa. The destroyers USS *Monssen* (DD-798) and USS *Mertz* (DD-691) were screening the fast carrier group when the *Monssen* made a sonar contact at 900 yards. Both destroyers moved in for the attack. The *Monssen* dropped three patterns of thirteen depth charges, whilst the *Mertz* dropped another three patterns. The *Monssen* dropped a final two patterns that probably destroyed the RO-56 as nothing was heard from the submarine again, and she was presumed lost with all seventy-nine hands off Okinawa.

RO-57

Surrendered in 1945.

RO-58

Surrendered in 1945.

Japanese submarine RO-58. (*Author*)

RO-59

Surrendered in 1945.

RO-60

The RO-60 sank on 29 December 1941 after running into the reef outside Kwajalein.

Japanese submarine RO-66. (*JMSDF*)

RO-66

Sank on 17 December 1941 after colliding with the RO-62 off Wake Island.

RO-100

The American Operation Shoestring II – the invasion of Bougainville by Rear Admiral Theodore S. Wilkinson's Third Amphibious Force, Task Force 31 – started on 1 November 1943 and landed Lieutenant General Alexander A. Vandegrift's 1st Marine Amphibious Corps at Cape Torokina, Empress Augusta Bay, Bougainville,

RO-100 class submarine caught on the surface by an Allied reconnaissance aircraft. (*USN*)

Solomons. Later that month the RO-100 departed Truk on her seventh patrol in the Bougainville area. The last signal from the submarine reported that the RO-100 was in the northern passage approaching Buin, west of Oema Island, Solomons. As the RO-100 approached the north channel to Buin on 25 November 1943, a mine exploded beneath her port side amidships hull. The explosion threw the captain and the lookouts that were standing on the bridge into the sea. The order to abandon the rapidly sinking boat was given, but whilst trying to reach Buin sharks attacked some of the survivors. Of the fifty crewmen, only twelve managed to survive.

RO-101

On 10 September 1943 the RO-101 departed Simpson Harbor, Rabaul, on its eighth war patrol south-east of San Cristobal, Solomons. At the entrance to Indispensable Strait, Guadalcanal, an unknown submarine attacked a convoy of two cargo ships en route to Espiritu Santo. The convoy's escorts, an old four-stack minelayer the USS *Montgomery* (DD-121) and the destroyer USS *Saufley* (DD-465), sighted a torpedo wake. Because the *Montgomery*'s sound gear was not working, the *Saufley* began to track the torpedo's wake and made a sonar contact at 3,000 yards. For the next three and one-half hours, the *Saufley* made five depth-charge attacks. Then the submarine surfaced obviously damaged and the destroyer's 5in gun batteries and machine guns opened fire on her conning tower. By this time a PBY-5 Catalina patrol bomber of VP-23 had joined in the attack and dropped two depth charges. The first one missed, but the second scored a direct hit. The submarine – probably RO-101 – disappeared, and minutes later the crew of the destroyer heard a heavy underwater explosion followed by a huge plume of water. Some hours later a diesel oil slick covering a square mile of the ocean was spotted together with a large amount of debris. The RO-101 was declared lost with all fifty-four members of the crew.

Japanese submarine RO-101. (*JMSDF*)

RO-102

The RO-102 was another of the Japanese submarines that just disappeared without trace. Some reports say that two PT boats sank her, but this has never been confirmed. Her last report was on 9 May 1943.

RO-103

The circumstances surrounding the loss of RO-103 are unknown. One suggestion was that it was sunk by a mine in one of the minefields laid by USS *Breese* (DM-18), USS *Preble* (DM-20) and USS *Gamble* (DM-15) as they were known to have been operating in that area. The RO-103's last report was on 28 July 1943.

RO-104

On 8 May 1944 US Naval Intelligence intercepted radio traffic that indicated that the Japanese had established a new submarine picket line between Truk and the Admiralty Islands to intercept American aircraft carriers. The destroyers USS *England* (DE-635), USS *Raby* (DE-698) and USS *George* (DE-697) were dispatched and left Purvis Bay, off Florida Island, Solomons, north of the Admiralty Islands. In the meantime the RO-104 had been spotted on the surface by a patrol plane, which directed the hunter-killer group to the submarine. Closing fast the *Raby* made a radar contact at four miles. The submarine's radar detector picked up the *Raby's* radar emissions so the RO-104 increased her speed from 5 to 8 knots and crash-dived. The *Raby* made a sound contact and attacked with four successive salvos of Mark 10 Hedgehog projector charges. Half an hour later the first sound contact with the submarine was lost. The *George* then arrived and made its first Hedgehog attack, but with no result and then lost contact, so the three destroyers formed a ring to reacquire the target. Then the *England* was ordered in and fired two full salvos of forty-eight Hedgehogs. On the second attack, the crew heard a tremendous underwater explosion. They immediately followed up with a pattern of thirteen depth charges set from 350ft to 450ft. Some minutes later the first pieces of debris came to the surface, along with a spreading oil slick. A boat recovered assorted debris including a dozen fragments of deck planking (some still containing bolts), cork stoppers, small pieces of wood with Japanese characters, a bottle cork and a sample of oil. The RO-104 was presumed lost with all fifty-eight hands.

RO-105

After sinking six submarines (I-16, RO-106, RO-104, RO-116, RO-108 and RO-105) between 18 May and 31 May 1944, the destroyers USS *England* (DE-635), USS *Raby* (DE-698) and USS *George* (DE-697) had put into Seeadler Harbour at Manus Island on 27 May, to refuel and replenish their supply of ahead-thrown Mark 10 Hedgehog projector charges from the escort destroyer USS *Spangler* (DE-696). The escort carrier USS *Hoggatt Bay* (CVE-75) and destroyers USS *Hazelwood*

(DD-531) and USS *McCord* (DD-534) then joined the hunter-killer group. North of the Admiralty Islands, the *Hazelwood* made a radar contact at 15,000 yards but the contact – a submarine – dived. The destroyer then made a sonar contact and attacked with depth charges. Some hours later the *Raby* and *George* took over from the *Hazelwood* and made several Hedgehog attacks. A number of hits were made, but with no result. The following morning the *Spangler* and the *England* arrived to assist. The *Spangler* fired a salvo of Hedgehogs with no success. Then the USS *England* made sonar contact and fired a salvo of twenty-four Hedgehogs. The Hedgehogs' explosions were followed by a shattering underwater blast followed some hours later by a large oil slick spreading across the surface. The RO-105 was the sixth submarine sunk by the USS *England* in 13 days. The RO-105 was declared lost with all hands on 31 May 1944.

RO-106

On 16 May 1944 the RO-106 left Truk on her eleventh war patrol to form a picket line north of the Admiralty Islands to warn of American invasion forces approaching the Palaus. Two days later US Naval Intelligence intercepted radio traffic that indicated that the Japanese had established a new submarine picket line between Truk and the Admiralty Islands with the intention of intercepting American aircraft carriers. The destroyers USS *England* (DE-635), USS *Raby* (DE-698) and USS *George* (DE-697) departed Purvis Bay, off Florida Island, Solomons as a hunter-killer group to attack the picket line. Just north of the Admiralty Islands, the *George* reported a contact at 14,000 yards on her SG radar. This was confirmed shortly after when a blip appeared on the *England's* radar screen that looked like a surfaced submarine. The *George* and *Raby* were ordered to close and the *England* to move to the north-east, to box the target in. Closing to within 4,000 yards, the *George's* searchlights were switched on illuminating a surfaced submarine. The submarine immediately crash-dived. The *George* made a sonar contact and attacked with a salvo of thrown-ahead Mark 10 Hedgehog bombs, but all were misses. The *England* joined in, made a sonar contact and attacked with Hedgehogs, but also missed. The *England* turned and headed back just as the submarine reversed course to meet the destroyer bow on. The *England* unleashed another salvo of Hedgehogs, this time the crew heard at least three underwater explosions at 275ft and contact was lost. Some time later a large slick of oil mixed with debris came to the surface; the RO-106 was sunk with all hands.

RO-107

The invasion of New Georgia by Rear Admiral Richmond K. Turner's Third Fleet Amphibious Force on 30 June 1943, supported by land-based aircraft, landed Marines and Army troops on Rendova and other islands in the New Georgia area of the Solomons. The same day the RO-107 left Rabaul to patrol off Rendova on her third war patrol. Confirmation of this was sent back to her base and this was the RO-107's last message to be received from the Rendova area. The destroyer USS *Taylor* (DD-468) was with Task Force 31 and had been screening the landing of supplies and troops, and monitoring the evacuation of the wounded off Rice Anchorage, Kula Gulf, New Georgia Island. During the early morning, the *Taylor* obtained radar and visual contact on a surfaced Japanese submarine and immediately attacked with gunfire and depth charges. A number of gunfire hits were scored on the submarine before it crash-dived and contact was lost. She was never heard from again. The submarine – probably the RO-107, was never identified but Japanese records showed that she had been operating in the area. The *Taylor* never claimed the sinking. The RO-107 was presumed lost with all forty-two hands.

RO-108

On 18 May 1944, the RO-108, like the RO-104 and RO-106, was ordered to form part of a picket line between Truk and the Admiralty Islands to intercept the American aircraft carriers. The US Navy had intercepted radio traffic that indicated that the Japanese had established a new submarine picket line there. The destroyers USS *England* (DE-635) and USS *Raby* (DE-698) were part of a hunter/killer group and sent to attack the picket line. The two destroyers were patrolling near Seeadler Harbour, Manus Island just north of the Admiralty Islands, when the *Raby* made a radar contact at 14,000 yards. At the same time the *England* also made a radar contact and closed on the contact. When the range was down to 4,100 yards, the target – a submarine – dived. The *England* switched to sonar and made contact at 1,700 yards. The *Raby* made the first run but was unsuccessful. Then the *England* fired a barrage of twenty-four ahead-thrown Mark 10 Hedgehog projector charges. The next morning, whilst looking for survivors, the destroyers saw that the sea was littered with debris and a large diesel oil slick. The RO-108 with deemed to be sunk with all fifty-three hands.

RO-109

April 1st 1945 saw Vice Admiral Raymond A. Spruance's Fifth Fleet, including more than 40 aircraft carriers, 18 battleships, 200 destroyers and over 1,000 support ships, surround Okinawa. Then Lieutenant General Simon B. Buckner Jnr's US Tenth Army (7th, 77th and 96th Infantry, and 2nd and 6th Marine Divisions) made amphibious landings and took the island from Lieutenant General Ushijima Mitsuru's 32nd Army. The following day the RO-109 left Sasebo on her tenth war patrol for an area east of Okinawa. The RO-109 was scheduled to arrive in an area 20 miles south of Okinawa by 20 April but, after her initial contact just after leaving, there was no further communication. 165nm south-south-west of Okino-Daito Jima the fast transport USS *Horace A. Bass* (APD-124) was escorting a seventeen-ship convoy from Guam to Okinawa, when a sonar contact was made at 1,250 yards. The *Horace A. Bass* dropped five depth charges on the submarine (probably the RO-109) that commenced a series of evasive manoeuvres attempting to jam its attacker's sonar with sound impulses. Following the detonations, contact was lost. Sound contact was regained at about 900 yards and the fast transport made another attack with five depth charges, but the submarine evaded the depth charges by diving deeper. After a number of successive attacks debris and oil was spotted on the surface, but before she was able to confirm a 'kill', the *Horace A. Bass* was ordered to abandon the chase and rejoin the convoy. The RO-109 was presumed lost with all sixty-five hands off Okinawa.

RO-110

On 14 December 1943 in the Bay of Bengal, south-east of Madras, India, the RO-110 detected and attacked an American convoy, damaging one vessel with a spread of torpedoes. A few seconds after the strike, the RO-110 was rammed by another vessel, probably from the same convoy. The ramming crushed one of her periscopes and demolished the roof of her conning tower. The crew managed to plug the leaks and stop the flooding. Suffering considerable damage the patrol was terminated and RO-110 headed back to Penang reporting one vessel as 'probably sunk'.

The RO-110 returned to Penang but discovered that there were no spare periscopes and a new one had to be brought in from Singapore. With the periscope replaced the RO-110 left Penang on her second war patrol to raid enemy communications in the Bay of Bengal. This was the last time there was any contact with the submarine. Patrolling in the Bay of Bengal, 200 miles north-east of Madras, India, the RO-110 attacked a convoy en route from Colombo, Ceylon to Calcutta, India on 11 February 1944. The 6,274-ton British merchant SS *Asphalion* received two torpedo hits that flooded her No. 3 hold and engine room. Six sailors were killed and ten others wounded. The survivors abandoned the crippled vessel but she remained afloat and was later towed to port. The escorting 1,200-ton Indian gunboat HMIS *Jumna* and the Australian minesweepers HMAS *Ipswich* and HMAS *Launceston* detected the RO-110 by Asdic and attacked her with depth charges. Some time later, several underwater explosions were heard followed by a large amount of oil and debris appearing on the surface. There were no survivors.

RO-111

At the beginning of June 1944 the RO-111 left Truk on her fifth war patrol for an area north of the Admiralty Islands. The RO-111 sent a regular situation report while moving in a patrol line south of Truk, but that was the last communication received from the submarine. On 10 June just north of the Admiralty Islands a Grumman FM-2 'Wildcat' fighter from the escort carrier USS *Hoggatt Bay* (CVE-75) sighted an oil slick. The escort destroyer USS *Taylor* (DD-468), one of the carrier's screening escorts, was detached to investigate. The destroyer made a sonar contact and dropped two patterns of depth charges, but without any apparent effect. The *Taylor* stopped to get a better sonar echo and then without warning a submarine surfaced about 2,500 yards ahead. The destroyer opened fire with her main 5in armament and 40mm AA guns. At least ten 5in shells and many 40mm rounds hit the submarine. Within minutes the submarine, probably the RO-111, had sunk by the stern. The *Taylor* immediately dropped a pattern of depth charges over the oil slick, followed minutes later by two heavy underwater explosions. There were no survivors.

RO-112

With the American invasion of Luzon at the beginning of January 1945 well underway, Vice Admiral Miwa ordered the RO-115, RO-46, RO-112 and RO-113 to prepare to participate in the evacuation of the stranded pilots from the Aparri area on Luzon, Philippines. All the above submarines were also ordered to land their deck-gun ammunition and reserve torpedoes at Takao prior to the rescue mission. Just off Camiguin Island, Luzon Strait, Philippines, the submarine USS *Batfish*'s (SS-310) SJ radar picked up a contact at 8,000 yards and her AN/APR-1 radar detector also detected radar emissions. Some minutes later the *Batfish* made a visual contact on a submarine running on the surface at 1,300 yards but the contact was broken when the target submerged. Still tracking the submarine, the *Batfish*'s soundman heard a submarine blowing tanks. The RO-112 surfaced again, and again the *Batfish* detected radar emissions and her SJ radar made contact at 8,650 yards. For the next hour the American submarine closed the range. With the range down to 6,000 yards, the USS *Batfish* dived to radar depth and at 880 yards, fired four bow torpedoes set to run at 4ft on a 100-degree starboard track using a 1-knot speed spread. The first torpedo hit and disintegrated the submarine – probably RO-112 – which sank almost immediately with all hands.

RO-113

On 9 February 1945 the RO-113, like the RO-112, departed Takao for Batulinao, northern Luzon, Philippines to evacuate stranded pilots and return them to Takao. Just off Babuyan Island, Luzon Strait, Philippines, the USS *Batfish* (SS-310) was on patrol on the surface when the submarine's SJ radar picked up a contact at a range of 10,700 yards. Moving at flank speed the *Batfish* quickly reduced the range to 7,150 yards, but the target submerged and contact was broken. Some time later the RO-113 resurfaced and was picked up by the *Batfish*'s APR radar detector at a range of 9,800 yards. At 6,800 yards range, the *Batfish* dived on the target's track and came up to radar depth. The *Batfish* fired a spread of three stern torpedoes at the target. The first torpedo hit and a large yellow ball of fire was seen through the periscope as the RO-113 blew apart and sank immediately. Because the it sank so quickly torpedoes two and three missed. The RO-113 was presumed lost with all fifty-nine crewmembers off Luzon.

RO-114

The RO-114 left Saipan on 11 June 1944 on her first war patrol. On her arrival at her assigned station she reported in; this was the last communication received from the RO-114. On 15 June 1944 the American Operation Forager (the invasion of Saipan) took place and Vice Admiral Richmond K. Turner's Task Force 52 landed Marine Lieutenant General Holland M. Smith's V Amphibious Corps. Communications between Takagi's Advance Expeditionary Force (Sixth Fleet) were disrupted by the invasion and command of the Sixth Fleet's submarines passed to ComSubRon 7's Rear Admiral Ōwada Noboru at Truk. Ōwada ordered most of the Sixth Fleet's submarines, including RO-114, to withdraw from the Marianas and be reassigned to patrol in the Marianas area. The destroyers USS *Wadleigh* (DD-689) and USS *Melvin* (DD-680) of Task Group 52.4 were on a screening patrol when they made strong sonar contacts with a submarine. Both destroyers attacked with depth charges and sank the submarine – probably RO-114 as she was known to be operating in the area at the time. The RO-114 was presumed lost, with all fifty-five crew, in the Philippines area.

RO-115

The RO-115 left Singapore on its fifth war patrol to the area west of Luzon. There was no communication received from the submarine from that day. Three American destroyers, the USS *Bell* (DD-587), USS *O'Bannon* (DD-450) and USS *Ulvert M. Moore* (DE-442) were patrolling off Mindoro to intercept Japanese transports attempting to take supplies and men to Luzon. The light cruiser USS *Boise* (CL-47), also operating in the area, made a surface radar contact. The *Bell* also picked up the contact on her SG radar at 9,250 yards. The *Bell* and *O'Bannon* were detached to investigate the contact. They picked the target on sonar and attacked with depth charges, but then lost contact. The *Ulvert M. Moore* was sent to assist. In the meantime the *Bell* had picked up the target on her sonar and made another depth-charge attack that resulted in a large oil slick. Some hours later the destroyer USS *Jenkins* (DD-447) arrived to relieve the *Bell* and took charge of the hunt. An hour later the *Ulvert M. Moore*, which was still on station, launched the first of five barrages of twenty-four ahead-thrown Mark 10 Hedgehog projector charges over the oil slick. The *Ulvert M. Moore*'s last Hedgehog barrage is presumed to have sunk the submarine, most likely the RO-115, as more oil mixed with debris came to the surface. A signal intercepted later to the RO-115 was ordering it to proceed to Takao, Formosa, by 6–8 February latest. She was tasked to participate in the evacuation of the stranded IJNAF pilots from Luzon, Philippines. The submarine did not respond to that signal. Another decoded message timed said, 'Submarines RO-112 and RO-113 left Takao on 9th and 10th respectively and were due to arrive at Batulinao on 12th and 14th. RO-115 has not yet returned to Takao from her operating area. There were no replies from any of the submarines contacted.

RO-116

On 31 March 1944 the RO-116 and RO-117 left Japan on their first war patrol to intercept an enemy task force reported in the Palau area. Following a fruitless mission, the RO-116 returned to Japan and was re-assigned to SubDiv 51 of Rear Admiral Noboru's Ōwada (SubRon 7 in Vice Admiral Takagi Takeo's Sixth Fleet (Submarines), and sent to Saipan. After taking on supplies the RO-116 left Saipan to join a picket line north of the Admiralty Islands to warn of American invasion forces approaching the Palaus. In the meantime the US Navy had intercepted radio traffic that indicated that the Japanese had established a new submarine picket line between Truk and the Admiralty Islands to intercept American carriers. The destroyers USS *England* (DE-635), USS *Raby* (DE-698) and USS *George* (DE-607) departed Purvis Bay, off Florida Island, Solomons as a hunter-killer group to attack the picket line. Just north of the Admiralty Islands, the *George* made a radar contact at 14,000 yards, but the contact disappeared. The *England* made a sonar contact resulting in the submarine commencing evasive action. The destroyer went into the attack and after two aborted attack runs, fired a salvo of twenty-four ahead-thrown Mark 10 Hedgehog projector charges. At least three hit and sank the RO-116. The submarine was presumed lost with all fifty-six hands.

RO-117

On 15 June 1944, with the invasion of Saipan well under way after Vice Admiral Richmond K. Turner's Task Force 52 had landed Marine Lieutenant General Holland M. Smith's V Amphibious Corps on Saipan, command of the Japanese Sixth Fleet's submarines passed to Rear Admiral Ōwada at Truk. He ordered most of the Sixth Fleet's submarines, including RO-117, to withdraw from the Marianas and ordered them to assume a new position south-east of Tinian, in the area between RO-111 and RO-113. As the submarines made their way to their new positions 350 miles south-east of Saipan, a Consolidated PB4Y-1 Liberator of VB-109 based at Eniwetok made radar contact with a surfaced submarine. Diving into attack the Liberator dropped a stick of bombs causing severe damage to a submarine and minutes later it sank. Messages from the Sixth Fleet Headquarters were sent but never acknowledged, and it was assumed that the RO-117 was lost with all fifty-five hands in the Saipan area. The RO-117 was lost on 17 June 1944.

RO-500

Surrendered 1945. This submarine was formerly the German U-511. As the RO-500 there were no recorded successes.

RO-501 (U-1224)

In a ceremony in a submarine pen at Kiel, Germany, the U-1224, a Type IXC/40 U-boat, was handed over to the IJN. It was commissioned in the IJN as RO-501 the crew of fifty-two having been trained for six months at the U-boat school in the Baltic on handling the submarine. On 30 March 1944 the RO-501 left Kiel carrying a cargo of mercury, lead, steel, uncut optical glass and aluminium in her keel together with drawings, models and blueprints necessary to construct a Type IXC U-boat. In addition to submarine-related materials there were a full set of Messerschmitt Me-163 'Komet' rocket interceptor blueprints. At the end of April 1944 just west of the Azores, the RO-501 refuelled from the U-488. The captain of the RO-501, Lieutenant Commander Norida Sadatoshi, sent a coded signal from a planned reporting position. This was to be the last signal sent by the submarine. The signal was detected by high frequency/direction finding equipment aboard a hunter-killer group situated in the Atlantic Narrows, 500 miles west of the Cape Verde Islands. The USS *Francis M. Robinson* (DE-220) was a member of the escort carrier USS *Bogue*'s (CVE-9) hunter-killer group with four other destroyer escorts. The *Francis M. Robinson* was on an ASW patrol making 17 knots when her sonar operator detected a target that he classified as a submarine at 825 yards. The *Bogue* turned away whilst the *Francis M. Robinson* deployed a 'Foxer' (noisemaker) to decoy any possible acoustic-tracking torpedoes that the submarine may have fired. The destroyer then fired a barrage of twenty-four ahead-thrown Mark 10 Hedgehog projector charges, followed by five salvos of Mark 8 magnetic influence depth charges. Four massive underwater explosions were heard and recorded. The RO-501 sank in 2,900ft of water. US Naval Intelligence decoded the German naval attaché's message about the whereabouts of the RO-501 but Berlin had been out of communication with U-1224 before 7 June. Another message later stated that the RO-501 would be refuelled by the I-8 in the Indian Ocean but by this time she had already been sunk.

Appendix 2

Japanese Submarine Successes in the Second World War

I-1

On 3 March 1942 in the Indian Ocean, 250 miles north-west of Shark Bay off Western Australia, the I-1's lookouts sighted smoke from the 8,806-ton Dutch armed cargo vessel MV *Siantar* escaping to Australia from Tjilatjap, Java. The I-1 submerged and fired a torpedo at the *Siantar*, but missed, so it surfaced off the *Siantar's* port beam and opened fire with its forward deck gun. The *Siantar* immediately went to full speed and returned fire from her 75mm deck gun, which jammed after the first shots. The second shell from I-1 brought down the radio antenna of the Dutch merchant ship. A fire then broke out and the crew abandoned ship. Following some thirty direct hits, the I-1 fired a second torpedo. Ten minutes later, the Dutch merchant ship sank by the stern. Twenty-one of the crew were killed and thirty-seven rescued by the Dutch steamer SS *Van Spielbergen*.

I-2

On 11 March 1942, the I-2 sighted the 4,360-ton British armed freighter the SS *Chilka* on a voyage from Calcutta to Padang. The I-2 surfaced on *Chilka's* port quarter and opened fire with both deck guns. The *Chilka* returned fire, but was hit fourteen times in 25 minutes. Three officers, three lascars and one gunner were killed in the engagement. After his only gun was disabled, the captain ordered the engines stopped and signalled his surrender. The I-2 ceased firing and allowed the survivors to abandon ship. The SS *Chilka* sank soon afterwards. The fate of the survivors is not known.

I-3

Early in the morning of 7 April 1942, 150 miles south-west of Colombo, the I-3 sighted five Allied merchant ships sailing eastward and one merchant and a tanker on a westbound course. After a fruitless chase lasting several hours the I-3 chanced on the 4,872-ton British armed steam merchant SS *Elmdale* en route from Karachi to Colombo. The I-3 fired a total of thirty-nine 5.5in shells and four torpedoes, scoring just fourteen shell hits, and none with the torpedoes, and failed to finish off her target. The following day, 300 miles off Colombo, the I-3 came across the British armed merchant ship the SS *Fultala* sailing from Calcutta to Karachi with

8,000 tons of coal. After receiving one Type 89 torpedo hit the 5,051-ton merchant sank. Her entire crew were rescued.

I-4

On 14 December 1941, the I-4 was off Cape Makapuu, Oahu, when it saw and attacked the 4,858-ton Norwegian freighter SS *Høegh Merchant*. The I-4 torpedoed *Høegh Merchant* and hit her on her starboard side. A fire broke out and ten minutes later the I-4 fired another torpedo, which struck the ship close to the same location. Within a few minutes the *Høegh Merchant* went down. Her crew and passengers were rescued by the minesweeper USS *Trever* (DMS-16), which had answered her distress call and later transferred them to the Coast Guard cutter *CG-403*, by which they were taken to Honolulu.

The I-4 claimed a second success on 6 April 1942 when she came across the 6,617-ton US steamer SS *Washingtonian* en route from Suez to Colombo. The I-4 fired two Type 96 torpedoes at the steamer. The torpedo was sighted 500 yards away, bearing down on the port side and so the steamer commenced a slow turn, but then received two hits. The fuel tanks were set on fire and within minutes the flames engulfed the entire ship. With the ship listing 25 degrees to port, ten officers, twenty-nine men and two passengers cleared the ship in two lifeboats. The survivors were able to reach the Maldives the following day.

The I-4's third and last success was on 29 September 1942 when it was patrolling surfaced off San Cristobal. The lookouts on the I-4 reported a 7,000-ton cargo ship on the port bow escorted by a solitary destroyer. The I-4 dived and started an approach at 5 knots. When in position two Type 96 torpedoes were fired at the freighter, set at 10ft. Seven minutes later, the first torpedo hit the stern. The second torpedo hit the target, but failed to explode. The ship, the 7,447-ton USS *Alhena* (AK-26), was being escorted by the USS *Monssen* (DD-436), en route from Guadalcanal to Espiritu Santo. She had been hit by a torpedo in the vicinity of No. 5 hold, opening a 45ft hole on both sides of the stern. Several fires had broken out and the *Alhena* was dead in the water. The ship developed a 10-degree stern list. Thinking the target was doomed the I-4 dived to 165ft and departed the area before the destroyer could react. The *Alhena* drifted throughout the night and the next day, until she was first taken in tow by the *Monssen* and later by the fleet tug USS *Navajo* (AT-64), arriving at Espiritu Santo on 7 October. Later the I-4 surfaced and reported the 'sinking' of the *Alhena* to ComSubRon 3 and the C-in-C, Sixth Fleet.

I-5

The I-5 was the first of the submarines that carried one floatplane. A hangar was fitted on the port and starboard side of the conning tower: one contained the fuselage and twin floats, the other, the wings. But without a catapult the assembling and launching of the aircraft was both time-consuming and extremely difficult so it was quickly removed. The I-5's first taste of action was almost its last when it was attacked by so-called 'friendly fire' whilst on patrol. On 25 February 1942, whilst running on the surface, the I-5 was spotted by a Mitsubishi C5M Type 98 'Babs', escorted by nine A6M2 'Zeke' fighters from the 3rd NAG Ambon detachment. Misidentifying the submarine as Dutch, the fighters repeatedly strafed the I-5, inflicting serious damage to the conning tower and causing the signal rockets located in there to explode and catch fire. The CO of the I-5 and two of her officers were seriously wounded and the I-5 was forced to abort her patrol. After extensive repairs the I-5 was on patrol in the Indian Ocean when it was claimed she had sank an unknown sailing ship with fire from her deck gun. This was its only unconfirmed success before being sunk by the USS *Wyman* (DE-38) with Hedgehog bombs in July 1944.

I-6

On 11 January 1942 the I-6 sighted the carrier USS *Saratoga* (CV-3) steaming at 15 knots to rendezvous with USS *Enterprise* (CV-6). The I-6 fired three Type 89 torpedoes with three-second intervals from 4,700 yards. One of them hit the *Saratoga* port amidships, flooding three of her boiler rooms and killing six firemen. The carrier heeled first to starboard, then to port, taking on 1,100 tons of water and losing headway. Escorting destroyers commenced a counter-attack, but failed to locate the submarine. The I-6 reported two hits on a Lexington-class carrier, claiming her as probably sunk. The *Saratoga* was not sunk but put out of action for six months. The I-6 was the second scouting submarine to be fitted with aircraft-carrying capabilities, which included a catapult built into the after deck. Whilst patrolling off Bombay it sank two British steamers, the SS *Clan Ross* (5,897 tons) and the SS *Babadur* (5,424 tons).

I-7

On 4 March 1942 off Cocos Island the I-7 surfaced and shelled and sank the unarmed Dutch 865-ton merchant ship SS *Merkus* en route from Tjilatjap to Bombay. The crew managed to reach Sumatra. The I-7 was the only submarine at the time that carried an aircraft. On 3 April the I-7 struck again and sank the British motor ship MV *Glenshiel* (9,415 tons). The destroyer HMS *Fortune* rescued the crew. On 14 July 1942 the I-7 torpedoed, shelled and sank the 2,722-ton USAT freighter SS *Arcata* en route from Bethel, Alaska, to Seattle. Once the *Arcata*'s bridge was hit, the crew and the passengers abandoned ship. The I-7 ceased firing after life rafts were spotted.

I-8

The I-8 was involved in one of the worst atrocities by a submarine crew in the Second World War. On 26 March 1944, the Dutch-registered merchant ship SS

Tjisalak, was torpedoed by the I-8 whilst sailing from Melbourne to Ceylon with 103 passengers and crew. The atrocities are described in the main text. On 30 March 1944 the 6,589-ton SS *City of Adelaide* was sunk by the I-8 followed on 29 June by sinking the 6,042-ton merchant ship SS *Nellore* off Addu Atoll. Two months later, I-8 was involved in another atrocity when she torpedoed the 7,176-ton American Liberty ship SS *Jean Nicolet*. This atrocity is also described in the main text

I-9

On 11 December 1941, the I-9 sank the 5,645-ton unarmed merchant ship SS *Lahina* with shellfire. The crew then abandoned ship but re-boarded the following morning. However, within an hour the ship exploded and sank.

I-10

Just hours after Japan had declared war on America, the I-10 sank an unarmed ship flying the Panamanian flag, the SS *Donerail*. There were only eight survivors from the crew and passengers. During June and July 1942 the I-10 sank the following cargo ships: the *Atlantic Gulf* (2,639 tons), *Melvin H. Baker* (4,999 tons), *King Lud* (5,224 tons), *Queen Victoria* (4,937 tons), *Express* (6,736 tons), *Nymphe* (4,504 tons), *Hartismere* (5,498 tons) and *Alchiba* (4,427 tons). The I-10 carried three survivors from the Norwegian tanker *Alcides* sunk on 23 July off the eastern coast of Madagascar.

I-11

In July 1942 the I-11 sank three ships on successive days. The first was the 5,482-ton merchant ship SS *G. S. Livanos*, the second the 3,290-ton freighter SS *Coast Farmer* and the 7,176-ton Liberty ship SS *William Dawes*. Then in August of that year the I-11 torpedoed the US merchant ship SS *Matthew Lyon* but failed to sink her.

I-12

The I-12 attacked the 7,176-ton American Liberty ship SS *John A. Johnson* on 29 October 1944 with two torpedoes, which broke the freighter in half and was abandoned. The I-12 surfaced and shelled both sections of the ship. Then the submarine rammed one lifeboat and made its way among the remaining lifeboats, the crew spraying the survivors with machine-gun and pistol fire, killing six men. Later that same day the USS *Argus* (PY-14) picked up the remaining survivors.

I-13

No recorded successes.

I-14 (aircraft-carrying submarine)

No recorded successes.

I-15
No recorded successes.

I-16
The I-16 sank four cargo ships, the SS *Susak* (3,889 tons) on 6 June 1942, SS *Agios Georgios IV* (4,847 tons) on 8 June 1942, SS *Supetar* (3,748 tons) on 12 June 1942 and SS *Eknaren* (5,243 tons) on 1 July 1942,

I-17
On 20 December 1941 8 miles west of Cape Mendocino lookouts on the surfaced I-17 spotted the 6,912-ton Socony-Vacuum Oil Company tanker SS *Emidio* en route from Seattle to Ventura. Despite the choppy seas, the I-17 overtook the fleeing tanker, firing six shells and scoring five hits in rapid succession. Within 30 minutes most survivors had cleared the now-stationary tanker in two lifeboats and one workboat. The appearance of two bombers forced the I-17 to crash-dive. Whilst submerged I-17 fired two torpedoes; one of them hit *Emidio*'s starboard side at the stern, killing two sailors in the engine room. A few hours later the tanker sank. Two days later the I-17 claimed a second tanker victim when it torpedoed the SS *Larry Doheny*, but it was later found that the torpedo had exploded prematurely causing almost no damage to the tanker. One of the first attacks on the American mainland was carried out by the I-17 when it shelled the Ellwood oil fields off Santa Barbara. A claim for the sinking of the oil tanker *William H. Berg* proved to be false. On 24 May 1943 the I-17 torpedoed the 10,138-ton Panamanian-flagged armed tanker SS *Stanvac Manila* en route from New York to Noumea. The tanker carried fuel and, as deck cargo, six PT boats. The torpedo hit the tanker in the port quarter and the tanker sank by the stern. *PT-165* and *PT-173* were lost with the ship. The I-17 was lost on 10 August 1943.

I-18
The I-18 sank four cargo ships, SS *Mundra* (7,341 tons) on 6 July 1942, SS *Wilford* (2,158 tons) on 8 June 1942, USS *Alchiba* (6,761 tons) on 1 July 1942 and SS *De Weert* (1,805 tons) on 1 July 1942. There was some debate over the *Alchiba*: some sources said that she was only damaged other said she was sunk, but yet another source said that she was scrapped in 1948.

I-19
The I-19 claimed a couple of unconfirmed successes before claiming the 5,698-ton timber carrier SS *Absaroka on 25 December 1941* with two torpedoes. The first one missed, but the second hit the *Absaroka*'s starboard hold throwing three sailors into the sea. Within minutes, the ship settled up to her main deck and the lifeboats were lowered. The USS *Amethyst* (PYC-3), aided by several Army bombers, arrived on

The destroyer USS *O'Brien* being hit by a torpedo from the I-19. In the background can be seen the aircraft carrier USS *Wasp* burning after being torpedoed by the same submarine. (*USN*)

the scene and dropped a pattern of thirty-two depth charges. The *Absaroka* was kept afloat by her cargo of timber and re-boarded and beached near Fort MacArthur. On 15 September 1942 the I-19 had her first big success, the aircraft carrier USS *Wasp* (CV-7). The task force was intercepted 250 miles off Guadalcanal and *Wasp* was hit by three torpedoes, starting an uncontrollable fire. She was later scuttled by five torpedoes from the USS *Lansdowne*. Also hit was the battleship USS *North Carolina* (BB-55) as was one of her escorts, the destroyer USS *O'Brien* (DD-415), damaging her severely. The I-19's next success came on 2 May 1943 when just off the Fiji Islands, the I-19 torpedoed and damaged the 7,181-ton American freighter SS *William Williams*. The torpedo put a hole 40ft by 30ft wide in her port side. The crew abandoned ship, but when the submarine did not come back, most of the crew re-boarded her and made Suva, Fiji. On 16 May 1943, again off Suva, the I-19 torpedoed and sank the 7,181-ton American freighter SS *William K. Vanderbilt*. The I-19 surfaced and machine-gunned the lifeboats, killing one man. On 3 August 1943 the I-19 torpedoed and severely damaged the 7,176-ton American Liberty ship SS *M. H. De Young* that was en route to Espiritu Santo with road scrapers, cranes, trucks, and other heavy equipment. The *De Young* was hit in the engine room but remained afloat because of barge pontoons that were stowed in her holds. Later, she was towed to Nukualofa, Tongatabu by the oil tanker SS *Quebec* but was found to be beyond repair. The destroyer USS *Radford* (DD-446) sank the I-19 in November 1943.

I-20

The I-20 sank eight ships; one oil tanker, *British Loyalty* (6,993 tons), beached on 10 May 1942, and seven cargo ships, SS *Johnstown* (5,086 tons) on 3 June 1942, SS *Christos Markettos* (5,209 tons) on 5 June 1942, SS *Mahronda* (7,926 tons) on 8 June 1942, SS *Hellenic Trader* (2,052 tons) on 12 June 1942, SS *Clifton Hall* (5,063 tons) on 12 June 1942, SS *Goviken* (4,854 tons) on 19 June 1942 and SS *Steaua Romana* (5,311 tons) on 30 June 1942. Also torpedoed by the I-20 was the American tanker *W.S. Rheem* but she managed to reach port under her own power.

I-21

The I-21, under the command of Commander Matsumura Kanji, was without doubt one of the most successful of all Japanese submarines. On 24 December 1941 it sank two oil tankers, the *Montebello* and the *Idaho*. Then on 5 May 1942 it claimed another tanker, the *John Adams* (carrying 2,000 tons of fuel), and the Greek merchant ship the SS *Chloe*. In an act of compassion, Commander Matsumura gave the survivors in the lifeboats supplies and provided them with a bearing for Noumea. On 12 June the I-21 sighted a convoy of eight ships and torpedoed and sank the freighter SS *Guatemala*. Then on 9 November the I-21 attacked the American Liberty ship USS *Edgar Allan Poe* (IX-103) After hitting the ship with a torpedo the I-21 surfaced with the intention of finishing her off with gunfire, but although most of the crew had left in lifeboats a gun deck crew remained aboard and shelled the submarine causing some minor damage. The I-21 dived and left the area. The *Edgar Allan Poe* was later taken under tow but was deemed to be beyond repair. On 18 January 1943 the I-21 sighted the Australian freighter SS *Kalingo* and torpedoed her. After allowing the crew to leave in lifeboats the freighter was sunk with another torpedo. Some hours later the I-21 sighted the Liberty ship USS *Peter H. Burnett* (IX-104) and fired two torpedoes into her and then left. The Liberty ship was later towed by the minesweeper USS *Zane* (DMS-14) and corvette HMAS *Mildura*. Most of the cargo was salvaged, but the *Peter H. Burnett* was a total loss. On 8 February 1943 the I-21 struck again. This time it was the 4,812-ton British freighter SS *Iron Knight* en-route from Whyalla to Newcastle. Two days later off Port Macquarie, Australia, the I-21 torpedoed and sank the American Liberty ship SS *Starr King* en-route from Sydney to New Caledonia with 7,000 tons of Army supplies. The Australian destroyer HMAS *Warramunga* rescued the survivors but had to abandon its attempt to tow the crippled freighter. On 11 November 1943 the I-21 attacked a convoy and torpedoed the American freighter SS *Cape San Juan* en-route to Townsville, Australia with 1,348 American troops aboard. Sixteen men were killed when the torpedo hit and another 114 drowned after they abandoned the ship. Survivors were picked up by the destroyers USS *Edwin T. Meredith* (DD-434), USS *McCalla* (DD-488) and USS *Dempsey* (DE-26). Aircraft from the USS *Chenango* (CVE-28) sank the I-21 on 29 November 1943.

The SS *Starr King* sinking after being torpedoed by the I-21. (*Author*)

I-22

No recorded successes.

I-23

No recorded successes although there were two claims.

I-24

The I-24's first success was on 3 June 1942 27 miles east of Sydney, when she fired two torpedoes at the 4,812-ton Australian merchant SS *Iron Chieftain* that was en route from Newcastle to Whyalla with a cargo of coke and materials for a shipyard. One torpedo struck her portside amidships. Her heavy load dragged her to the bottom in about five minutes. The I-24 claimed to have hit and sunk the 7,748-ton British merchant ship SS *Orestes* with gunfire, but this was proved later not to have been the case. The I-24 was rammed and sunk on 7 June by the sub-chaser USS *Larchmount* (PC-487).

I-25

The I-25 was one of the few Japanese submarines equipped with a reconnaissance aircraft. Whilst off the coast of Oregon the I-25 torpedoed the tanker SS *Camden* which later sank whilst under tow. This was followed by the sinking of the 7,038-ton tanker SS *Larry Donheny* which, it is claimed, burst into flames and sank. Although having claimed to have sunk a number of other ships, none were ever confirmed.

I-26

On 7 December 1941 just 300 miles off San Francisco, the I-26, under the command of Lieutenant Commander Toshio Kusaka, spotted the 2,140-ton Army-chartered steam schooner SS *Cynthia Olson* carrying a cargo of Army supplies en route from Tacoma, Washington to Honolulu, Hawaii. At dawn, the ship's nationality was established and the I-26 fired a warning shot. Twenty-nine more shells were fired and the *Cynthia Olson* was sunk. She was the first American merchant to be sunk by a Japanese submarine in the Second World War. Her next victim was on 7 June 1942 when she fired a single Type 89 torpedo at the 3,286-ton American armed cargo steamer MV *Coast Trader* carrying 1,250 tons of newsprint. The torpedo hit on the starboard side and the freighter sank stern-first. On 31 August the I-26 carried out an unsuccessful attack on the aircraft carrier USS *Saratoga* but only managed to inflict some minor damage. On 13 November the I-26 came upon the USS *San Francisco* (CA-38), which was part of a large task force, and fired three torpedoes. All three missed the *San Francisco* but hit the USS *Juneau* (CLAA-52) on her port side amidships near where she was hit the previous night. A minute later, a magazine explosion blew the *Juneau* in half and killed most of her crew. The 8,473-ton cruiser sank in about 20 seconds. Eight days later only ten men had been rescued, but not one of five Sullivan brothers was amongst the survivors. Their deaths were to bring in a rule that siblings were not allowed to serve together.

On 11 April 1943 the I-26 attacked a convoy. Three torpedoes were fired at the 4,732-ton Yugoslavian armed merchant SS *Recina* bound from Whyalla to Newcastle with a cargo of iron ore. After a hit to starboard the steamer sank in less than a minute, taking thirty-two men with her. The Australian sloop HMAS *Moresby* rescued ten survivors. Ten days later on 24 April 1943 the I-26 launched three torpedoes at the 2,125-ton Australian armed merchant ship SS *Kowarra* on its way from Bowen to Brisbane with a load of sugar. Following a boiler explosion the steamer broke in two and sank within 45 seconds of being hit.

On 2 January 1944 I-26 fired four torpedoes at the 7,176-ton American Liberty ship USS *Albert Gallatin*. Most of the torpedoes missed. The I-26 surfaced and opened fire on the *Gallatin* with her deck gun. The *Gallatin* sank 60 miles off the Arabian coast. On 13 March 1944 off Karachi, India, the I-26 torpedoed the 8,298-ton American tanker SS *H. D. Collier*, operated by Standard Oil of San Francisco (Chevron), en route from Iran to Bombay with 103,000 barrels of gasoline and kerosene. Her crew abandoned ship and she sank. On 21 March 1944 the I-26 torpedoed and sank the 8,117-ton Norwegian tanker SS *Grena* en route from Aden to Abadan. One week later on 29 March 1944 the I-26 torpedoed the 7,176-ton American Liberty ship SS *Richard Hovey* which was en-route from Bombay to the United States. Three torpedoes hit the *Hovey* and the I-26 surfaced and opened fire with her deck gun, the ship was abandoned as she sank. The I-26 then started to machine-gun the lifeboats and the rafts. The captain of the *Richard Hovey*, Hans

Thorsen, and three other crewmen were taken aboard the submarine. Miraculously only eight of the crew were killed, the remaining members of the crew drifting for 16 days before being rescued by a British cargo ship. The destroyer USS *Richard M. Powell* (DE-403) later depth-charged and sank the I-26.

I-27

Another of the most successful Japanese submarines was the I-27. Her first victim on 3 June 1942 was the Australian 3,353-ton armed ore carrier SS *Iron Crown* en route from Whyalla to Port Kembla with a cargo of iron ore. The I-27 tracked the *Iron Crown* and sent a torpedo into her port side, abaft the bridge, and in less than a minute the ore carrier had sunk. On 2 October 1942 in the Gulf of Oman, near Masirah Island, the I-27 torpedoed the 7,174-ton British armed steamer SS *Ocean Vintage* sailing with 9,300 tons of general cargo. After receiving one hit the steamer sank. In the Indian Ocean on 20 March 1943 the I-27 torpedoed the 7,132-ton British armed merchant SS *Fort Mumford*, loaded with 6,649 tons of war supplies for the Mediterranean, on her maiden voyage from Vancouver, Canada. The crew abandoned ship, but only one of them survived and was later rescued by an Arab dhow. On 7 May 1943 in the Gulf of Oman the I-27 torpedoed the 6,608-ton Dutch motor vessel MV *Berakit* en route from Colombo to Durban. The submarine surfaced and sank the merchant ship with gunfire. One month later on 3 June 1943 whilst still in the Gulf of Oman, the I-27 torpedoed the 4,897-ton American armed freighter SS *Montanan* and sank her. Some of the survivors were picked up by a dhow, the remaining survivors landed on Masirah Island. Still patrolling in the Gulf of Oman, the I-27 torpedoed the 4,696-ton British armed tanker SS *British Venture* en route from Abadan to Bombay with a cargo of kerosene and gas oil. Two minutes after being torpedoed the tanker was ablaze and sank. Two days later the I-27 torpedoed the 1,974-ton Norwegian armed steamer SS *Dah Puh* carrying a cargo of bitumen. Following the explosion the steamer broke in two; the stern sank immediately and the bow several hours later.

Moving into the Indian Ocean, at the beginning of July 1943, the I-27 attacked a convoy en route from Abadan, Iran to Montevideo, Uruguay and torpedoed the 6,797-ton American freighter SS *Alcoa Prospector*. The Royal Indian Navy corvette HMIS *Bengal* took on board the survivors. The next day, the freighter, still afloat, was re-boarded by her crew as Anglo-Iranian oil company tugs arrived and towed the damaged freighter into Bandar Abbas, Iran. On 9 September 1943 the I-27 torpedoed the 5,151-ton British armed motor vessel SS *Larchbank* that was carrying 7,394 tons of general cargo and military stores, including four tanks, eight amphibious craft, and railway iron. The *Larchbank* sank within two minutes. The following day, 10 September 1943, in the Gulf of Aden, the I-27 torpedoed the 7,219-ton British Liberty ship SS *Sambo*, on her maiden voyage with nitrate and general cargo. On 18 November the I-27 torpedoed and sank the 7,176-ton British Liberty ship SS

Sambridge on her maiden voyage with 365 tons of general cargo and 1,000 tons of sand ballast. Ten days later the I-27 torpedoed and sank the 4,824-ton Greek steamer SS *Athina Livanos*. On 2 December she torpedoed and sank the 4,732-ton Greek steamer SS *Nitsa* en route from Calcutta to Aden. The following day off the coast of Somalia the I-27 torpedoed and damaged the 7,126-ton Canadian-built British freighter SS *Fort Camosun* but later proceeded on to Calcutta.

On 4 February 1944 the I-27 sighted a large convoy accompanied by a large cruiser, a corvette and two anti-submarine cutters. The I-27 moved into the attack and a large transport, the SS *Khedive Ismail*, received a torpedo hit to her starboard side engine room and started to list to starboard. Approximately five seconds later a second torpedo struck the boiler room forward, directly below the ship's funnel, causing a major explosion inside the ship. Once on her beam-ends, *Khedive Ismail* broke in two and sank. The escorts immediately went into the attack on the I-27 and after a pattern of intense depth-charging the I-27 was forced to the surface where she was finished off with a torpedo from one of the escorts. There were no survivors.

I-28
No recorded successes.

I-29
On 2 September 1942 the I-29 torpedoed and sank the British freighter SS *Gazcon*. The following day she carried out an attack on the British freighter SS *British Genius* but was unsuccessful and the ship escaped with just minor damage. Then on 10 September in the Arabian Sea, the I-29 torpedoed and sank the British freighter SS *Haresfield* en route from Aden to Colombo. One week later in the Gulf of Aden, the I-29 torpedoed, shelled and sank the British freighter SS *Ocean Honour*. On 22 September whilst patrolling in the Indian Ocean the I-29 torpedoed and sank the American freighter SS *Paul Luckenbach* about 800 miles from the coast of India. On 23 November 1942 in the Gulf of Aden, the I-29 torpedoed and sank the British India Company passenger/cargo liner SS *Tilawa* on her way from Bombay to Mombasa and Durban with 6,472 tons of cargo. Of 958 people on board, 252 passengers and 28 crew were lost. The cruiser HMS *Birmingham* rescued the survivors. Still in the Gulf of Aden, the I-29 torpedoed, shelled and sank the Norwegian fleet oil tanker SS *Belita* as she was en-route from Abadan to Mombasa with 9,000 tons of oil for the Admiralty.

I-30
No recorded successes.

I-31
On 12 May 1943, the I-31 claimed to have scored one of Japan's major successes during the war: the sinking of the American battleship USS *Pennsylvania*

(BB-38). This, however, turned out to be untrue, and was part of Japan's propaganda programme to claim the sinkings of major ships by their submarines. The I-31 did attack the *Pennsylvania* and did fire a torpedo, but it missed and the submarine was tracked down and within hours had been forced to the surface by depth charges and sunk by gunfire from the USS *Edwards* (DD-619).

I-32
The I-31, like the I-32, claimed to have sunk an important ship when it attacked the 8,482-ton Australian troop transport HMAS *Katoomba*. The I-32 surfaced and attempted to attack the ship with gunfire but was unsuccessful, and the transport escaped at flank speed. Again the propaganda machine was at work.

I-33
No recorded successes.

I-34
No recorded successes.

I-35
Once again the Japanese propaganda machine was at work when it was claimed that the I-35 had sunk the American light cruiser USS *Santa Fe* (CL-50). No other successes were recorded or claimed.

I-36
The I-36's successes were due to the *Kaiten*s she launched when on 12 January 1945 they badly damaged the ammunition ship USS *Mazama* (AE-9) and sank *LCI-600* (Landing Craft Infantry). There were a number of other claims made but none were ever confirmed.

I-37
The I-37's successes started in June 1943 when on the 16th she torpedoed and shelled the 8,070-ton armed British tanker SS *San Ernesto*. The tanker failed to sink and after the crew had abandoned her she was left to drift. It finally grounded on an island off Sumatra some 2,000 miles away. Her second victim was the 7,167-ton Liberty ship SS *Henry Knox*. Torpedoed and then sunk by shellfire, the crew of the *Henry Knox* were allowed to leave in their lifeboats. On 23 October north-west of Madagascar, the I-37 torpedoed and sank the 3,404-ton Greek merchant ship SS *Faneroment*. Then on 27 November the I-37 torpedoed the 9,972-ton Norwegian armed tanker MV *Scotia* that had detached from a convoy. Another torpedo hit the starboard engine room and the ship broke in two. Her next victim was the 7,118-ton British armed steam tanker MV *British Chivalry*. She received

two torpedo hits to starboard, disabling her engines and killing six sailors. The I-37 then surfaced and sank the now abandoned tanker with gunfire. Two lifeboats with survivors were ordered alongside and interrogated. The captain of the submarine, Commander Hajime Nakagawa. ordered the crew to open fire on the survivors. A total of thirteen British sailors were killed and five wounded. Thirty-seven days later twenty-nine sailors and nine gunners were rescued by the British merchant SS *Delane*. On 26 February 1944, the I-37 sighted the 5,189-ton British armed motor vessel MV *Sutlej*. The I-37 fired two torpedoes and one torpedo hit the port side between holds Nos. 1 and 2 and the ship sank. The survivors escape in a lifeboat and several rafts. The I-37 surfaced and illuminated the surrounding area with a searchlight. One of the survivors, a teenage Indian boy, was found clinging to the submarine's rudder and taken aboard. After receiving information about the ship's cargo and destination, Commander Nakagawa ordered his crew to open fire on the survivors. A total of forty-one sailors and nine gunners were killed. On 29 February 1944 the I-37 fired two torpedoes at the 7,005-ton British armed cargo steamer SS *Ascot*. After one hit to her engine room the steamer was dead in the water. Four sailors were killed in the blast whilst fifty-two survivors boarded a lifeboat and a raft. The I-37 surfaced and following a brief interrogation of the survivors sank the cargo ship by shellfire and then sank the lifeboat and raft with all its occupants. Only four sailors and three gunners were rescued on 3 March by the Dutch steamer SS *Straat Soenda*. The destroyer USS *McCoy Reynolds* (DE-440) sank the I-37 on 19 November 1944.

I-38
No recorded successes.

I-39
No recorded successes.

I-40
No recorded successes.

I-41
The I-41 was used mainly as a supply submarine but on 3 November 1944 it carried out a torpedo attack on the American light cruiser USS *Reno* (CL-96) and although claiming her to be sunk, it only managed to cause her slight damage. It also claimed to have sunk an *Essex* class aircraft carrier but there was no confirmation of such an attack.

I-42
No recorded successes.

I-43

No recorded successes.

I-44

The I-44 was a *Kaiten*-carrying submarine and although there are no successes recorded for her, it is thought that one of her *Kaiten*s might have scored a victory but this is not officially recorded.

I-45

The I-45's one and only success was on 28 October 1944 with the torpedoing and sinking of the USS *Eversole* (DE-44). The submarine surfaced and began machine-gunning the survivors in the water but quickly dived again when two more American destroyers suddenly appeared on the scene. Two hours later, after a series of depth-charge attacks, the I-45 was sunk with all hands.

The aircraft-carrying submarine I-45. (*USN*)

I-46

No recorded successes.

I-47

The I-47 was a *Kaiten*-carrying submarine so any recorded successes were down to her *Kaiten*s. Although there were a number of claims made by the submarine, none were ever confirmed.

I-48

Like the I-47, the I-48 was also a *Kaiten*-carrying submarine and no successes were credited to the *Kaiten*s.

I-49, I-50, I-51, I-52, I-53, I-54, I-55 and I-56
All cancelled.

I-57 (See I-157)
No recorded successes.

I-58 (See also I-158)
The I-58 was one of the submarines converted to carry *Kaiten*s. Her first contact with an enemy ship was with the American cruisers the USS *Indianapolis* (CA-35). The cruiser was not equipped with sonar or hydrophones, which made her vulnerable to submarine attack. A request for a destroyer escort was denied, so the *Indianapolis* began the trip from Guam to Leyte unescorted; the first major warship to do so during the war without equipment to detect enemy submarines. On 29 July 1945 the *Indianapolis* was zigzagging at 17 knots in overcast weather when she was spotted by the I-58. A spread of six Type 95 torpedoes with two-second intervals, set to the depth of 4m, was fired. Three equally-spaced hits on the starboard side were observed. Then the cruiser stopped and started to list to starboard and down by the bow. The submarine captain decided another attack was necessary and dived to 100ft to open the range, reloading his two forward torpedo tubes. In less than an hour the *Indianapolis* capsized and sank by the bow. After surfacing, a new check revealed no further traces of its victim. The I-58 departed the area at full speed, heading north while recharging its batteries. Besides what the *Kaiten*s may have attacked – none of which were confirmed – this was the only major success for the I-58.

The I-58 at Sasebo loading supplies. (*Author*)

I-59

The I-59 had three successes, the first on 20 January 1942 when it torpedoed the 4,184-ton Norwegian freighter SS *Eidsvold* off Christmas Island. The second was on 25 January 1942 when it entered Sabang Roads, Philippines and sank British merchant ship the 1,811-ton SS *Giang Sen*, and took some of her crew prisoner. Then on 1 March 1942 in the Indian Ocean, the I-59 torpedoed and sank the 1,035-ton Dutch passenger ship MV *Rooseboom*. About 250 lives were lost, mainly British military personnel and a few civilians including a woman and two children from Malaya. With all but one of the lifeboats wrecked, eighty people crammed on to a lifeboat designed to hold twenty-eight, with a further fifty hanging on to the outside of the lifeboat. By the time the lifeboat had drifted over a thousand miles back to the Sumatra coast, there were just two passengers and three crewmembers left alive. On 20 May 1942 the I-59 was re-numbered the I-159 but there were no more recorded successes.

I-60

No recorded successes.

I-61

No recorded successes.

I-62

See I-162.

I-63

No recorded successes – scrapped in 1940.

I-64, I-65, I-66, I-67, I-68 and I-69

All re-numbered to I-164, I-165, I-166, I-167, I-168 and I-169.

I-64 (I-164)

The I-64's first success was on 22 January 1942 when it sank the 4,482-ton Dutch merchant SS *Van Overstraten*. The I-64 fired two torpedoes at her but missed. It then surfaced and shelled the Dutch ship, killing four members of the crew. The captain and crew abandoned ship and the I-64 sank the ship with a third torpedo. One week later whilst on patrol in the Indian Ocean the I-64 torpedoed and sank the 5,049-ton American merchant ship the SS *Florence Luckenbach*. On 30 January the I-64 torpedoed, shelled and sank the 2,498-ton Indian merchant ship SS *Jalatarang*. The following day it shelled and sank the 4,215-ton Indian merchant ship SS *Jalapalaka*. On 13 March still on patrol in the Indian Ocean the I-64 torpedoed, shelled and sank the 1,513-ton Norwegian merchant SS *Mabella* off

Japanese submarine I-164 with the submarine tender *Heian Maru* at Paramushiro in the Kurile Islands. (*JMSDF*)

the coast of Coromandel near Madras. Shortly after this the I-64 was re-numbered the I-164. The submarine had no more successes and was sunk on 17 May 1942 by the USS *Triton* (SS-201).

I-65 (I-165)

In January 1942 the I-65 torpedoed, shelled and sank the 1,003-ton Dutch steamship SS *Benkoelen* that was en route from Soemenep to Cheribon. The American destroyer USS *Paul Jones* (DD-230) rescued her survivors the next day. Then on 14 January 1942 the I-65 torpedoed and sank the 5,102-ton British-Indian armed merchant SS *Jalarajan* that was en route from Singapore to Calcutta. On 9 February 1942 in the Indian Ocean, the I-65 torpedoed and damaged the 6,693-ton British converted boom carrier SS *Laomedon*. One week later the I-65 torpedoed and sank the 4,681-ton Danish/British merchant ship SS *Johanne Justesen*. Some days later the I-65 torpedoed and sank the 5,280-ton British merchant ship SS *Bhima*. These were its last recorded successes as the I-65.

I-66 (I-166)

On 24 December 1941 the I-65 sighted a surfaced fleet-type submarine off her starboard bow and identified it as a Dutch submarine. The I-66 commenced a submerged approach and fired a single torpedo. The K-XVI Type submarine broke in two and sank with all thirty-six hands. Then on 11 January 1942 the I-66 torpedoed the 6,211-ton US Army Transport USAT *Liberty* en route from Tanjong Priok (Batavia) carrying rubber and explosives originating from the Philippines as deck cargo. The heavily-damaged freighter was left dead in the water and the USS *Paul Jones* (DD-230) and the Dutch destroyer HNLMS *Van Ghent* attempted to tow her to Singaraya, Bali, but due to the steadily increasing flooding the ship was finally beached off Tulamben, north-east Bali, and later capsized. Ten days later on 21 January 1942 the I-66 torpedoed the 3,193-ton Panamanian-flagged merchant ship SS *Nord* en route from Calcutta to Rangoon, Burma, with 2,500 tons of coal. The following day the I-66 torpedoed the 2,358-ton British passenger-cargo steamer

Dutch submarine K-XVI. (*Author*)

SS Chak Sang. The I-66 then surfaced and sank the crippled ship with gunfire. Five crewmembers were lost, but sixty-one survivors were rescued later. On 4 February the I-66 torpedoed and shelled the British Straits Steamship Company's 2,076-ton steamer SS *Kamuning*. The crippled steamer sank while being towed to Trincomalee. These were the last recorded successes as the I-66.

I-70

There are no recorded successes for the I-70. It was the first Japanese boat to be sunk in the Pacific War.

I-71 (See also I-171)

During the evening of 9 January 1942 off the Hawaiian Islands, the I-71 attacked a three-ship convoy bound from Kahului, Maui for Hilo, Hawaii. One of the ships was

USAT *General Royal T. Frank*. (*US Army*)

Japanese submarine I-171 (I-71). (*Author*)

the 622-ton Army transport USAT *General Royal T. Frank* carrying army recruits and a small freighter SS *Kalae* with a barge in tow. The I-71 torpedoed the *Frank* and she exploded and sank in thirty seconds. There were no survivors.

I-72

On 19 December 1941 the I-72 torpedoed the 5,113-ton American merchant ship SS *Prusa* that was en route from Honolulu to Baltimore. The torpedo wrecked the engines and she sank within a few minutes. The US Coast Guard rescued fourteen men in a lifeboat in the vicinity of the sunken ship; the captain and ten others were picked up near Fiji after 31 days. On 23 January 1942 the I-72 spotted the 7,383-ton oil tanker USS *Neches* (AO-3) proceeding unescorted to a refuelling rendezvous with Task Force 11's USS *Lexington* (CV-2) that was steaming to conduct an air raid on Wake Island. The I-72 fired a torpedo that hit the *Neches* amidships, but failed to detonate. A second torpedo hit the ship on her starboard side, aft on her stern and destroyed her engine room. A third torpedo hit the *Neches* on the port side. The I-172 then surfaced to finish the job with its deck gun, but the *Neches*'s crew returned fire from her 5in and 3in guns. Two hours later the *Neches* sank by the bow with the loss of fifty-seven crew. The I-72 was later re-numbered the I-172 and had no more successes. There were 126 survivors from the *Neches*.

I-73

No recorded successes.

I-74 to I-85

All re-numbered I-174 to I-185.

I-121

No recorded successes.

I-122

No recorded successes.

I-123

No recorded successes.

I-124

On 10 December 1941 the I-124 torpedoed and sank the 1,228-ton British steamer SS *Hareldawins* en route from Hong Kong to Singapore. The master of the steamer was taken as a POW. This was her only recorded success.

I-156

The I-56 was renumbered the I-156 in May 1942. As the I-56 on 11 December 1941, she shelled and sank the 1,186-ton Norwegian merchant ship SS *Hai Tung* en route from Bangkok, Siam (now Thailand) to Singapore with a cargo of rice and general supplies. There were no survivors. One month later she struck again when she shelled and sank the 2,626-ton British freighter SS *Kwangtung* on 4 January 1942. The following day the I-56 shelled the 8,169-ton Dutch merchant SS *Tanimba* but the armed merchantman fired back and the I-56 dived to escape damage. On 8 January 1942 the I-56 torpedoed the 3,050-ton Dutch steamer SS *Van Rees*. Five sailors were killed in the torpedo explosion and the I-56 surfaced, captured and questioned the survivors regarding their cargo and destination. Later that evening the I-56 shelled and sank the 2,263-ton Dutch passenger ship SS *Van Riebeeck*. Thirteen sailors were killed in the attack; the Dutch minelayer HNLMS *Willem Van Der Zaan* rescued the survivors. There were no more recorded successes.

The I-156 entering harbour. (*Author*)

I-157

No recorded successes

I-158

On 9 January 1942 in the Java Sea, west of Bawean Island, the I-58 first shelled and then torpedoed and sank the Dutch merchant ship SS *Camphuys*. The American destroyer USS *Paul Jones* (DD-230) rescued the survivors. The following month, whilst still on patrol in the Java Sea, the I-58 torpedoed and sank the Dutch passenger ship SS *Pijnacker Hordijk*. On 25 February the Dutch merchant ship SS *Boeroe* was en route to Perth, Australia when the I-58 fired two torpedoes, both hit and the *Boeroe* sank slowly, enabling all of her 70-man crew to escape. Three days later the I-58 torpedoed and damaged the British tanker SS *British Judge*. All these successes were claimed when the submarine was designated as that I-58 and then it was renumbered the I-158 in May 1942. No more successes were recorded.

I-159 (See also I-59)

No recorded successes as the I-159.

I-160 and I-161

Not built.

I-162 (See also I-62)

On 31 January 1942 24 miles west of Colombo, Ceylon, the I-162 attacked the 9,463-ton British tanker SS *Longwood*, but failed to sink her and the tanker made it to Colombo, albeit seriously damaged. On 10 March 1942 whilst on patrol in the Indian Ocean, the I-62 shelled and sank the 235-ton British sailing ship *Lakshmi Govinda*. Three days later the I-62 torpedoed and damaged the 8,012-ton British motor tanker SS *San Cirilo* but the tanker managed to make Colombo two days later. Then in October 1942 the I-162 torpedoed the Soviet armed timber ship SS *Mikoyan* en route from Calcutta to Karachi with a general cargo. The ship received one hit between the holds Nos. 1 and 2 and went dead in the water and the crew abandoned ship. Some hours later the *Mikoyan* sank. Two days later the I-162 torpedoed the 5,597-ton British armed steamer SS *Manon* en route from Calcutta and Vizagapatam to Colombo with 7,100 tons of coal. The merchant ship sank and eight sailors were killed. On 4 March 1944 the I-162 torpedoed, shelled and sank the 7,127-ton British armed merchant ship SS *Fort McCloud*. This was the last recorded success and although the I-162 claimed more, none were substantiated.

I-164

No recorded successes as the I-164. (See I-64.)

I-165 (See also I-65)

On 25 August 1942 in the Indian Ocean, the I-165, under the command of Commander Tsuruzo Shimizu, torpedoed and sank the 5,237-ton British armed merchant ship SS *Harmonides* en route from Calcutta to Trincomalee. One month later on 24 September the I-165 torpedoed and sank the 5,549-ton American armed freighter SS *Losmar* en route from Port Said to Colombo. A total of twenty-seven sailors were lost. The 10,286-ton British armed merchant ship SS *Perseus* was the next victim when the I-165 struck her with a torpedo on the port side. She started to sink by the stern. Ten minutes later a second torpedo hit and then a third. The *Perseus* sank with no loss of life. Her radio operator got off an SOS before she sank and a PBY Catalina arrived soon after. Later, a Royal Indian Navy corvette rescued the entire crew. On 18 March 1944 the I-165 torpedoed the 3,916-ton British armed merchant SS *Nancy Moller* enroute from Durban with a cargo of coal to Colombo, Ceylon. She went down rapidly after two hits to the port side. I-165 surfaced about 50 yards from the lifeboats and attempted to establish the identity of the ship. Six men from one boat were ordered aboard the submarine and taken POW. The I-165 then circled the wreckage of the *Nancy Moller*, spraying it and the survivors, who had taken to the lifeboats and rafts, with machine-gun fire. A total of thirty sailors and two gunners were killed. Four days later, the British light cruiser HMS *Emerald* rescued the ship's master, twenty-seven sailors and four gunners.

I-166 (See also I-66)
On 1 October 1942 the I-166 landed three Indian National Army insurgents off Calcutta and the same day shelled and damaged the 1,201-ton Panamanian-flagged armed merchant SS *Camila*. The burning merchant ship was beached, but became a total loss. Then on 23 November whilst on patrol the I-166 torpedoed and sank the 5,332-ton British armed merchant ship SS *Cranfield* en route from Calcutta to Suez. Nine sailors were lost, but sixty-four sailors and three gunners manage to reach the coast of Travancore, India in the lifeboats. These were the last recorded successes of the I-166.

I-167
No recorded successes.

I-168
On 6 June 1942 one of I-168's lookouts spotted the USS *Yorktown* (CV-5) about 12 miles away. Alongside the *Yorktown*, which had been crippled by an air attack, was the destroyer the USS *Hammann* (DD-412), which was in the process of putting a salvage party aboard the carrier. The *Hammann* was secured to the *Yorktown*'s starboard side providing power for the carrier's pumps and foam to fight the fires. Undetected, the I-168 penetrated the destroyer and cruiser screen and from 1,900 yards, fired two torpedoes followed by two more three seconds later. The first torpedo hit the *Hammann* and broke her back and she sank in about four minutes. As she went down, her depth charges exploded and killed 81 of her 241-strong crew. The next two torpedoes struck the USS *Yorktown* below the bridge. The aircraft carrier later sank. There were no more recorded successes.

I-169

On 25 July 1942 the I-169 torpedoed the 9,227-ton Dutch freighter SS *Tjinegara* being operated by the US Army as a troopship. She was hit by several torpedoes and was sunk. This was the I-169's only success.

I-170

No recorded successes.

I-171 (See also I-71)

No recorded successes.

I-172 (See also I-72)

No recorded successes.

I-173

No recorded successes.

I-174

After claiming to have sunk the 3,303-ton SS *Point San Pedro*, the 4,113-ton US Army transport USAT *Edward Chambers* and the 176-ton American Liberty ship USS *John Bartram* (none of which were confirmed), the I-174 came upon a convoy of transports. The submarine fired two torpedoes at two overlapping ships. The second ship in the fourth column was the 5,551-ton USAT *Portmar*, fully loaded with fuel and ammunition. The 5,000-ton Landing Ship Tank *LST-469* astern of *Portmar* moved aside to allow the transport room to manoeuvre. The first of I-174's torpedoes hit the LST's starboard side, the blast destroying the steering gear and killing twenty-six men. Despite the severe damage *LST-469* was eventually towed back to Sydney for repairs. Moments after the explosion on the LST, *Portmar's* lookouts sighted torpedo tracks. Before the ship could manoeuvre she was hit by a second torpedo on her starboard side. Seven minutes after being hit, the *Portmar* was abandoned and sunk. She was the last ship sunk by IJN submarines on the eastern coast of Australia.

I-175

On 23 July 1942 the I-175 torpedoed and damaged the stern of the 3,279-ton Australian merchant ship SS *Allara* bound from Cairns, Queensland to Sydney with a cargo of sugar. The ship received one hit and settled by the stern; she was abandoned, but did not sink. She was later re-boarded and towed to Newcastle. The following day, near Sydney, the I-175 torpedoed and damaged the 3,345-ton Australian merchant ship SS *Murada*. Four days later the I-175 torpedoed and sank the 2,795-ton French merchant ship SS *Cagou* carrying nickel ore. On

3 August off Moruya, New South Wales, the I-175 shelled and damaged the 233-ton Australian trawler SS *Dureenbee*. The crew abandoned the sinking trawler. On 24 November the I-175 had been diverted to intercept American warships and came across the battleship USS *New Mexico* (BB-40) and the escort carrier USS *Liscombe Bay* (CVE-56) preparing her planes for a dawn launching. The I-175 fired four torpedoes at the carrier. One torpedo hit the carrier on the starboard side aft of the after engine room and detonated the bomb storage magazine, totally destroying the stern. Within 30 minutes the *Liscombe Bay* listed to starboard and sank. This was the last recorded success of the I-175.

I-176
Whilst patrolling 300 miles south of Truk, lookouts on the I-176 spotted a 'PERCH-class' submarine, the USS *Corvina* (SS-226) on the surface in the process of recharging her batteries. The I-176 crash-dived and reached a firing position on *Corvina*'s starboard quarter at a distance of 2,700 yards. The I-76 fired three torpedoes from her bow tubes and 25 seconds later two heavy explosions were heard. The *Corvina* blew up and sank with all eighty-two hands. This was the only recorded success of the I-176.

I-177
On 6 April 1943, 20 miles southeast of Cape Byron, near Brisbane, the I-177 sank the 8,724-ton British freighter SS *Limerick*. Her escort dropped two depth charges but they caused the I-177 no damage. Then on 14 May 1943 the I-177 was cruising on the surface east of Brisbane when it spotted the 3,222-ton hospital ship HMAHS *Centaur* en route from Sydney via Cairns to Port Moresby, New Guinea with 333 persons aboard. The I-177 fired a single torpedo, which set the ship on fire. In just three minutes the *Centaur* sank in 1,787ft of water. The I-177 surfaced but took no action for or against the survivors. The destroyer USS *Mugford* (DD-389) picked up some of the survivors later. These were the only successes recorded for the I-177.

I-178
On 27 April 1943 off Port Stephens, Australia the I-178 torpedoed and sank the 7,176-ton American Liberty ship USS *Lydia M. Childs* which was bound for Australia with a cargo of Army tanks. This was the only recorded success of the I-178.

I-179
No recorded successes.

I-180
On 29 April 1943 the I-180 sank the 2,239-ton Australian merchant ship SS *Wollongbar*. Only five of her thirty-seven crewmen survived and were later

rescued by the trawler *XLCR*. One week later the I-180 attacked the 2,137-ton Norwegian merchant ship SS *Fingal* that was en route from Sydney to Port Darwin with general cargo and ammunition. The *Fingal* was hit by one torpedo on her port side and then another in the engine room. She went down within a minute. Two hours later, her escort destroyer USS *Patterson* (DD-392) picked up nineteen survivors of her crew of thirty-one. The I-180 claimed hits on other ships but only these two were confirmed.

I-181
No recorded successes.

I-182
No recorded success – lost on first patrol.

I-183
No recorded successes.

I-184
No recorded successes.

I-185
No recorded successes.

I-201
No recorded successes.

I-202
No recorded successes.

I-203
No recorded successes.

RO-33
On 6 August 1942 in the Gulf of Papua, north-east of Murray Island, the RO-33 spotted the Australian 300-ton motor vessel MV *Mamutu* carrying 103 passengers, a crew of 40, and general cargo. The submarine surfaced and started shelling the vessel from her 3in deck gun. The first shell destroyed the radio room; the second shot hit the bridge, killing the ship's captain. The blazing wreck went dead in the water and as the RO-33 passed the sinking vessel it fired its machine gun, killing a number of survivors struggling in the water. At the end of August the 3,310-ton merchant ship MV *Malaita*, escorted by the destroyer HMAS *Arunta*, was torpedoed by RO-33. The torpedo hit the *Malaita* below the bridge on her starboard side and she took on a heavy list to starboard. The crew abandoned the ship fearing that she

was about to capsize, but later re-boarded her. The *Malaita* was taken under tow back to Port Moresby. No other successes recorded.

RO-34
The RO-34 made a number of claims of vessels sunk but none were confirmed.

RO-35
Lost on first war patrol. No recorded successes.

RO-36
No recorded successes.

RO-37
No recorded successes.

RO-38
No recorded successes.

RO-39
No recorded successes.

RO-40
No recorded successes.

RO-41
On 3 October 1944 35 miles east of Morotai Island, the RO-41 attacked the two escort carriers of Task Group 77.1.2, the USS *St. Lo* (CVE-63) and USS *Fanshaw Bay* (CVE-70). The RO-41 fired four of its torpedoes at the two aircraft carriers. Four explosions were heard. Three of the torpedoes missed the two carriers, although one hit the escort destroyer USS *Shelton* (DE-407) in the stern. The RO-41 reported one CV sunk and one CV damaged. The RO-41 also claimed to have sunk the American submarine USS *Kete* (SS-369) but this was never confirmed.

RO-42
On 14 January 1944 the RO-42 torpedoed the 800-ton harbour craft USS *YO-159*. US forces later scuttled the badly damaged fuel-oil barge. The RO-42 however reported that they had sunk a 10,000-ton fleet tanker. This was the RO-42's only success.

RO-43
No recorded successes.

RO-44
No recorded successes

RO-45
No recorded successes.

RO-46
No recorded successes.

RO-47
No recorded successes

RO-48
No recorded successes.

RO-49
No recorded successes.

RO-50
On 10 February 1945 the RO-50 fired a four-torpedo salvo at an enemy convoy sailing in a single column escorted by the destroyer USS *Isherwood* (DD-520). *LST-577* was in a group a few thousand yards to starboard of the destroyer and was hit by one of the torpedoes. One-third of *LST-577* was blown clean off including the entire bridge. Another LST then took the remnants of the LST in tow and proceeded to depart the area. This was the RO-50's only confirmed success.

RO-51–RO-54
Never assigned.

RO-55
No recorded successes.

RO-56
No recorded successes.

RO-57–RO-60
Used as training submarines.

RO-61
On 30 August 1942 the RO-61 entered Nazan Bay in the Aleutian Islands on a slow cautious approach, then from 875 yards, fired a spread of three torpedoes at what was identified as the 1,766-ton *Barnegat*-class seaplane tender USS *Casco* (AVP-12). The first one missed the *Casco* and landed on the beach. The third

torpedo also missed but the second hit *Casco*'s forward engine room and damaged the tender severely. The crew beached the ship to prevent her from sinking. This was the RO-61's only success.

RO-62
No recorded successes.

RO-63
No recorded successes.

RO-64
On 11 December 1941 the RO-64 closed to within 2,200 yards of Howland in the Phoenix Islands, and opened fire with her deck gun. The island was said to be an American seaplane base. They targeted the wireless and weather station, runways, depots, barracks and the lighthouse. As a result of her one-hour shelling, a number of buildings were set ablaze and there were several casualties among the locals. The RO-64 later turned her attention and gun on to Baker Island, as did the RO-68, which joined her. This was the RO-64's only recorded attack.

RO-65
No recorded successes.

RO-66
No recorded successes. Lost when in collision with the RO-62.

RO-67
No recorded successes.

RO-68
No recorded successes.

Japanese submarine RO-69 later re-numbered RO-30. Seen here at sea with her battle flag fluttering on the stern. (*JMSDF*)

RO-69
Served as a training submarine throughout the Second World War.

RO-100
No recorded successes.

RO-101
No recorded successes.

RO-102
No recorded successes.

RO-103
On 23 June 1943 off the eastern tip of San Cristobal Island, the RO-103 sighted a convoy of three transports protected by three destroyers. Going into the attack the RO-103 torpedoed and sank the 7,440-ton USS *Aldura* (AK-72) and then torpedoed the 7,176-ton Liberty ship USS *Deimos* (AK-78), while both were in convoy en route to Guadalcanal. The *Deimos* was so badly damaged that she was scuttled by the destroyer USS *O'Bannon* (DD-450).

RO-104
No recorded successes.

RO-105
No recorded successes.

RO-106
On 18 July 1943 off New Georgia, Solomons the RO-106 torpedoed and sank the 1,625-ton *LST-342*. This was its only confirmed success.

RO-107
No recorded successes.

RO-108
On 3 October 1943 the RO-108 spotted three destroyers off Finschafen, New Guinea and moved into attack. The destroyers, the USS *Henley* (DD-391), USS *Reid* (DD-369) and USS *Smith* (DD-378), were on an ASW sweep off Finschafen, New Guinea. The RO-108 fired a salvo of torpedoes at the three destroyers. The *Smith* spotted the three torpedo wakes and combed them, so that one torpedo passed 500 yards to port and the other 200 yards to starboard. The *Henley* also spotted and evaded two of the torpedoes, but a third hit her port side and exploded, destroying

her boilers and breaking her keel. Six minutes later, the *Henley* broke in half and sank stern-first. The RO-108's captain reported two destroyers sunk. The *Henley* was its only confirmed success.

RO-109
No recorded successes.

RO-110
On 2 February 1944 the RO-110 departed Penang on her second war patrol to raid enemy communications in the Bay of Bengal. In the Bay of Bengal the RO-110 attacked Convoy JC 36 en route from Colombo, Ceylon to Calcutta, India. The 6,274-ton British merchant ship SS *Asphalion* was hit by two torpedoes that flooded one of her holds and her engine room. The survivors abandoned the crippled vessel, which was later towed to port. This was the RO-110's only recorded success.

RO-111
In December 1943 the RO-111 attacked the British convoy JC 30 en route from Swansea to Calcutta, comprising twelve ships. The 7,934-ton armed cargo ship SS *Peshawur* received one torpedo hit and sank two hours later. Then on 16 March 1944 in the Bay of Bengal, the RO-111 attacked a convoy en route from Calcutta to Colombo, Ceylon. The RO-111 torpedoed the 3,962-ton Indian armed troopship *SS El Mdina*, which broke in two and sank within minutes.

RO-112
No recorded successes.

RO-113
On 6 November 1944 the RO-113 torpedoed and sank the 3,827-ton British merchant SS *Marion Moller* whilst on patrol in the Bay of Bengal. She was the last Allied vessel torpedoed by IJN submarines in the Indian Ocean. In the December the RO 113 claimed to have sunk two more transport ships and the British submarine HMS *Thule* but none of these were confirmed.

RO-114
No recorded successes.

RO-115
No recorded successes.

RO-116
No recorded successes.

RO-117
No recorded successes.

Japanese submarine RO-500 (ex-U-boat U-511). (*Author*)

RO-500 (U-511)

Formerly the German submarine U-511, it had success whilst as a U-boat but no recorded successes as the RO-500.

RO-501 (U-1224)

Formerly the German submarine U-1224. No recorded successes.

I-351

No recorded successes.

I-361

No recorded successes.

I-362

No recorded successes.

I-363

One merchant ship claimed but none confirmed.

I-364

No recorded successes – sunk on first patrol.

I-365

No recorded successes.

I-366

The I-366 claimed three American transports sunk, but these were never confirmed.

I-367

No recorded successes.

I-368
No recorded successes.

I-369
No recorded successes.

I-370
No recorded successes.

I-371
No recorded successes.

I-372
No recorded successes.

I-373
No recorded successes.

All of the I-300 class submarines were used as either transport submarines or converted to carry *Kaitens* (human torpedoes).

I-400 (Aircraft-carrying submarines)
None of the I-400 class submarines saw action.

The I-401 in Tokyo Bay. (*USN*)

I-501 (ex U-181)
Only successes were as a U-boat.

I-502 (ex U-862)
Only successes were as a U-boat.

I-503

Formerly the Italian submarine UIT-24. No recorded successes.

I-504

Formerly the Italian submarine UIT-25. No recorded successes.

JAPANESE AIRCRAFT-CARRYING SUBMARINES

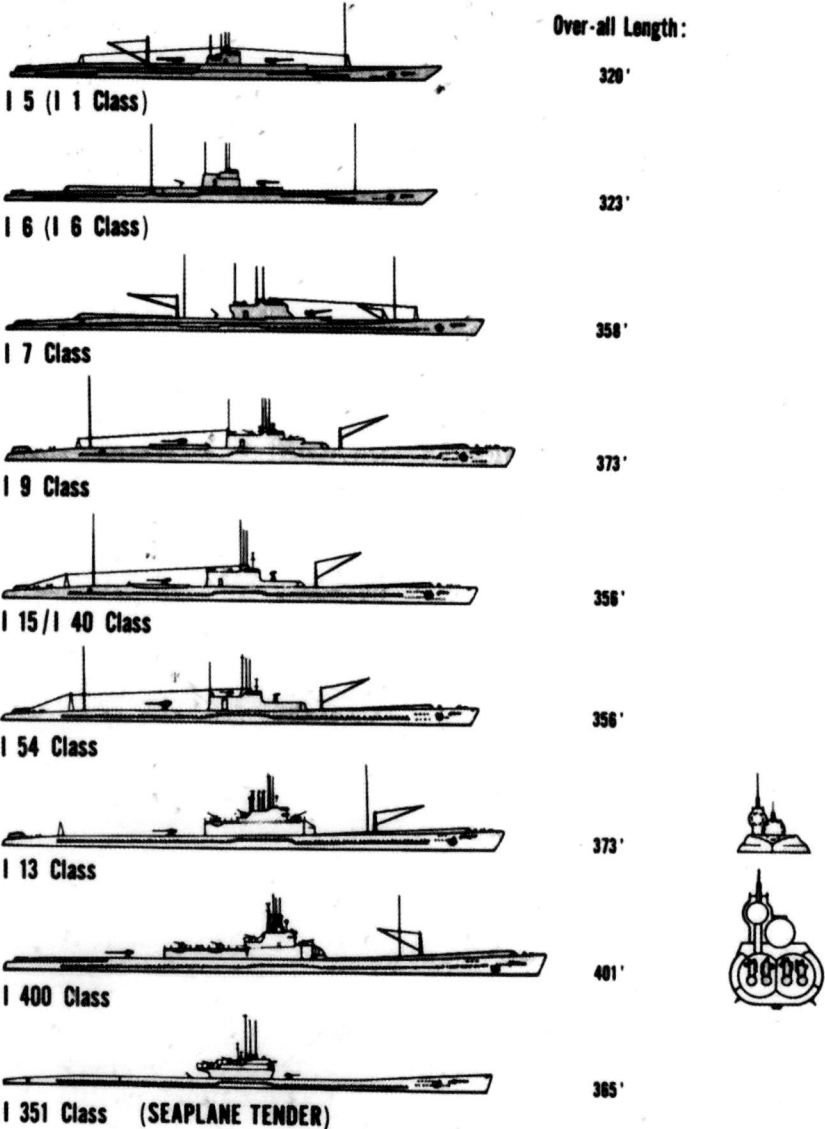

Over-all Length:

I 5 (I 1 Class) — 320'

I 6 (I 6 Class) — 323'

I 7 Class — 358'

I 9 Class — 373'

I 15/I 40 Class — 356'

I 54 Class — 356'

I 13 Class — 373'

I 400 Class — 401'

I 351 Class   (SEAPLANE TENDER) — 365'

SCALE: 1" equals 100'

List of Japanese aircraft-carrying submarines. (*Author*)

Japanese Submarine Specifications

Holland 1, 2, 3, 4, 5

Length:	67ft (20.4m)
Beam:	11.75ft (3.63m)
Draft:	10.25ft (3.12m)
Engine:	180hp shaft driven petrol engine
	70hp electric motor
Speed:	8 knots on surface
	7 knots submerged
Depth:	125ft
Displacement:	105 tons on surface
	130 tons submerged
Range:	185 nautical miles on surface
Crew:	13 officers and men
Torpedo tubes:	One 18in (457mm) in the bow
Torpedoes:	Two

Holland 6

Length:	73.25ft (22.4m)
Beam:	11.75ft (3.63m)
Draft:	7ft (2.1m)
Engine:	250hp shaft driven petrol engine
	22hp electric motor
Speed:	8.5 knots on surface
	4 knots submerged
Depth:	125ft
Displacement:	57 tons on surface
	63 tons submerged
Range:	185 nautical miles on surface
	12 nautical miles at 4 knots submerged
Crew:	15 officers and men
Torpedo tubes:	One 18in (457mm) in the bow
Torpedoes:	One

Holland 7

Length:	84.5ft (25.7m)
Beam:	11.75ft (3.63m)
Draft:	8ft (2.4m)
Engine:	250hp shaft driven petrol engine
	22hp electric motor
Speed:	8.5 knots on surface
	4 knots submerged
Depth:	125ft
Displacement:	57 tons on surface
	63 tons submerged
Range:	185 nautical miles on surface
	12 nautical miles at 4 knots submerged
Crew:	4 officers and men
Torpedo tubes:	One 18in (457mm) in the bow
Torpedoes:	One

Vickers (HA-1) 8, 9, 10, 11, 12.

Length:	142ft (43.3m)
Beam:	13.5ft (4.1m)
Draft:	11.25ft (3.4m)
Engine:	600hp shaft driven petrol engine
	300hp electric motor
Speed:	12 knots on surface
	8.5 knots submerged
Depth:	125ft
Displacement:	266 tons on surface (Nos 8, 9)
	321 tons submerged
	291 tons surfaced (Nos 10, 11, 12)
	326 tons submerged
Range:	600 nautical miles on surface
	60 nautical miles at 4 knots submerged
Crew:	26 officers and men
Torpedo tubes:	Two 18in (457mm) in the bow
Torpedoes:	Two

Vickers (HA-6) 13

Length:	126.75ft (38.6m)
Beam:	12.5ft (4.1m)
Draft:	11.35ft (3.8m)
Engine:	1160hp shaft driven petrol engine
	300hp electric motor

Speed:	10 knots on surface
	8 knots submerged
Depth:	125ft
Displacement:	304 tons on surface
	340 tons submerged
Range:	600 nautical miles on surface
	60 nautical miles at 4 knots submerged
Crew:	26 officers and men
Torpedo tubes:	Two 18in (457mm) in the bow
Torpedoes:	Two

Schneider-Labeufs Type (Nos 14, 15)

No. 14 was later taken back by the French Navy.
No. 15 became HA-10.

Length:	186.5ft (56.6m)
Beam:	17ft (5.2m)
Draft:	9.25ft (3.0m)
Engine:	2 x 2000hp diesel
	850hp electric motor with 2 shafts
Speed:	17 knots on surface
	10 knots submerged
Depth:	125ft
Displacement:	457 tons on surface
	665 tons submerged
Range:	2,050 nautical miles at 10 knots on surface
	60 nautical miles at 4 knots submerged
Crew:	32 officers and men
Torpedo tubes:	6 x 18in (457mm) in the bow
Torpedoes:	Eight
Armament:	Originally a machine gun but later replaced with a 3in deck gun.

O-1 (Ex-German UE II Type [U-125]

Length:	269ft (81.6m)
Beam:	24.3ft (7.42m)
Draft:	13.8ft (4.22m)
Engine:	2 x 2,400hp diesel
	1,200hp electric motor with 2 shafts
Speed:	14.5 knots on surface
	7 knots submerged
Depth:	245ft (75m)

Displacement: 1,164 tons on surface
                1,152 tons submerged
Range: 11,470 nautical miles at 8 knots on surface
                35 nautical miles at 4 knots submerged
Crew: 4 officers and 36 men
Torpedo tubes: 4 x 18in (457mm) in the bow
                2 internal mine tubes
Torpedoes: Eight
Mines: 42
Armament: 2 x 3in deck guns.

O-2 (Ex-German U-46)
Length: 213.5ft (65.0)
Beam: 20.3ft (6.2m)
Draft: 12ft (3.7m)
Engine: 2 x 2,000hp diesel
                1,200hp electric motor with 2 shafts
Speed: 15.5 knots on surface
                9.5 knots submerged
Depth: 165ft (50m)
Displacement: 725 tons on surface
                940 tons submerged
Range: 11,420 nautical miles at 8 knots on surface
                51 nautical miles at 5 knots submerged
Crew: 4 officers and 32 men
Torpedo tubes: 6 x 19.7in (50cm) in the bow
                2 internal mine tubes
Torpedoes: Eight
Armament: 1 x 5.9in deck gun.

K (Kirai-sen) Type I-121, I-122, I-123 and I-124.
Length: 279.5ft (85.0)
Beam: 24.5ft (7.5m)
Draft: 14.5ft (4.3m)
Engine: 2 x 2,400hp diesel
                1,100hp electric motor with 2 shafts
Speed: 14.5 knots on surface
                7 knots submerged
Depth: 200ft (60m)
Displacement: 1,383 tons on surface
                1,768 tons submerged

Range:	8,000 nautical miles at 12 knots on surface
	40 nautical miles at 7 knots submerged
Crew:	8 officers and 65 men
Torpedo tubes:	4 x 21in (53cm) in the bow
	2 internal mine tubes
Torpedoes:	12
Mines:	42
Armament:	1 x 5.9in deck gun.

J (Junsen) Type I-1, 1-2, 1-3 and 1-4.

Length:	320ft (97.5m)
Beam:	30.5ft (9.2m)
Draft:	16.5ft (5.0m)
Engine:	2 x 6,000hp diesel
	2,600hp electric motor with 2 shafts
Speed:	18 knots on surface
	8 knots submerged
Depth:	265ft (80m)
Displacement:	2,135 tons on surface
	2,791 tons submerged
Range:	25,000 nautical miles at 10 knots on surface
	60 nautical miles at 3 knots submerged
Crew:	8 officers and 60 men
Torpedo tubes:	6 x 21in (53cm), 4 in the bow, 2 in the stern
Torpedoes:	20
Armament:	2 x 5.5in deck gun.

KD3A/B Type

Length:	330ft (100m)
Beam:	28ft (8.0m)
Draft:	15.75ft (4.8m)
Engine:	2 x 6,800hp diesel
	1,800hp electric motor with 2 shafts
Speed:	20 knots on surface
	8 knots submerged
Depth:	200ft (60m)
Displacement:	1,800 tons on surface
	2,300 tons submerged
Range:	10,000 nautical miles at 10 knots on surface
	90 nautical miles at 3 knots submerged
Crew:	8 officers and 52 men
Torpedo tubes:	8 x 21in (53cm), 6 in the bow, 2 in the stern

Torpedoes: 16
Armament: 1 x 4.7in (120mm) deck gun.

B1 Type Submarine
Length: 356ft (108.7m)
Beam: 30.5ft (9.3m)
Draft: 16.7ft (5.1m)
Engine: 2 x 12,400hp diesel
                2,000hp electric motor with 2 shafts
Speed: 23.5 knots on surface
                8 knots submerged
Depth: 330ft (100m)
Displacement: 2,584 tons on surface
                3,654 tons submerged
Range: 14,000 nautical miles at 16 knots on surface
                96 nautical miles at 3 knots submerged
Crew: 94 officers and men
Torpedo tubes: 6 x 21in (53cm) in the bow
Torpedoes: 17
Armament: 1 x 4.7in (120mm) deck gun
Aircraft: One Yokosuka E14Y1 seaplane

YU-class Submarine (Army)
Length: 134ft (40.85m)
Beam: 18.5ft (4.1m)
Draft: 9ft (2.8m)
Engine: 1x 400hp diesel
                75hp electric motor with 1 shaft
Speed: 10 knots on surface
                5 knots submerged
Depth: 330ft (100m)
Displacement: 2,584 tons on surface
                3,654 tons submerged
Range: 1,500 nautical miles at 8 knots on surface
Crew: 13 officers and men
Torpedo tubes: None
Armament: 1 x 37mm anti-aircraft gun

I-400
Length: 400ft (122m)
Beam: 39.3ft (12m)
Draft: 22.9ft (7m)

Engine:	4 x 10-cylinder 2,250hp diesels
	2 electric motors 1,600 kw
Speed:	18.7 knots on surface
	6.5 knots submerged
Depth:	300ft (100m)
Displacement:	3,530 tons on surface
	3,223 tons submerged
Range:	37,500 nautical miles at 14 knots on surface
	60 nautical miles at 3 knots submerged
Crew:	21 officers and 170 men
Torpedo tubes:	4 x 18in (50cm) in the bow
	2 internal mine tubes
Torpedoes:	Eight
Armament:	One 5.5in Type 11 rear deck gun
	Ten 25mm Type 96 anti-aircraft guns
Aircraft:	Three Aichi Sieran M6A1 special attack aircraft
Wing Span:	40ft 2¾in (12.6m)
Length:	38ft 2¼in (11.6m)
Height:	15ft 0½in (4.58m)
Weight Empty:	7,277lb (3,301kg)
Weight Loaded:	8,907lb (4,040kg)
Max. Speed:	295mph
Ceiling:	32,480ft (9,900m)
Range:	739 miles (642 nautical miles.)
Engines:	One 1,400hp Aichi Atsuta 31,
	12-cylinder,vee liquid-cooled
Armament:	One flexible rear-firing 13mm machine gun
Crew:	Pilot and Observer in tandem.

Kaiten Type 1

Length:	48ft 5ins (14.75m)
Diameter:	3ft 3ins (1m)
Weight:	8.3 tons
Engine:	Wet heater double action 2-cylinder 550hp diesel
Propellant:	Kerosene and oxygen
Maximum Range:	42nm (78km)
Cruising Speed:	12 knots (22km/h)
Maximum Speed:	30 knots (56km/h)
Maximum	
Operating Depth:	250ft (80m)
Warhead:	3,420lb (1,550kg)

Bibliography

Boyd, Carl, and Akihiko Yoshida, *The Japanese Submarine Force and World War Two* (Airlife, UK, 1995).

Hashimoto, Mochitsura, *Sunk: The Story of the Japanese Submarine Fleet 1942–1945* (Cassel & Company, London, 1954).

Ishimaru, Lieutenant Commander Tota, *Japan Must Fight Britain* (Hurst and Blackett, London, 1936).

Januszewski, Tadeusz, *Japanese Submarine Aircraft* (Stratus, Poland, 2002).

Naval Aviation News, Washington Navy Yard, Washington D.C. USA.

Polmar, Don, and Norman Carpenter, *Submarines of the Japanese Imperial Navy* (Conway Maritime Press, London, 1986).

Rohwer. Jurgen, *Axis Submarine Successes of World War Two* (Naval Institute Press, Annapolis, Maryland, 1968)

Sakai. Henry, Nila, Gary, and Takai, Koji, *I-400* (Hikoki Publications, 2006).

Treadwell, Terry C., *Strike From Beneath the Sea* (History Press, 2009).